AN ANNOTATED CORPUS OF THREE HUNDRED PROVERBS, SAYINGS, AND IDIOMS IN EASTERN JIBBALI/ŚḤƏRέT

An Annotated Corpus of Three Hundred Proverbs, Sayings, and Idioms in Eastern Jibbali/Śḥərέt

Giuliano Castagna
with a contribution by Suhail al-Amri

https://www.openbookpublishers.com

©2024 Giuliano Castagna

This work is licensed under an Attribution-NonCommercial 4.0 International (CC BY-NC 4.0). This license allows you to share, copy, distribute, and transmit the text; to adapt the text for non-commercial purposes of the text providing attribution is made to the authors (but not in any way that suggests that they endorse you or your use of the work). Attribution should include the following information:

Giuliano Castagna, *An Annotated Corpus of Three Hundred Proverbs, Sayings, and Idioms in Eastern Jibbali/Śḥarɛ́t*. Cambridge, UK: Open Book Publishers, 2024, https://doi.org/10.11647/OBP.0422

Further details about CC BY-NC licenses are available at http://creativecommons.org/licenses/by-nc/4.0/

All external links were active at the time of publication unless otherwise stated and have been archived via the Internet Archive Wayback Machine at https://archive.org/web

Any digital material and resources associated with this volume will be available at https://doi.org/10.11647/OBP.0422#resources

Semitic Languages and Cultures 26

ISSN (print): 2632-6906
ISSN (digital): 2632-6914

ISBN Paperback: 978-1-80511-384-3
ISBN Hardback: 978-1-80511-385-0
ISBN Digital (PDF): 978-1-80511-386-7

DOI: 10.11647/OBP.0422

Cover image: Dhofar Inscription KMH 1-8, Raxyut, Oman. Photo by Giuliano Castagna, CC BY-NC.
Cover design: Jeevanjot Kaur Nagpal

The main fonts used in this volume are Charis SIL, Scheherazade New and Abyssinica SIL.

CONTENTS

Acknowledgements vii

1. Introduction 1
   1.0. Limitations of the Study 4
   2.0. The Modern South Arabian Languages 5
   3.0. Jibbali/Śḥərε̄t 6
   4.0. The Place of Jibbali/Śḥərε̄t within Modern
          South Arabian 10
   5.0. Glottonymy 14
   6.0. Dialectal Areas 18
   7.0. Language Varieties at the Basis of This Study 20
   8.0. Paremiological Remarks 20
   9.0. Sources 24
   10.0. Grammatical Features of Jibbali/Śḥərε̄t 28
   11.0. Methodology and Presentation 44
   12.0. Glossing 47

2. Proverbs and Linguistic Analysis 49
　1.0. Al-Shahri Collection 49
　2.0. *Muʿǧam Lisān Ẓufār* 172
　3.0. *Jibbali Lexicon* 193
　4.0. Elicited Entries 204

3. Conclusions 215
　1.0. Phonetics and Phonology 215
　2.0. Morphology 218
　3.0. Lexis 219
　4.0. Arabic Translation of *Jibbali Lexicon* and Elicited Entries 227

Bibliography 231
Index 241

ACKNOWLEDGEMENTS

I would like to express my gratitude to Beijing Normal University and the Research Centre for History and Culture for funding this study and generously contributing to the publication expenses.

It would not have been possible to carry out this study without the valuable contribution of the many Dhofari informants who provided comments and remarks on the data. I would like to dedicate this study to them, in the hope that they will keep and pass down the incredibly rich and ancient culture of Dhofar through the coming generations.

This publication owes much to the comments and remarks provided by Prof. Janet Watson, who took the trouble to read an early draft of this study. All the remaining shortcomings and inconsistencies are, of course, my own responsibility.

Finally, I would like to mention a very special person who, for the last three years, has helped me cope with the highs and lows of being myself: my daughter Clemi, who showed me what 'love at first sight' means. Whatever happens, we'll never feel lonely again.

1. INTRODUCTION

This book is the first scholarly work exclusively devoted to the study of proverbs (that is, *paremiology*) in the Jibbali/Śḥərε̄́t language, and the first monograph[1] to explore this aspect of lexicography in a Modern South Arabian language.

Jibbali/Śḥərε̄́t proverbs bear witness to a thousand years of the history of Dhofar which scholars have little other means of analysing, due to the virtual non-existence of historical records.

Dhofar (Arabic ظفار *ḍufār*, Jibbali/Śḥərε̄́t ضفول *ṣɔfɔ́l*), is historically one of the names by which the medieval settlement of al-Baleed and subsequently the whole area of Ṣalalah (the capital of the governorate of Dhofar, Oman) has been called (al-Shahri 1994, 23). In time, however, it came to designate a much larger square area in the south of the Sultanate of Oman, sharing borders with the Republic of Yemen and the Kingdom of Saudi Arabia. The present-day governorate of Dhofar comprises the Indian Ocean coast from Ras Sharbithat in the north-east to Ras Darbat Ali in the south-west, as well as a big part of the Omani Negd, a gravel desert, and borders Saudi Arabia and the Rubʿ al-Khali (the empty quarter) to the north: according to al-Shahri (1994, 23–24), this area was traditionally called فيجير اعوفر *figír ʕɔfər* 'the red

---

[1] There exists a journal article about a collection of 101 proverbs in the Mehri language (Sima 2005). Specifically, this rather concise paper focuses on the presentation of proverbs, idioms, and expressions in the Hawf dialect, Yemen. See also below (p. 45).

land'. The present work is concerned with the Jibbali/Śḥərέt-speaking area, which is described below (pp. 6–7) and falls entirely within the borders of the Dhofar governorate. Since the beginning of Sultan Qaboos's reign in 1970 and the consequent modernisation, Dhofar has been an integral part of the Sultanate, thus ending centuries of colonial attitudes towards this land on the part of the sultans of Muscat and Oman. Before 1970, Dhofar (and Oman at large) was largely isolated from the rest of the world: items were produced with locally available materials through processes established since time immemorial. Agriculture, fishing, and livestock rearing represented the main sources of livelihood for the great majority of Dhofaris, and although the Maria Theresa dollar was used as a currency, barter was widely practised. Travel was hazardous, and the only means of transport available to the people of the land was the camel (or one's own feet); indeed, cars were an uncommon sight in Dhofar before Sultan Qaboos's modernisation, as reported by Watson (2013).

In light of the above facts and considering the pre-literate status of the old Dhofari society, it is no wonder that the intergenerational transmission of a substantial body of traditional knowledge would need to be ensured: this includes several oral poetic genres, lullabies, nursery rhymes, games, riddles, and proverbs.

A linguistic analysis of the rather vast proverb collection that constitutes one of the chapters of Ali Ahmad Mahash al-Shahri's seminal work *The Language of Aad*—لغة عاد (al-Shahri 2000) is the topic of a journal paper entitled 'A Collection of Jibbali/Śḥərέt Proverbs from Ali al-Shahri's Publication *The Language of Aad*'

1. Introduction

(Castagna 2022a). It was not until the end of the painstaking correction process of this article[2] that G. Castagna fully realised the importance of Jibbali/Śḥərḗt proverbs in terms of linguistic analysis: not only do proverbs preserve archaic linguistic features, understanding of which has the potential to enhance our knowledge of the Modern South Arabian languages greatly, but they also offer insights into the culture of pre-modernisation Dhofar. For example, the analysis of al-Shahri's collection yielded some personal names which had not been published in previous literature: personal names are of particular interest, as gradual assimilation into the mainstream Islamic society of Arabia means that Dhofaris forsook their native anthroponyms in favour of Arabic/Islamic names.

The case for this corpus therefore became compelling, and so too did the involvement of a native speaker of Jibbali/Śḥərḗt. Some of the sources from which this work draws are written, and do not come with audio recordings, so S. al-Amri got involved in the early stages of this project with the aim of providing audio recordings of the proverbs. However, it became clear from the outset that his linguistic insights, patience, and natural linguistic sensitivity would be greatly beneficial to the whole process. The two authors then proceeded to work together, mostly via videoconferencing and voice messages, almost every day in mid-2023, until the end of the write-up. S. al-Amri ensured that his contribution was faithful to the tradition: he often double-checked the

---

[2] G. Castagna can hardly find the right words to thank the anonymous reviewer, whose solid scholarship and unwavering patience in reviewing his article made possible the very existence of this study.

nominal and verbal forms reported in this work, as well as the overall meaning of the expressions, with linguistically authoritative elders, and his own friends and family. G. Castagna carried out the linguistic analysis of the lexical material found in the proverb collections and undertook the write-up. The result of this collaboration is this volume, with a total of 300 entries including proverbs, idioms, and formulaic expressions in Jibbali/Śḥərɛ́t, which, despite being far from exhaustive and not taking into account the many dialectal and lexical variants that surely exist, offers an overview of different proverb genres and, through them, a peek into everyday life in pre-modern Dhofar. Furthermore, the pieces of linguistic information gleaned from the proverbs, which are described in the conclusion chapter, shed light, albeit in a limited fashion, on certain characteristics of the language.

1.0. Limitations of the Study

The main limitation of this study is its being based on two speakers only. This, coupled with the fact that they both speak an eastern variety of the language, means that the results and conclusions found in the final chapter must not be viewed as representative of the whole language. Similarly, the expressions collected here are likely to be but a fraction of the entire body of Jibbali/Śḥərɛ́t proverbs, sayings, idioms, and formulaic expressions. An extensive survey, encompassing the whole Jibbali/Śḥərɛ́t-speaking area, would be the bare minimum action to be taken to obtain a comprehensive corpus. Hence, in documentary terms, this work is of some interest in the field of *eastern* Jibbali/Śḥərɛ́t linguistics and lexicology, and any conclusions in regard to the whole language should be carefully reflected upon and backed by a greater range of relevant data. It is, however, hoped that future research will enrich and expand the data presented here with new insights from other areas of Dhofar and a greater number of speakers.

2.0. The Modern South Arabian Languages

The so-called Modern South Arabian languages (henceforth optionally called MSA languages, MSA, or MSAL) are six currently unwritten Semitic languages, five of which are spoken in the southern part of the Arabian Peninsula, while the remaining one is spoken on the Island of Soqotra and a few islets that surround it.

These languages are endangered, three of them having far less than 1,000 speakers. In spite of having been in contact with Arabic for many centuries, probably since before the great Islamic conquests, all MSA languages were vital as recently as the 1930s (Thomas 1939), so the reasons for their gradual loss must be sought not only in the prestige, both political and religious, of Arabic (which is spoken by virtually every speaker of an MSA language), but also in the mass emigration towards oil-rich countries like Kuwait, Qatar, and Saudi Arabia that took place during the 1970s and the 1980s, triggering a need for social and linguistic adaptation within the expatriate communities. However, at present, this process seems not to be threatening these languages as much as it did in the past, since many individuals who had spent a number of years working in the oil industry in other Gulf countries came back to their ancestral abodes and resumed the use of their ancestral languages when Oman began to exploit its oil reserves. In spite of this, MSA languages are now additionally being threatened by the interference of Arabic as a language of entertainment, education, and communication. This state of affairs greatly influences the younger generations, including the present-day child-bearing generation.

One of the features that sets Modern South Arabian apart from most other Semitic subgroups is the lack of historical records.

The documentation of these languages was initiated in the late 1970s by Miranda Morris, and the proceedings of these projects have been deposited in the Endangered Languages ARchive (ELAR) for Mehri (Watson and Morris 2016a), Jibbali/Śḥərέt (Watson and Morris 2016b), Ḥarsūsi (Eades and Morris 2016), Baṭḥari (Morris 2016a), and Hobyōt (Morris 2016b).

3.0. Jibbali/Śḥərέt

Recent estimates of the number of Jibbali/Śḥərέt speakers are in the region of 30,000 ~ 50,000 (Rubin 2014, 3); these figures, however, might not take into account a considerable number of semi-competent users living in Ṣalalah who are normally not fond of being labelled as speakers of this language. The area in which Jibbali/Śḥərέt is spoken stretches from Dhalkut, near the Oman–Yemen border, to Hasik,[3] at the western end of the Kuria Muria bay, and includes the inland part of this region, whose mountain

---

[3] According to Suhail al-Amri, as well as other informants, most of the Dhofari inhabitants of Hasik are competent both in Jibbali/Śḥərέt and Mehri.

ranges run roughly parallel to the coast, as well as the island of al-Hallānīyya, the only inhabited island of the Kuria Muria archipelago (officially called Ǧuzur al-Ḥallānīyāt). The oldest reliable attestation of the language is found in a divorce formula uttered, and duly recorded, in the presence of a Qadi at Zafar (modern-day Ṣalalah) in the sixteenth century (Serjeant and Wagner 1959). However, before that, travellers to the modern-day Jibbali/Śḥərɛ́t-speaking area detected and recorded some anomalies in the local language: for example, Ibn al-Mujawir, a thirteenth-century Arab merchant and traveller, described the inhabitants of the mountains of Dhofar (as well as those of Soqotra and Masira) as "having their own language which none can understand but they" (Smith 2008, 269). The existence of the language was brought to the attention of western scholarship by Fulgence Fresnel, a French diplomat in Jeddah, in 1838. Although an increasingly growing number of scholarly works have been devoted to it since its discovery, only in 2014 was the first full-fledged grammatical description of Jibbali/Śḥərɛ́t published (Rubin 2014).

A Semitic language, Jibbali/Śḥərɛ́t exhibits the typical traits of this language family:

- A comparatively large sound inventory;
- SVO ~ VSO word order;
- Two grammatical genders and three numbers;[4]

---

[4] The dual number is obsolescent in both the verbal and the nominal system.

- Cross-agreement in gender between a low numeral (3 to 10) and the counted noun;
- An extensive system of 'internal plural' patterns;
- A large number of verbal classes, derived from a basic class by means of prefixation, infixation, and vowel lengthening;
- A rich verbal morphology, employing suffix and prefix conjugation.

Furthermore, Jibbali/Śḥərɛ́t exhibits the traits of the Modern South Arabian sub-branch of Semitic, namely:

- Its inventory includes a lateral fricative/affricate series, and glottalised stops and affricates;
- The presence of two prefix conjugations: the imperfective and the subjunctive, alongside the suffix conjugation of the perfective;
- The presence of a conditional mood;[5]
- The presence of a $-(v)n$ suffix in the imperfective of some verbal classes, whose origin and development remain obscure to date;
- [n]-prefixed verbs have a strong tendency to occur with non-triliteral roots;[6]

---

[5] However, in the case of Jibbali/Śḥərɛ́t, "Conditional forms are rare. They appear almost exclusively in the apodosis of unreal (counterfactual) conditional sentences" (Rubin 2014, 152).

[6] However, in Jibbali/Śḥərɛ́t this prefix is not found exclusively with quadriliteral roots, but also with reduplicated quinqueliterals of the patterns $C^1C^2C^3C^2C^3$ and $C^1C^2C^3C^4C^4$, as well as with triliteral roots with an infixed long vowel (Castagna and al-Amri forthcoming).

- Consonant gemination is only marginally phonemic;
- A rich vocabulary which features Semitic and Afro-Asiatic lexical items that are absent or obsolescent elsewhere, alongside a considerable number of items of uncertain or unknown origin (Kogan 2015).

Finally, some of the characteristics exhibited by this language are peculiar to the eastern MSA languages (that is, a subgroup of the MSA languages made up of Jibbali/Śhərε̄t and Soqotri), including:

- 'Internal' feminine for non-triliteral adjectives, e.g., bərġɔ́l 'obese (M.SG.)' vs bərġél 'obese (F.SG.)' (MLZ, 125), raʕbɔ́b 'tall and well-built (M.SG.)' vs raʕbéb 'tall and well-built (F.SG.)' (MLZ, 383), ḥalkḷɔ́ḳ 'matte (M.SG.)' vs ḥalkḷéḳ 'matte (F.SG.)' (Castagna and al-Amri forthcoming);
- The loss of the t- prefix in the morphology of some verbal classes;
- Weak phonological load of vowel quantity;
- Presence of the nominal and verbal reduplicated quinqueliteral pattern $C^1C^2C^3C^2C^3$, e.g., khanhanút تُصنع الحزن 'pretence of sadness' (MLZ, 81), ḥalkḷɔ́ḳ 'matte' (Castagna and al-Amri forthcoming), ənḥadəbdab احدودب 'to become hunchback' (MLZ, 223).[7]

---

[7] This is a third person (that is, M.SG., M.PL., and F.PL., but not F.SG.) of an n-prefixed (N-stem) verbal form.

4.0. The Place of Jibbali/Śḥərέt within Modern South Arabian

There is a growing consensus among Semitic scholars that MSAL should be divided into two branches: a western branch comprising Mehri, Ḥarsūsi, Baṭḥari, and Hobyōt, and an eastern branch comprising Jibbali/Śḥərέt and Soqotri (Dufour 2016; Kogan 2015; Lonnet 2006; 2008; 2009; Morris 2007; Rubin 2015). Simeone-Senelle (2011) considers Jibbali/Śḥərέt and Soqotri two separate subgroups, whilst arguing in favour of a subgroup containing the remaining four languages.

This subgrouping was first proposed by Bertram Thomas (1939, 11), who admittedly lacked formal training in linguistics. He stated that the languages could be classified into two groups: Mehri, Ḥarsūsi, and Baṭḥari in the first group, and Jibbali/Śḥərέt in the second one,[8] on the basis of the high degree of intercomprehensibility among speakers of the former three, and the lack thereof between them and speakers of the latter (1939, 5–6).

In time, as more evidence from fieldwork became available, this division of MSAL could be backed, above all, with morphological and lexical data. The following table illustrates some of the isoglosses relevant to MSA subgrouping:[9]

---

[8] At Thomas's time, Hobyōt was not known, and although Soqotri was, it is not mentioned.

[9] Rubin (2015) describes these isoglosses in detail. See also Kogan (2015) for the lexical isoglosses.

Table 1: Modern South Arabian subgrouping isoglosses

	Mehri	Ḥarsūsi	Baṭhari	Hobyōt	Jibbali/Śḥərɛ́t	Soqotri
[h] ~ [ḥ] - broken plurals	X	X	X	X		
[h] ~ [ḥ] - article	X	X	X	10		
apophonic feminine in quadri-quinqueliteral adjectives					X	X
'future participle'	X	X	X			
loss of t- in some verbal classes					X	X
preservation of *w	X	X	X	X		
phonemic vowel length	X	X	X	X		
lexical isoglosses[11]	+	+	+	+	−	−

As can be observed, Jibbali/Śḥərɛ́t shares a number of isoglosses with Soqotri, versus the rest of Modern South Arabian:

- Quadriliteral and quinqueliteral adjectives form the feminine by internal vowel modification, rather than by suffixation of the common Semitic feminine morpheme -(v)t;

---

[10] Hobyōt does not have a definite article.

[11] Although lexicon is not, *per se*, a reliable indicator of genetic relationship, it is taken into account here alongside more reliable evidence from other linguistic subdomains. Mehri, Ḥarsūsi, and Baṭhari on the one hand, and Jibbali/Śḥərɛ́t and Soqotri on the other hand, appear to share a significant number of core lexical items, whilst Hobyōt seems to be somewhere in between the two groups (Kogan 2015, 597; Rubin 2015, 328).

- The *t-* prefix in the verbal system has been lost in certain verbal classes;
- Proto-Semitic *w has been lost in a number of environments, either by shifting to [b], especially in Jibbali/Śḥərέt, or disappearing altogether;
- Vowel length is only marginally phonemic;
- Jibbali/Śḥərέt and Soqotri share a great number of lexical items not found in the western sub-group.

Whether these isoglosses result from shared innovation or shared retention remains a matter of debate. Individually, the MSAL exhibit several innovations, as well as archaisms. The principal criterion that guides subgrouping in Semitic is, however, shared morphological innovation (Kogan 2015, 3). In this regard, the same author (2015, 389–95) identifies a number of characteristics that he describes as shared innovations of the MSAL, namely:

- The above-mentioned *-n* suffix in the imperfective of some verbal classes (see above p. 8);
- The conditional, similarly characterised by an *-n* suffix;
- The diachrony of the *š-* prefix in the so-called Š1 and Š2 verbal classes;
- The external feminine plural marker *-Vtən*;
- The so-called *a*-replacement, whereby a substantial number of nominals are pluralised by replacing the vowel between the second and third root consonants in the singular with */a/*.

To these, Dufour (2016, 404–6) adds the following features:

- The innovative nature of proto-MSAL accent;
- Glide- and guttural-triggered allomorphy;
- The so-called idle glottis effect (Bendjaballah and Ségéral 2014; see also below p. 35).

As for the internal subgrouping of the MSAL, most scholars agree on the following figure (Rubin 2015, 313).

Figure 1: Subgrouping of MSAL

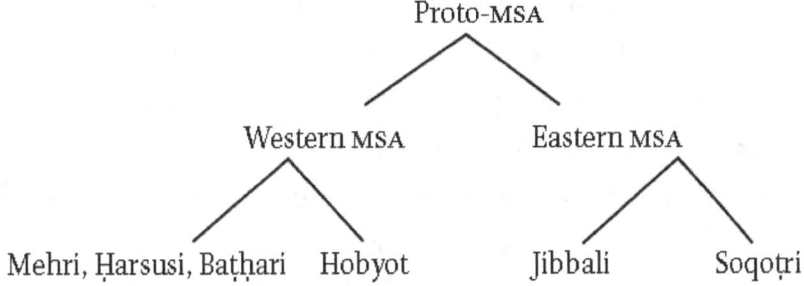

However, in view of the areal phenomena in the MSAL-speaking area, that is, the wandering tribes coming into contact and then separating again, the figure should be slightly modified as follows, to reflect this state of affairs.

Figure 2: Subgrouping of MSAL with shared areal phenomena

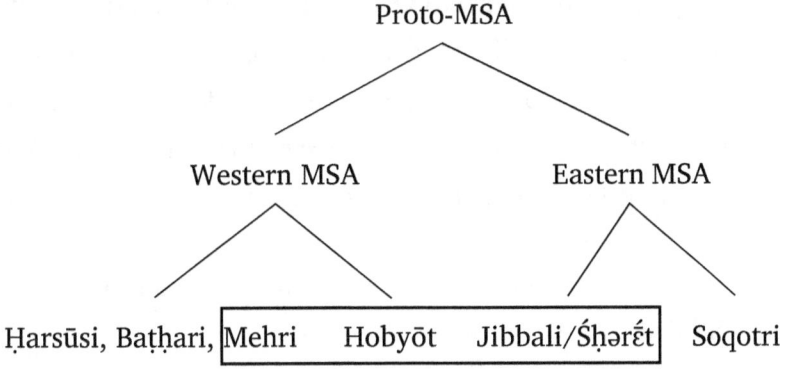

5.0. Glottonymy

MSAL linguistics is a relatively new field, but intensive fieldwork and research in recent decades have made it possible to arrive at a satisfactory level of description of the languages, at least synchronically. That being said, many unknowns remain: the past phases of the languages are, at present, undocumented and, probably, undocumentable. The glottonyms too are far from straightforward, except (perhaps) for the languages with few speakers. For a start, Mehri is called by native speakers variously *Məhrəyyet*, *Mahriyōt*, or *Mehrīyət* according to the geographical area. Modern South Arabian itself is but a label contrasting with Ancient South Arabian: the total lack of historical records means that it is impossible to name this subgroup of Semitic according to a more accurate criterion, be it geographical (e.g., *Ṣayhadic*), or deriving from an endonym (e.g., *Akkadian, Hebrew, Arabic*). When it comes to the language at the core of the present work, things become considerably more complex: the ethnic groups whose members speak it natively are the *Ḥaklī* (alternatively known as *Qara* in Arabic), the *Śḥarī* (known as *Šaḥra* in Arabic), and also some sections of the *Kaṯīrī*, the *Mašāyix*, the *Barʕima*, the *Hikman* (Peterson 2004), and the *Baṭāḥira* (Gasparini 2018, 11). Historically, a number of glottonyms have been associated with this language: the native *Gəblɛ́t*, *Śḥarɛ́t*, and *Əḥkilyɔ́t*[12] on the one hand, and, on the other hand, their widely used Arabic counterparts

---

[12] *Aḥkilyút* is believed to be the ancient name of the Hobyōt language by its speakers (Morris 2017, 22).

Gibbālī ~ *Ǧibbālī*,[13] *Šaḥrī*, and *Ḥaklī* ~ *Qarāwī*. Another glottonym, *Šxawri* ~ *Šḥawri*, used for the first time in the *Südarabische Expedition* material concerned with this language (Bittner 1913), is a misnomer resulting either from a misinterpretation on the part of the scholars or, more probably, an attempt of their informant to mock the language.[14]

The native term *əḥkilyɔ́t*, its Arabic rendition *Ḥaklī*, and the Arabic alternative designation *Qarāwī* are the glottonyms used in the earliest accounts of the language (Fresnel 1838; Carter 1845). *Ḥaklī* is the name of the people who are traditionally held to have come to Dhofar from the west some time in the past, and seized the lands and wealth of the *Šaḥrī*, who were (and are, by many, still held to be) the original inhabitants of Dhofar. The *Ḥaklī* are said to have been speakers of Mehri who, in time, adopted the language of the *Šaḥra*. The latter became weak (Arabic *ḍaʕīf*) and were forbidden to bear arms or intermarry with the dominant tribal (Arabic *qabīlī*) people. Johnstone (1972, 17) states that this could shed light on the origin of the enigmatic poetic register of this language, as the invaders would have composed poetry in Mehri upon their arrival in Dhofar, and would then have gradually started to incorporate their newly acquired language into their poetry, giving rise to a mixed language. Today, the ethnonym

---

[13] The realisation of */g/ as [g], [gʲ], or [d͡ʒ] is a dialectal feature.

[14] The person in question, Muḥammad bin Sālim al-Kaṭīrī, was an Arab, but he was perfectly bilingual in Jibbali/Śḥərɛ́t (Lonnet 2017, 278). Given his higher social standing, as an Arab, he might have attempted to mock the language by using a term derived from the root √šxr, with the general meaning of 'weakness'; cf. *šaxər* 'old man' (JL, 264).

Ḥaklī designates a Dhofari tribal confederation consisting of the following Jibbali/Śḥərɛ́t-speaking tribes: ʕAḵʕāḵ, ʕAmri, Gabúb, Kəšúb, Ḳitán, Maʕʕni, Šammás, Ṭəbɔ́k (personal fieldwork). The members of these tribes do not (any longer) use *Əḥkilyɔ́t/Ḥaklī* as a glottonym, and normally refer to the language as *Jibbali/Gəblɛ́t*. However, they also use, and are in general comfortable with, *Šaḥrī/Śḥərɛ́t*.[15] Conversely, the *Šaḥrī* unsurprisingly favour the glottonym *Šaḥrī/Śḥərɛ́t*, and generally consider *Jibbali/Gəblɛ́t* a disrespectful and derogatory term. Of course, reactions to the use of the *Jibbali/Gəblɛ́t* glottonym do vary: milder reactions can be expected of the *Šaḥra* inhabiting al-Ḥallānīyah,[16] whilst passionate and sometimes fierce reactions are typical of the *Šaḥra* of the mainland, on the grounds of their claim of being the original speakers of the language, as well as the original inhabitants of Dhofar.

Hence, the glottonymic situation discussed above can be summarised as follows. Two glottonyms are currently in use: *Jibbali/Gəblɛ́t* and *Šaḥrī/Śḥərɛ́t*. The non-*Šaḥra* tribes tend to favour *Jibbali/Gəblɛ́t*, but do not consider *Šaḥrī/Śḥərɛ́t* offensive, whereas the *Šaḥra*-affiliated speakers tend to use *Šaḥrī/Śḥərɛ́t* and consider *Jibbali/Gəblɛ́t* incorrect or outright offensive.

Regrettably, there are no safe options in terms of glottonymy: someone will be offended, or at the very least annoyed, by the use of either *Jibbali/Gəblɛ́t* or *Šaḥrī/Śḥərɛ́t*.

---

[15] However, there are exceptions. During one interview, the interviewee, a member of the ʕAmri tribe, became angered by the fact that I had used the glottonym *Śḥərɛ́t*.

[16] This conclusion was formed on the basis of personal communications.

1. Introduction

This state of affairs has remained unchanged for a long time, and the existing literature offers little to no discussion (Hofstede 1998, 15; JL, xi; al-MaʕsanI 2003; Morris 2017, 20–21; Rubin 2014, 10–11). However, a commonality of many scholarly descriptions of this issue is the fact that the Arabic glottonym and ethnonym *Šaḥrī* is considered to be merely a rendition of the native term *Śḥərí*, a *nisbah* adjective derived from *Śḥɛ(h)r* 'green area of the mountain, countryside' (JL, 250), 'monsoon-affected mountain' (Morris et al. 2019, 77), جبل 'mountain' (MLZ, 504), whilst *Jibbali* (M.SG.) and *Gəblḗt* (F.SG.) both mean 'of the mountains', respectively in Arabic and in the language under discussion.[17]

---

[17] Morris (2017, 21) states that the the Baṭāḥirah associate the glottonym *Śḥərḗt* with the Śḥarȯ "Incorrectly, as 'Śḥerḗt' simply means '(language) of the śḥɛr', that is, the mountains affected by the annual monsoon. The belief that Śḥerḗt is/was the language of the Śḥarȯ peoples is widespread and the cause of much social tension today, and is one reason that Gəblḗt or Jibbāli (an arabisation of Śḥerḗt) has come to be preferred as a less controversial name for this language." Whilst this might be the case, this statement makes one wonder why the Śḥarȯ themselves insist that the correct glottonym is *Śḥərḗt*, and why they consider *Šaḥrī*, which is their tribal *nisbah* is Arabic, an acceptable Arabic exoglottonym. If 'Śḥerḗt' simply means '(language) of the śḥɛr', then why are the Śḥarȯ outraged by the use of *Ǧibbālī* '(language) of the mountains'? When questioned about glottonymy, ʕAli Aḥmad Mahāš al-Šaḥrī, the Dhofari author who wrote one of the sources from which the present study draws (al-Shahri 2000), and staunch advocate of the glottonym *Šaḥrī/Śḥərḗt*, usually affirms "mountains don't speak!" (personal communication).

That *Jibbali* and *Gəblέt* are cognate can be observed on the basis of both the regular sound correspondences (Arabic √ǧbl regularly corresponds to MSAL √gbl) and the matching semantics. Whilst *Šaḥrī* and *Śḥərέt* also exhibit regular sound correspondences (Arabic √šhr corresponds to MSAL √śḥr), the same does not apply to semantics: the above-mentioned meaning of *Śḥɛ(h)r* does not precisely match its alleged Arabic etymological cognate root √šhr, which has the general meaning of 'soot' (Wehr 1976, 457).

It must, however, be mentioned that some Dhofaris, not necessarily belonging to the *Šaḥra* tribes, state that *Šaḥrī/Śḥərέt* is the correct glottonym, regardless of tribal loyalties, and *Jibbali/Gəblέt* is but a recent invention.

In light of the above, the use of the compound glottonym Jibbali/Śḥərέt has presented itself as the most sensible choice. As strange and artificial as it may sound, especially in live speech, it nevertheless ensures a fair treatment of all the stakeholders, and bears witness to the rich and complex pre-history of this language.

6.0. Dialectal Areas

There exists a certain degree of consensus about the division of the Jibbali/Śḥərέt-speaking area into three main dialectal areas, commonly referred to as east, centre, and west (JL, xii; al-Shahri 2007, 76-77; Rubin 2014, 11–13), which roughly correspond to the three mountain ranges running parallel to the coast of Dhofar: Jabal Samḥān, Jabal Qara, and Jabal Qamar. The *Muʕǧam lisān Ḍufār* goes into further detail, describing six dialectal areas: (1) the dialect of the Ḥallāniyāt islands (Kuria Muria); (2) the dialect of eastern Dhofar, comprising the region of Ṣalūt, the province of

Sadḥ, and the eastern part of the province of Mirbāṭ; (3) the dialect of the eastern part of Jabal Qara, comprising the entirety of Ṭawi Aʕtair territory and the eastern part of the province of Ṭāqa; (4) the central-eastern dialect, comprising Medinat al-ḥaqq and the rest of the province of Ṭāqa; (5) the central-western dialect, spoken in the western part of the province of Ṣalalah; and (6) the western dialect, spoken in the provinces of Raxyūt and Ḍalkūt (MLZ, 66). According to the author of MLZ (67), furthermore, a seventh dialect exists: the poetic language of Dhofar, which exhibits marked lexical differences from everyday speech.

Notwithstanding the existence of dialectal areas, the majority of scholars and speakers of Jibbali/Śḥərέt agree that dialectal variation is not prominent enough to hinder communication. It is, however, felt to be revealing of a speaker's geographical origin (MLZ, 66).

As for the relationship between dialectal variation and tribal affiliation, it is not mentioned by any study to the best of the authors' knowledge. However, it is worth mentioning that the presence/absence of certain linguistic traits once thought to be a feature of the central dialects, e.g., the distinctiveness of alveopalatal sibilants, has been found in other geographical areas too (Bellem and Watson 2017). This, coupled with sporadic mentions of inter-tribal variation,[18] calls for further investigation in the field of Jibbali/Śḥərέt dialectology.

---

[18] JL (29) records a verb bɔsɔ́ṭ, normally meaning 'to eat; to smooth out a pile of food', with the additional meaning of 'to drink milk' only for the Kathiri tribe.

7.0. Language Varieties at the Basis of This Study

The audio recordings of the proverbs which constitute the subject of this work come from two varieties of eastern Jibbali/S̃ḥərέt, namely those spoken by Ali al-Shahri (a native of Ṭawi Aʕtair), and Suhail al-Amri (a native of Sadḥ). The common traits of these varieties include a clearly audible palatalisation of /g/, which is realised as [gʲ] in most environments, and an unsystematic assimilatory phenomenon which determines, within a word, the quality of an unstressed vowel on the basis of the quality of the stressed vowel, a trait that might lead one to postulate vowel harmony. However, a more comprehensive analysis of the relevant tokens in context would be needed in order to do so, and the fact that this phenomenon is far from predictable casts additional doubt on the viability of this hypothesis (Castagna 2022a, 82–83). Another trait that the two varieties share is the pausal realisation of /l/ as [ɭ] (Castagna 2022a, 84). However, more research is needed to determine the exact boundaries of this isogloss.

8.0. Paremiological Remarks

As this is a collection of proverbs, sayings, and idioms,[19] one must spend a few words on the paremiological aspect of this piece of research.

Proverbs can be semantically labelled as linguistic utterances which "summarize everyday experiences and common observations in a concise and figurative way. They have been created and used for thousands of years and passed as expressions

---

[19] In actuality, it is a *compendium* of four collections.

of wisdom and truth from generation to generation" (Hrisztova-Gotthardt and Varga 2015, 1). *Paremiology* (that is, the study of proverbs) is a relatively recent discipline that has gained a substantial following in the last few decades. However, "the history of compiling proverb dictionaries is probably as old as the first systems of writing that emerged in ancient Mesopotamia (Sumer, the Akkadian Empire, Assyria, Babylonia) and ancient Egypt more than five millennia ago" (Petrova 2015, 245).

Since the early days of paremiology, scholars have been trying to define *what* a proverb is, and what sets it apart from regular phraseology. The most famous definition, and the most controversial one, is the following: "An incommunicable quality tells us this sentence is proverbial and that one is not. Hence no definition will enable us to identify positively a sentence as proverbial" (Taylor 1962, 3). As the field acquired new insights and more scholars made their contributions to paremiology, the concept of *proverbial markers* became current in the works of many proverb scholars. In Mac Coinnigh's (2015, 112) words: "Scholars have identified a range of devices which operate in ensemble to effect the concept of proverbial style, amongst which the most important are parallelism, ellipsis, alliteration, rhyme, metaphor, personification, paradox, and hyperbole." Furthermore, there are a "set of optional syntactic devices that occur in proverbs, particularly synactic [*sic*] parallelism, parataxis, and inverted word order" (Mac Coinnigh 2015, 113).

In addition to this, it is important to mention that there exist a number of proverbial genres that are encountered cross-linguistically. Among those mentioned by Mac Coinnigh, the following are common in the present collection:

- Better X than Y[20]
- No X, no Y
- X is X
- The so-called Wellerism[21]

For linguists, proverbs are of particular interest and importance, as they "unite features of the lexeme, sentence, set phrase, collocation, text and quote. They illustrate interesting patterns of prosody, parallelism, syntax, lexis and imagery" (Norrick 2015, 8), and "often contain archaic and dialect words and structures" (Norrick 2015, 21). When dealing with a language like Jibbali/Śḥərɛ́t, whose prehistory is unknown due to the lack of written records, proverbs open a window on some features of the language which have become obsolete in the course of its history.[22] However, it is also important to point out that proverbs do change, grammatically speaking, and their form in not immutable. Nevertheless, recognisability does not require complete im-

---

[20] According to Mac Coinnigh, this formula is "one of the most widely dispersed" (2015, 117).

[21] An ironic proverbial statement possessing the following structure: "a statement (often a proverb) + a speaker + context (phrase or subclause)" (Mac Coinnigh 2015, 120).

[22] A good example of this is the contents of entries **(92)** and **(149)** of the al-Shahri collection, which feature a mixed Jibbali/Śḥərɛ́t–Mehri language: this is likely a holdover from a time of widespread bilingualism (Johnstone 1972).

mutability of proverb form. Listeners continue to identify proverbs in spite of lexical and grammatical variation because proverbs are "strongly coded" (Norrick 2015, 12).

From a Euro-western point of view, proverbs often exhibit "folksy, rural, pre-industrial connotations" (Norrick 2015, 18). However, in the case of Jibbali/Śḥərɛ́t proverbs, this statement does not hold true, as the elements contained in them are often felt as vivid and real by its speakers, a good number of whom still practise traditional activities. By the same token, Mac Coinnigh's (2015, 130) statement that "there appears to be a clear preference for simple indicative statements over the majority of other forms in modern English-language proverbs" does not apply to the present collection.

It will be of value to trace definite boundaries to the scope of the present work: this is, for the most part, a presentation of proverbs and a linguistic analysis of them. Thus, the reader will encounter few cross-cultural comparisons with other linguistic areas[23] or remarks about the semiotic features of the token analysed. Instead, this work focuses on description of the linguistic features of the proverbs, that is, phonetics, phonology, morphology, and syntax.

Finally, the definition of "proverb collection" used here needs to be clarified. According to Kispál (2015, 229):

> On the one hand, there are proverb collections where proverbs can be interpreted within the framework of the prototype theory, i.e., they interpret proverbs in a broader sense,

---

[23] Although they are not completely absent: see the elicited proverbs collection below, pp. 204–13.

and with this in mind, they include better examples of the proverb category (e.g. The apple doesn't fall far from the tree) and worse examples too, i.e., proverbial comparisons (e.g. as busy as a bee), wellerisms (e.g. "Everyone to his own taste," as the farmer said when he kissed the cow), weather proverbs and superstitions (e.g. When it rains and the sun shines, the devil is beating his grandmother), even idioms (e.g. kick the bucket). On the other hand, there are proverb dictionaries where proverbs can be interpreted within the framework of features (sentence, rhyme, alliteration, ellipsis, moral authority, didactic intent et al.), i.e., they interpret proverbs in a narrow sense and so they codify only proverbs that are generally sentential statements (e.g. Still waters run deep; The shoemaker's son always goes barefoot; Too many cooks spoil the broth).

In view of the above, the present work falls within the first category, in that it presents not only sentential statements, but also the other categories mentioned by Kispál, as well as a good number of idioms.

9.0. Sources

The data analysed in this study proceed from four sources:

9.1. *The Language of Aad*—لغة عاد (2000)

This publication is bilingual, the English part being the translation of the Arabic part. Its contents include pictures and drawings of the Dhofar cave paintings and inscriptions,[24] as well as information about Shahri tribal divisions, land management, folk

---

[24] These undeciphered inscriptions, which are likely to be revealing of the linguistic past of Dhofar and the other adjacent areas where they

games, calendar, measurements, and song genres in the Jibbali/ S̱həré̱t-speaking area. The publication also contains an extensive collection of proverbs (210 items), which are analysed in the present work, further elaborating on the contents of Castagna (2022a). The book is (was)[25] sold with an accompanying audio cassette, containing, among other things, a recording of the proverbs made by Ali al-Shahri in person.

The proverbs and expressions are presented in the Arabic part of the book in the following format (al-Shahri 2000, 263):

أذيِيلِين أَنفاع بوشفاع

المعنى = فلان لا نفع منه ولا شفع

فلان لا يفيد ولا يتشفع لاحد, لا لنفسه ولا لغيره, فهو بدون فائدة. يطلق هذا المثل على الانسان الكسول الكثير النوم والجلوس, وعلى الانسان الذي لا يعمل اي عاطل عن العمل ولا يفيد احداً. فاذا احدهم سأل شخصاً عن هذا الشخص, قال المثل اعلاه والذي يفيد بان فلاناً بدون عمل لا لنفسه ولا لاهله اي ليس يه فائدة لنفسه او اهله.

The underlined portion of the text is proverb number **(72)** in the al-Shahri collection (see below p. 94), as presented in the text.[26] There follows its Arabic translation in the line immediately

---

are found, can be found in great numbers in the caves of the monsoon hills in Dhofar, as well as in the contiguous Mahrah governorate in Yemen and Soqotra. A few specimens from Oman proper have been found in recent years (al-Jawhari 2018).

[25] This publication has regrettably been out of print for 10 years.

[26] The highly idiosyncratic transcription system devised by al-Shahri, based on colour-coded Arabic letters to represent the sounds of Jibbali/

below. The longer text at the bottom is a description of the proverb in Arabic, which has not been reproduced in the present work for the sake of brevity. The English-language section of the book contains a rendition of each proverb in English, which has been faithfully reproduced in the present study, despite an evident lack of accuracy in the translation process. Where, however, this inaccuracy may hinder comprehension, a literal translation of the original Jibbali/Śḥərέt item is provided. It is important to point out that the analysis of this collection yielded a considerable number of terms previously unattested in Jibbali/Śḥərέt, as well as unattested variants of attested terms. These are summarised in Castagna (2022a, 84–86), and described in the conclusions chapter (see below, pp. 220–27).

9.2. *Muʕğam Lisān Ḍufār* (MLZ)—معجم لسان ظفار (2014)

This privately published Jibbali/Śḥərέt–Arabic dictionary was compiled by a local amateur lexicographer.[27] It is structured according to the Arabic alphabetical order, and the roots are coherently presented throughout the book. Although its arbitrary use of Arabic diacritics to render the linguistic sounds unknown to Arabic make it slightly difficult to use, it is, nevertheless, a good

---

Śḥərέt not found in Arabic, has not been reproduced in each individual entry, for the sake of the reader's comprehension and to ensure consistency throughout the publication. However, see the transcription table below for a key to this and the transcription systems used by the other collections.

[27] The name of this work is abbreviated to MLZ in this publication. See below (p. 231).

consultation tool, especially as it often succeeds in filling the gaps found in western lexica. The fact that it was compiled by a native speaker is of particular interest in terms of the insights into the traditions, tales, and legends connected with some of the lexical items presented in the volume, and of the occasional descriptions of dialectal variation. The proverbs contained in this dictionary are presented as in-context examples of some of the terms entered. Here is reproduced one such entry (MLZ, 434):

سّحِقْ : سُحق. أثار سخط غيره. وتأتي هذه الكلمة مرادفة لكلمة (مِحِقْ)
أي الذي يتحرش بالناس لإثارتهم وإغاظتهم فيقال : أذيلين محِق بسَحقَ.
فلان يتسبب في إثرة إغاظة الناس وسخطهم.

The underlined text is the Jibbali/Śḥərɛ̄t text of proverb number **(11)** of the MLZ collection (see below, p. 178) as presented in this work.[28] The text that follows is its translation in Arabic. The present work analyses 44 proverbs and expressions contained in MLZ.

9.3. *Jibbali Lexicon* (JL) (1981)

This work, alongside the Ḥarsūsi and Mehri lexica, represents the corollary of Johnstone's long periods of seminal fieldwork in the MSAL-speaking areas. The introduction contains a brief grammatical sketch of the language, which is considerably less extensive than the one in the Mehri Lexicon (Johnstone 1987; henceforth ML). The main body consists of the terms arranged by root in English alphabetical order. Philologically speaking, these

---

[28] The Arabic transcription system devised by the author of MLZ is given in the relevant section.

works often offer cognates in other MSA languages, but rarely do so with other Semitic languages outside Modern South Arabian. Similarly to MLZ, the proverbs and idioms found in JL are meant to provide an in-context example of the use of a given term (JL, 144):

> ḳɔ́ttəl to shrink: to feel dizzy after a knock on the head.
> yəḳətél ḥask! May your brain shrink! (a friendly curse)

The above-mentioned expression is analysed below (pp. 199–200) and presented as number **(16)** of the JL collection. The present work analyses 26 proverbs and expressions from JL.

9.4. Elicited Proverbs

Twenty entries have been obtained by elicitation. S. al-Amri came up with these proverbs, either on his own or with the aid of his acquaintances in his native Sadḥ and the nearby inland village of Gufa.

The text makes it clear when a Jibbali/Śḥərɛ́t proverb or expression has a counterpart in English or Arabic.

10.0. Grammatical Features of Jibbali/Śḥərɛ́t

What follows is a very short sketch of the grammatical features encountered in this study. This is meant as a quick reference for the reader and is by no means exhaustive. For further reference, see the relevant literature (JL; Rubin 2014; Dufour 2016; al-Kathiri and Dufour 2020, *inter alia*).

10.1. Sound Inventory and Transcription

Table 2: Jibbali/Śḥərɛ́t consonants

	Labial	Labiodental	Interdental	Dental/Alveolar	Lateral	Alveo-palatal	Guttural	Laryngeal/Pharyngeal
Stop	b			t d ṭ			k g ḳ	
Fricative		f	ṯ ḏ ṭ̱	s z ṣ	ś ź ṣ́	š s̃ z̃ ṣ̌	x ġ	h ḥ ʕ
Nasal	m			n				
Trill				r ṛ				
Approximant	w				l	y		

Table 3: Jibbali/Śḥərɛ́t vowels

	Back					Front
High	i					u
		e		ə	o	
			ɛ		ɔ	
Low				a		

Emphasis, that is, an umbrella term which describes certain phonologically distinct phenomena of secondary articulation in the Semitic languages, is said to be realised as ejectivity in Jibbali/Śḥərɛ́t. However, the extent to which ejectivity is actually perceived varies substantially according to the phoneme, speaker, and phonotactics (Rubin 2014, 27). On the whole, /ḳ/ seems to be the only phoneme which exhibits a consistently perceptible ejectivity, whilst in the other 'emphatic' sounds it is much weaker, and they can sometimes be partially voiced or pharyngealised.

Each of the sources from which the present study draws employs a different transcription system. In order to ensure consistency, it has been decided to use a single, largely phonetic, transcription system. The following tables summarise the above-mentioned systems (with regard to consonants and vowels, respectively), and how they relate to the one employed in this publication.

Table 4: Transcription systems across Jibbali/Śḥərέt studies—consonants

This study	The Language of Aad	MLZ	JL	This study	The Language of Aad	MLZ	JL
ʔ	أ, ء	أ, ء	ʼ	ṣ́	ض	ض	ź
b	ب	ب	b	ṭ	ط	ط	ṭ
t	ت	ت	t	ṭ̱	ظ	ظ	ḏ̣
ṯ	ث	ث	ṯ	ʕ	ع	ع	ʻ
g ~ gʲ	ج	ج	g	ġ	غ	غ	ġ
ž	red ج	ج̌	ž	f	ف	ف	f
ḥ	ح	ح	ḥ	ḳ	red ق	ق	ḳ
x	خ	خ	x	š̃	green ش	يۃ	š̃
d	د	د	d	k	ك	ك	k
ḏ	ذ	ذ	ḏ	l	ل	ل	l
r	ر	ر	r	ź	yellow ش	ڵ	ź
z	ز	ز	z	m	م	م	m
s	س	س	s	n	ن	ن	n
š	ش	ش	š	h	ه	ه	h
š̃	blue ش	بۡش	š̃	w	و	و	w
ś	red ش	ش̇	ś	y	ي	ي	y
ṣ	red ص	ص	ṣ				

Table 5: Transcription systems across Jibbali/Śḥərɛ̄t studies—vowels

This study	The Language of Aad	MLZ	JL
a, ā	ا, ‍ا, آ	ا, آ	a, ā
e, ē	ا, ‍ا, آ	ا, آ	e, ē
ɛ, ɛ̄	ا, ‍ا, آ	ا, آ	ɛ, ɛ̄
i, ī	اي, ي, ڍ	اي, ي	i, ī
o, ō	او, و, وو	او, و	o, ō
ɔ, ɔ̄	او, و, وو	او, و	ɔ, ɔ̄
u, ū	او, و, وو	او, و	u, ū
ə	/	/	ə
ᵊ	/	/	/

In addition to the above, al-Shahri's transcription employs a red ع to signify nasalisation of the preceding vowel, and a red ه for the devoicing/pre-aspiration of a sonorant in final position. In the transcription system employed in this work, these processes are indicated respectively by a tilde <~> above the nasalised vowel, and a circle under the sonorant in question (for example, [r̥]).

As for the sound inventory of Jibbali/Śḥərɛ̄t, it is worth clarifying the following:

- /g/ may be realised as [g] or [gʲ] both in al-Shahri's and S. al-Amri's dialects. However, the unmarked realisation seems to be [gʲ] in both dialects.
- The three sounds here transcribed as <s̃>, <z̃>, and <ṣ̃> make-up a cross-linguistically rare alveo-palatal labialised series (respectively voiceless, voiced, and 'emphatic'). These sibilants are articulated with a high degree

of contact between the tongue and the alveo-palatal region, and are accompanied by a protrusion of the lips (Bellem and Watson 2017). Only /š/ can be regarded as a full-status phoneme, besides being an allophone of /k/ in certain phonetic environments. [ž] is an allophone of /g/. [ṧ] is mostly an allophone of /ḳ/, but it does have a phonemic load.

- Regarding emphasis, see under Table 3 above.
- The three sounds here transcribed as <ś>, <ź>, and <ṣ́> are a series of lateral sounds: a voiceless and a voiced fricative, and a partially glottalised/voiced affricate respectively. Whilst /ś/ and /ṣ́/ are phonemic,[29] <ź> = [ɮ] is an allophone of /l/ in certain phonetic environments.
- The phoneme /ṯ/ is an 'emphatic' interdental voiceless fricative/affricate. As is the case with all 'emphatic' phonemes except /ḳ/, the ejective trait is rather weak, and it may become at least partially voiced (Watson and al-Kathiri 2022).
- /r/ has a retroflex allophone [ɽ] before coronal consonants.
- All sonorants (/l/, /m/, /n/, /r/) in final position may undergo a process variously described as devoicing (Rubin 2014, 37–38; Dufour 2016, 24–26) and pre-aspiration (Watson et al. 2023b). This phenomenon seems to be sub-

---

[29] They are cognates of Arabic ش and ض respectively, and are often found in Arabic loans.

ject to a considerable degree of inter-speaker (and dialectal) variation, as shown by the *Muʕǧam Lisān Ḏufār* (MLZ), which consistently points out that the speakers of the western dialect do not produce this phenomenon (MLZ *passim*). In this study, it was decided to use the devoicing diacritic (i.e., [n̥]) where relevant, while this phenomenon is being investigated from a dialectological perspective.

- The transcription system employed in this study uses <ᵊ> to describe an ultra-short transitional vowel which does not trigger any phonological processes and appears according to predictable patterns (Dufour 2016; Watson et al. 2023a).
- The neutral vowel /ə/ is prosodically lighter than the other vowels and cannot be stressed (al-Kathiri and Dufour 2020, 182).
- Jibbali/Śḥərέt vowels, with the exception of /ə/, have long (/ā/, /ɛ̄/, /ē/, /ī/, /ɔ̄/, /ō/, /ū/) and long-nasalised counterparts (/ã/, /ɛ̃/, /ẽ/, /ĩ/, /ɔ̃/, /õ/, /ũ/). However, vowel length, *sensu stricto,* is marginally phonemic: long and long-nasalised vowels are chiefly the result of phonological processes such as the intervocalic deletion of labials (see below). Long vowels are found in diminutive patterns (Johnstone 1973). However, this can be explained diachronically by the presence of diphthongs in Mehri where Jibbali/Śḥərέt has long vowels (Johnstone 1973).

As for the rest of the Jibbali/Śḥərέt sounds described above, they are phonetically akin to those of Arabic.

10.2. Phonological Processes

Jibbali/Śḥərέt is known for the complexity of its phonological and morphological processes in comparison to the other MSA languages and Semitic at large. The following is a rough sketch of the phonological processes commonly encountered in this study.

10.2.1. Intervocalic Deletion of Labials

When between two vowels, not including the ultra-short non-phonological vowel <ᵊ> (Dufour 2016), the voiced bilabial stop /b/ and the bilabial nasal /m/ are lost. In most cases, they are replaced by a long vowel and a long nasalised vowel respectively (Rubin 2014, 28, 30):

ḳɔ̄r 'grave' < *ḳebɔ́r
gū̃l '(male) camel' < *gemúl

Occasionally, [i] may precede the resulting long (or long nasalised) vowel (Rubin 2014, 28, 30).

10.2.2. /n/, /l/, and /r/ in Unstressed Syllables

These three phonemes cannot be realised at the onset of an open unstressed syllable (al-Kathiri and Dufour 2020, 183):

nbaʕ 'chase away' < *nibáʕ

Post-tonically, closed syllables also do not tolerate a sonorant at the onset:

yəśḵɔ́ṭɔrn 'they (M.PL) quarrel' < * yəśḵɔ́ṭɔrən

10.2.3. Nasals

When adjacent to a nasal, /n/ or /m/, /e/ is raised to [i] and /ɔ/ to [u] (al-Kathiri and Dufour 2020, 183):

ḏunúb 'tail' < *ḏɔnɔ́b
axnít 'to take out' < *axnét

10.2.4. Gutturals

/ḥ/, /x/, /ġ/, and /ʕ/ have a lowering effect on the adjacent vowels (al-Kathiri and Dufour 2020, 184), e.g., /ɛ/ is realised as [a]. Moreover, a full vowel becomes a short neutral vowel when it is part of an open syllable and precedes a guttural (al-Kathiri and Dufour 2020, 184):

šəʕíl 'strength' < *šɛʕil

10.2.5. Plain Voiceless Consonants

Unstressed vowels cannot stand between two plain (i.e., not 'emphatic') voiceless consonants (al-Kathiri and Dufour 2020, 185). This applies not only to Jibbali/Śḥərɛ́t, but also to the other MSA languages. This process has been labelled ©© or the 'idle glottis' effect in the literature (Bendjaballah and Ségéral 2014):

skɔf 'to sit' < *sɔkɔ́f[30]

10.2.6. Pre-consonantal /l/ and /r/ Deletion

These phonemes are lost in pre-consonantal position, especially in the core lexicon. In the case of /l/, the shift also occurs irregularly

---

[30] Compare ḳɔdɔ́r 'to be able'.

in the verbal system in stressed syllables (al-Kathiri and Dufour 2020, 185):

kɔb 'dog, wolf' < *kɔlb

šḥak 'to pour' (perfective 1.C.SG and 2.M.SG.) < *šḥalk < √šḥl

As for /r/, the phenomenon seems to be limited to core lexicon:

ḳun 'horn' < *ḳurn

10.3. Definiteness

The Jibbali/Śḥərέt definite article is a prefix commonly encountered in its basic form ɛ- ~ e-. It is attached to nouns to express definiteness, and is required when a personal suffix is attached:

e-dɔ́fərš 'his badness'

The definite article is prone to allomorphy, as is the case with most parts of speech in this language. It can manifest in the form of several allomorphs, some of which are not entirely predictable.

When attached to a term with an initial guttural consonant, it takes on the quality of the vowel that follows said consonant:

a-ʕáśər 'the friend'

ɔ-hɔ̄t 'the snake'

o-xofέt 'the window'

When attached to a word-initial vowel, the definite article emerges as a lengthening of this vowel:

īḏɛ́n 'the ear'

An initial semi-vowel /y/ normally geminates when the definite article is attached:

e-yyet 'the she-camel'

The definite article triggers the intervocalic deletion of labials (see above):

ɔ́b 'the door' < **e-bɔb*

ĩẓ́ḥɔ́t 'the salt' < **e-miẓ́ḥɔ́t*

The definite article can be omitted in some cases. This often happens before an initial sonorant. Despite the tendency of nouns beginning with a plain voiceless consonant not to take the definite article (Rubin 2014, 84), this study offers at least three counterexamples, respectively in entries **(96)** and **(162)** of the al-Shahri collection, and entry **(5)** of the MLZ collection:

e-ffudún 'the stone'

e-kkəʕéb 'crockery'

o-śúrəʕ 'the sails'

See also the gemination of the first consonant of the syntactically definite noun *kelṭ* in entry number **(206)** of the al-Shahri collection.

10.4. ε- as a Relativiser and a Genitive Exponent

In Jibbali/Śḥərɛ́t, the prefix ε- functions as a relativiser and a genitive exponent (in addition to ḏ-),[31] as well as being the basic

---

[31] The prefix ḏ- has been described as a Mehrism which can be used interchangeably with ε-. However, recent fieldwork points to a more

form of the definite article. As a relativiser and genitive exponent, it seems to behave morphophonologically like the definite article, at least in part:

> ɔ ġɔlɔ́b l-ōl-š ɔ l-eš miṭɔrˀ lɔ 'You cannot blame a person for keeping his own property' (entry **(83)** of the al-Shahri collection)

Here, the relativiser takes the form ɔ-, because of [ɔ] as the leftmost vowel in the following term ġɔlɔ́b, according to the same principle described above for the definite article. The same seems to apply to the genitive exponent:

> ɛḏīlín əntəktέk lhes e-ḳāḥáf o gʲūḏɛ́t 'so-and-so boils like a pot full of corn' (entry **(1)** of the MLZ collection)

In the above expression, the segment o gʲūḏɛ́t means 'of corn'. It is noteworthy that the assimilation of vowel quality described above for terms beginning with a guttural consonant also applies to /g/, despite Johnstone's exclusion of this phoneme from this phenomenon (JL, xxix–xxx).

10.5. Negation

The unmarked negator for both verbal and nominal phrases is the circumfix ɔ(l)… lɔ (Rubin 2014, 330):

> ɔ tékən lhes ɔ̄z ɛ nkśɔ́t lɛ-ɛnuf e-skinˀ lɔ 'don't be like a goat who found the knife' (entry **(7)** of the al-Shahri collection)

---

complex situation, whereby the two prefixes have their own respective functions, and only seldom overlap.

fɛ́kər ɔl ʕib lɔ 'poverty is no sin' (entry **(2)** of the elicited proverbs collection)

However, as described in the conclusions chapter, there exist several variants to this norm.

10.6. Independent Personal Pronouns and Personal Suffixes

Table 6: Jibbali/Śḥərɛ́t independent personal pronouns

	Singular	Dual	Plural
1.C.	he	(ə)ši	nḥa(n)
2.M.	hɛt	(ə)ti	tum̥
2.F.	hit		tɛn̥
3.M.	šɛ	ši	šum̥
3.F.	sɛ		sɛn̥

Dual personal pronouns are now largely obsolete, and do not appear in the expressions analysed in this study.

Table 7: Personal suffixes (for singular / plural nouns)

	Singular	Dual	Plural
1.C.	-i	-(ə)ši / -ɛ́ši	-(ə)n / -ɛ́n
2.M.	-(ə)k / -ɛ́k	-(ə)ši / -ɛ́ši	-(ə)kum / -ɔ́kum
2.F.	-(ə)š / -ɛ́š		-(ə)kən / -ɛ́kən
3.M.	-(ə)š / -ɛ́š	-(ə)ši / -ɛ́ši	-(ə)hum / -ɔ́hum
3.F.	-(ə)s / -ɛ́s		-(ə)sən / -ɛ́sən

These suffixes may express possession and the direct object of a verb (Rubin 2014, 48). The latter can also be expressed by attaching these suffixes to the pseudo-preposition (or direct object marker) *t-* (Rubin 2014, 54). When this is the case, the following forms result:

Table 8: Direct object marker + personal suffixes

	Singular	Dual	Plural
1.C.	tɔ	tɔ́s̃i	tun
2.M.	tɔk	tɔ́s̃i	tókum
2.F.	tɔs̃		tókən
3.M.	tɔš	tɔ́ši	tóhum
3.F.	tɔs		tósən

This rule is not invariable, and some exceptions do exist, especially with regard to the vowels. For example, some speakers from the Kuria Muria archipelago whose speech was recorded in the 1980s use [ə] instead of [ɔ]:

> *her ṭōron təš b-e-rɛbᵊreb i-núkaʕ* 'when we break it into the sea, it comes' (Castagna 2018, 139)

10.7. Jibbali/Śḥərɛ́t verbal classes

The following table (after al-Kathiri and Dufour 2020, 180) summarises the most productive verbal classes of Jibbali/Śḥərɛ́t.[32]

---

[32] The forms recorded correspond to the verbal morphology of a speaker of eastern Jibbali/Śḥərɛ́t from Gufa.

1. Introduction

Table 9: Jibbali/Śḥərε̄t verbal classes[i]

(For notes to Table 9, see p. 42.)

Verbal class	Gloss	Perfective Third person[ii]	Imperfective 3.M.SG.	Subjunctive 3.M.SG.
Ga	to be able	ḳɔdɔ́r	yəḳɔ́dər	yɔ́ḳdər
Gb	to shiver with fear	féḏər	yəfeḏɔ́r	yəfḏɔ́r
H1[iii]	to escape	əfflét	yəffelɔ́t	yέflət
H2	to cut the limbs of (a slaughtered animal)	əgúdəl	yəgúdələn	yəgɔ́dəl
H3	to distract	əġéfəl	yəġéfələn	yəġéfəl
H4	to separate	əbdéd	yəbdédən	yəbdéd
H5	to guide	ədelél	yədelélən	yədelél
T1	to become poor	fɔ́ṭkər	yəfteḳɔ́r	yəftéḳər
T2	to watch	əfterég	yəfterégən	yəfterɔ́g
Š1[iv]	to lack, miss	šəḳṣér	yəšḳeṣɔ́r	yəšέḳṣər
Š2	to bargain	šəḳέṣər	yəšḳέṣərən	yəšḳέṣər
ᵠH1[v]	to hurl	ġəḏfér	yəġɛḏefɔ́r	yəġáḏfər
ᵠN1	to fall down	əngərdéś	yəngērdɔ́ś	yəngέrdəś
ᵠH2	to stare haggardly	əṣenífər	yəṣenífərən	yəṣenéfər
ᵠN2	(of a camel) to roll in the dust	ənbəʕér	yənbəʕérən	yənbəʕér
ᵠY	to shriek	ṣəġirér	yəṣġirér	yəṣġír
ᵠNY	to go pale	ənʕifirér	yənʕifirér	yənʕáffər

Notes to Table 9

[i] For a thorough overview of the verbal paradigms, see Rubin (2014), Dufour (2016), and al-Kathiri and Dufour (2020).

[ii] 3.M.SG., 3.M.PL, and 3.F.PL forms of the perfective are identical.

[iii] Al-Kathiri and Dufour's transcription records the H-stems as Ȟ1, Ȟ2, Ȟ3, Ȟ4, and Ȟ5. The caron above the H means that the etymological /h/ of the prefixed morpheme of these verbal classes has disappeared in Jibbali/Śḥərέt.

[iv] In al-Kathiri and Dufour's transcription, the S of this and the following verbal class have a tilde < ~ > instead of a caron above. This is because the Jibbali/Śḥərέt prefix is a voiceless alveo-palatal labialised sibilant /š/ (Bellem and Watson 2017), rather than a plain voiceless palato-alveolar sibilant /š/.

[v] Q stands for quadriliteral. Hence these verbal classes apply to quadriliteral and quinqueliteral (true and reduplicated) roots.

According to al-Kathiri and Dufour (2020, 181), however, H4, H5, ᵂH2, and ᵂN2 stems are rare.

The above table does not take into account anisomorphic roots, that is (al-Kathiri and Dufour 2020, 186):

> When a root is used in a class where the number of slots in the patterns exceeds that of the consonants in the root, the last one or two consonants of the root are repeated to fill in the exceeding slots. But in such cases (i.e., when the root is 'too short' or anisomorphic), the pattern eventually selected will often differ from the default pattern for a given morphological cell.

Each of the above verbal classes tends to convey a certain nuance of meaning:[33]

- Ga- and Gb-stems represent the basic triliteral verb, with the Gb-stem comprising verbs of quality (Dufour 2016, 94).
- The H1-stem is primarily causative, but can also be purely lexical and not convey any causative meaning (Rubin 2014, 118).
- The H2-stem[34] comprises denominative verbs and is used to form the causative of intransitive verbs (Rubin 2014, 112).
- The H3-stem is similar in semantic value to the H2-stem (Dufour 2016, 94).
- The H4- and H5-stems are too rare to make generalisations as to their semantics.

---

[33] However, this principle is not universal.

[34] This verbal class is called D/L-stem in Johnstone's and Rubin's works.

- The Š1-stem conveys an array of semantic nuances, comprising causative-reflexive, causative-passive, reflexive, passive, and estimative, as well as a few lexical verbs (Rubin 2014, 122–23).
- The Š2-stem is mainly reciprocal, although this class also contains a few lexical verbs (Rubin 2014, 125–26).
- T1-stem verbs can be reciprocal, passive, intransitive, or reflexive. This class too includes a few lexical verbs (Rubin 2014, 128).
- The T2-stem seems to be in a derivational relationship with the H2-stem, whereby a T2-stem is often a passive, reflexive, or reciprocal of the corresponding H2-stem. This verbal class also contains many Arabic loans from forms V and VI (Rubin 2014, 131–32).
- Quadriliteral and quinqueliteral verbs usually describe complex, unusual, or extreme circumstances, events, and actions. The N-stems of quadriliterals and quinqueliterals are usually reflexives and intransitives.

11.0. Methodology and Presentation

Most of the proverbs, sayings and idiomatic expressions presented in this study have been extracted from the above-mentioned sources by means of careful perusal over a two-year period between 2021 and 2023. With regard to the al-Shahri collection, the tokens had already been analysed in Castagna (2022a), to which the present analysis owes much. However, new details regarding the al-Shahri collection emerged in the period between

2022 and 2023, thanks to S. al-Amri's work and invaluable insights. These have been implemented in the existing analysis. As for the other sources, which, unlike al-Shahri's, do not come with audio recordings, the selected tokens were recorded by S. al-Amri in the form of mobile phone voice notes, and subsequently analysed by both authors over the telephone or video-calls. When the written texts do not match S. al-Amri's rendition, this is made clear in the relevant entry.

Besides the paremiological interest of this study, nearly all the entries feature a brief grammatical commentary which describes the contents of the utterance in linguistic terms. Where relevant, the equivalent proverb in Mehri is provided: the Mehri proverbs are taken from Sima (2005) and the Mehri Lexicon (ML). The latter is Johnstone's Mehri lexicon. The former is a work of the late Austrian scholar Alexander Sima, who presents 101 proverbs in the Mehri dialect of Hawf, Yemen.[35] With regard to the transcription system used in this work, it resembles that of JL, except for the character <ä>, which is used to represent a front to central mid-high vowel.[36] In terms of presentation, each

---

[35] An interesting (and apparently inexplicable) feature of Sima's proverb collection *vis-à-vis* al-Shahri's is that in both collections the entries are presented in exactly the same order. Some sort of traditional citation order presented itself as the most intriguing (and not unlikely) explanation for such a coincidence. However, when contacted by S. al-Amri, Ali al-Shahri denied the existence of such a citation order and stated that the presentation order in his collection is totally random.

[36] See Sima (2009, 10–22) for a description of Sima's transcription system.

source is treated differently. Here follows a summary of the presentation styles used for each source:

- The Language of Aad

    (entry number)
    Proverb transcription in Jibbali/Śḥərε̄t
    Original English translation (from the text)
    الترجمة باللغة العربية (Arabic translation)

- MLZ

    (entry number) reference
    Proverb transcription in Jibbali/Śḥərε̄t
    المثل الجبالي\الشحري بالنسخ الاصلي (Proverb in the original Arabic transcription)
    الترجمة في اللغة العربية (Arabic translation)
    English translation

- JL

    (entry number) reference
    Proverb transcription in Jibbali/Śḥərε̄t
    Original English translation

- Elicited proverbs

    (entry number)
    Proverb transcription in Jibbali/Śḥərε̄t
    المثل الجبالي\الشحري (Proverb in Arabic transcription)
    English translation

The MLZ and elicited entries have been translated into English by the authors, whereas those from al-Shahri and JL are presented with their original English translation. An Arabic translation for the JL and elicited entries is provided below (§4.0). The Mehri proverbs presented as equivalents of Jibbali/Śḥərέt items are reported with Sima's German translation.

12.0. Glossing

1 = first person
2 = second person
3 = third person
M = masculine
F = feminine
C = common gender
SG = singular
PL = plural

As mentioned above, the 3.M.SG., 3.M.PL., and 3.F.PL. of the perfective are identical in all verbal forms. Therefore, when encountered, they are labelled as 'third person' in this wor

2. PROVERBS AND LINGUISTIC ANALYSIS

1.0. Al-Shahri Collection

(1)
ɛ́bśér b-egḗdɛ́m b-egḗdɛ́m xarɔ́gʲ
Gaidam came, Gaidam died
ابشر بيجييدام ولكنه مات

This is said to describe a happy occasion which unexpectedly turns unhappy (al-Shahri 2000, 74, 242).

Egḗdɛ́m is a masculine personal name with no clear equivalent in Arabic, which can be compared with Jibbali/Śḥərɛ́t *gɔdəm* 'piece of bread' (JL, 71), Mehri *godəm* 'id.' (ML, 114), and Soqotri *gódim* 'morceau' (LS, 103). As far as onomastics is concerned, we find *gdm* as a personal name in Safaitic (al-Manaser and Macdonald 2017, 1452, 4302), and perhaps in the Sabaic lineage name *gdmn* (Robin 1981, 326).

The verbal form *ɛ́bśér* is a perfective third person of a H1-stem meaning 'to give good news' (JL, 29). The /g/ phoneme in *xarɔ́gʲ*, a perfective third person of a Ga-stem meaning 'to die' (JL, 304) is realised with palatalisation, as it seems to be in most positions in the variety of Jibbali/Śḥərɛ́t spoken by al-Shahri, while it seems to be realised without palatalisation in *Gedam*.

In view of the meaning of the first verb, a better translation for the proverb is 'they gave good news about Egḗdɛ́m, and Egḗdɛ́m died'.

(2)

ɛ̄ bṣer ɔ yɔ́xɔ́f

He who sees the reality of life, never settles

من عرف وتحقق فانه سيغادر ولن يحل

If someone has been mistreated (or not treated well enough) by a host, they use this saying upon being asked why they are leaving (al-Shahri 2000, 74, 242). The verb transcribed here as *bṣér* is actually *ɛbṣér*, a perfective third person of a H1-stem < √bṣr meaning 'to see' (MLZ, 130: أبصر. رأى), and is not recorded in JL. Therefore, *ɛ bṣér* is to be interpreted as **ɛ ɛbṣér* = relativiser + third-person singular of a perfective H1-stem verb.

The verb *yɔ́xɔ́f* is an imperfective 3.M.SG. of a Gb-stem < √wxf meaning 'to come to a new place and settle' (al-Kathiri and Dufour 2020, 208–9). The prefixed negation *ɔ* without a suffixed *lɔ* is unexpected here (Rubin 2014, 332–34).

(3)

iblís her ɔ šeš ʕiśa lɔ idhɔ́r śɔ́ṭ ṭrut

If the devil can't find dinner, he lights two fires

إبليس اذا لم يجد عشاء يوقد نارين

This proverb is used as a remark about those living beyond their means, and often serves as an encouragement to them to moderate their excesses (al-Shahri 2000, 74, 242).

The cleft structure of this sentence is, as will be seen below, fairly common in this collection of proverbs. The verbal form *idhɔ́r* is an imperfective 3.M.SG. of a H1-stem meaning 'to make a big fire' (JL, 36). The noun *śɔ́ṭ* 'fire' (JL, 258) is grammatically feminine, as shown by the agreement with the feminine numeral *ṭrut* 'two' (cf. its masculine counterpart *ṭrɔh*).

This can also be found as إبليس هس أبْش عثئ لو دهر شّوط ثُرُت in MLZ (342).[1]

(4)

ɛ̄ bédər yəšɔ́ḳ

Who comes first, his animals drink first

من سبق غيره على الماء يسقي حيوانه قبل الاخرين اي من سبق لبق

This is said to praise someone's promptness at carrying out an action and this person's subsequent gain, in contrast to someone else who did not act as promptly and effectively (al-Shahri 2000, 74, 242), in a similar fashion to *The early bird catches the worm*.

The relativiser appears here as a long vowel ɛ̄ instead of the expected short vowel ɛ. The verbal form *bédər* is a perfective third person of a Gb-stem meaning 'to outrun' (JL, 23), or 'to precede' (MLZ, 118: سبق). The verbal form *išɔ́ḳ* is an imperfective 3.M.SG. of a weak III-y Ga-stem < √šky meaning 'to irrigate, to give a drink' (JL, 262), which exhibits the loss of the last root consonant in the imperfective that is typical of this verbal class (Rubin 2014, 202).

This expression is recorded by MLZ (118) as أبدر يْشُقَ.

The corresponding Mehri proverb is *ḏä-sbōḵ, yhäyḵ* 'Wer zuerst (an die Wasserstelle) kommt, tränkt (seine Tiere zuerst)' (Sima 2005, 72), whose German translation 'Whoever comes first (to the watering hole) waters (his animals first)' applies also to its Jibbali/Śḥərɛ̄t counterpart.

---

[1] The use of *hes* 'when' (Rubin 2014, 368) in this variant of the proverb, instead of *her* 'if', is noteworthy.

(5)

ɔ tšeṭeʕánanᵊ ʕar báʕlət ḳerún

Only the one who has horns can butt

لا تناطح إلا صاحبة القرون

This is used to refer to doing something beyond one's abilities (al-Shahri 2000, 74, 243).

The verbal form *tšeṭeʕanan* is an imperfective 3.F.SG. of a Š2-stem < √*ṭʕn* meaning 'to keep stabbing' (JL, 273). The suffix *-an* is found in the imperfective of H2, Š2, and T2 stems in the singular and plural forms, but not in the dual forms (Rubin 2014, 141–42).[2] Rubin further states that the vowel in this suffix is [ə]. However, Dufour (2016, 36) posits that there is a tendency to realise a secondary stress accent on the penultimate cv syllable in yes/no questions, protases, and topicalisation, which could result in a [ɛ] ~ [a][3] instead of the expected [ə], and indeed, the speaker's intonation in the recording does argue in favour of topicalisation of the verb.

The feminine noun *báʕlət* 'owner' (JL, 22) is one of the few terms in Jibbali/Śḥərɛ̃́t that can be used in the construct state (Rubin 2014, 88). The Mehri counterpart of this proverb is *täšdaḥrän ār ḏ-bīs ḳrōn* 'Es kann nur die (jenige Ziege) (mit den Hörnern) stoßen, die Hörner hat' (Sima 2005, 72), that is, 'Only the goat that has horns can strike', which also applies to the Jibbali/Śḥərɛ̃́t proverb.

---

[2] It is also found in some unproductive and obsolescent verbal classes, namely: H3, H4, H5, ᵠH2, and ᵠN2 (al-Kathiri and Dufour 2020, 180).

[3] It would be [a] in this case, due to the adjacent voiced pharyngeal fricative [ʕ].

(6)

ɔ tḵun ʕar ɛ irɔ̃t

Only the one who delivers the child can bring it up

لا تربي إلا من ولدت

This is a remark about situations where someone is supposed to take responsibility for something (chiefly parenthood and animal husbandry) but appears not to be up to the task.

According to JL (147), the first verbal form *tḵun* is an imperfective 3.F.SG. of a Ga-stem verb derived from the root √ḵnv,[4] meaning 'to rear, look after, bring up'. The second verb is a perfective 3.F.SG. of a Ga-stem verb derived from the root √brw 'to give birth' (JL, 28), which would normally emerge as *birɔ̃t*. In this case, [b] is elided because of the preceding relativiser ɛ.[5]

(7)

ɔ tékən lhes ɔ̃z ɛ nkɕɔ́t lɛ-ɛnuf e-skinᵊ lɔ

Don't be like a goat who found the knife

لا تكن كالغنمة التي نبشت على نفسها السكينة

This is used as a piece of advice to someone who is engaging in a dangerous activity that will likely result in trouble (al-Shahri 2000, 75, 243).

---

[4] In the *Jibbali Lexicon*, the root consonant v represents an unspecified vowel (JL, xxxvi).

[5] According to Rubin (2014, 29), the bilabial consonant deletion process may operate across a word/morpheme boundary when the second term is a particle with a pronominal suffix, or when a word once had a dual suffix. This case seems not to fall within either category.

This proverb employs a rather everyday register of the language that does not call for a detailed grammatical analysis. However, it is worth noting the coalescence of the definite article ɛ- and the term ɔz 'she-goat' (JL, 5) into ɔ́z. The negative command is realised as a negated verbal phrase employing the subjunctive 2.M.SG. form of a G-stem tékən 'to be' (JL, 138), as expected (Rubin 2014, 154). The verbal form nkś́ɔ́t is a perfective 3.F.SG. of a Ga-stem meaning 'to uncover'.[6] Thus, the phrase nkś́ɔ́t lɛ-ɛ-nuf means 'she uncovered against herself': the use of this verb followed by the preposition l- 'against' is malefactive and is probably best translated as 'she turned against herself'. The corresponding Mehri proverb is l-tᵃḳäʿ hīs ḥōz ḏīk ḏä-kᵃś́ōt la-ḥnäfs skīn lä 'Sei nicht wie jene Ziege, die gegen sich selbst (d.h. zu ihrem eigenen Unglück) ein Messer ausgegraben hat' (Sima 2005, 72).

(8)

ɔ təġɔ́rɔb her a-ʕáś́ərk ɛdᵊ laxálf ʕãš
You never know how good your friend is until he leaves you

لن تعرف قيمة صديقك حتى تستبدل به اخر

This proverb stresses the importance of good friends, and the regret of not recognising in time the qualities of someone who has left (al-Shahri 2000, 75, 244).

This is one of the 18 proverbs from al-Shahri's collection that were transcribed and partially analysed by Rubin (2014, 642–45). Rubin translates 'you don't know (the value of) your friend until you move away from him'. However, the presence of

---

[6] MLZ (939) does not record the Ga-stem stem from this root.

her 'if' (JL, 98) renders this interpretation doubtful. The term *ʕaśər* 'friend' is recorded by both JL (17) and MLZ (628) with a short vowel. The verbal form *laxalf* < √*xlf* 'to change, to leave behind', a subjunctive 2.M.SG of a H1-stem (JL, 299), exhibits the expected loss of the *t-* prefix typical of H1-stems and other verbal classes (Rubin 2014, 146; Testen 1992), and the vocalisation [a] triggered by the guttural first root consonant, in contrast to the open-mid front vowel [ɛ] in H1-stems of strong roots (Rubin 2014, 174).

This proverb is formally comparable with the Mehri proverb *tġōräb ḳīmät ḏ-rībāʿak lä, är at-tä thaxläf mänh* 'Du kennst den Wert deines Gefährten erst, wenn du dich von ihm trennst' (Sima 2005, 73), that is 'You don't know the value of your companion until you part with him', which translates the Jibbali/Śḥərɛ́t expression in a more suitable fashion.

Interestingly, the Arabic translation of the proverb employs the form X verb استبدل followed by the preposition ب, meaning 'to replace, substitute' (Wehr and Cowan 1976, 46), and اخر 'other'. Therefore, there is a possibility that the actual meaning of the proverb is 'you don't know the value of your companion until you replace him with someone else'.

(9)

ɔ ttek šinı̃t ʕar mən a-ʕeṭélk

The louse only bites you from your old clothes

لا تاكلك القملة إلا من ثوبك البالي القديم

This is said when trouble is caused by family or close friends (al-Shahri 2000, 75, 244).

The imperfective 2.M.SG prefix *t-* and the first root consonant of the verb *t-te*, which is a G-stem < √*twy* 'to eat' (JL, 273), coalesce, so that they are realised as a geminate [tː]. The term *ṣeṭél* actually means 'rotten rag; old cloth, old clothing' (JL, 8). Cf. the Mehri equivalent *attäywäk ār känmīt ḏa-xläḳak* 'Es frißt dich nur die Laus deines (eigenen) Kleides' (Sima 2005, 73).

(10)

ɔ tštéḳɛ ar ẽṣteḥɔ́t

Only those who had breakfast, drink

لا ترغب في الشرب إلا التي اكلت في الصباح

This proverb is used when evidence indicates that someone has eaten, despite that person affirming otherwise. The allusion to a milch animal is probably due to these animals being well fed (al-Shahri 2000, 75, 244).

The verbal form *tšteḳɛ* is an imperfective 3.F.SG. of a T1-stem < √*šky* meaning 'to drink' (JL, 262).[7] The term *ẽṣteḥɔ́t* < √*ṣbḥ*, a passive participle of a T-stem, *e-meṣteḥɔ́t* 'milch sheep' (MLZ, 534) is not recorded in JL.

(11)

e-gizᵊmétk ṭer fegʲᵊrɔ́

You swore on the Bedu

حنثك على عاتق البدو

---

[7] The perfective third-person form of this verb is *šuṣ̌i*, with the assimilation of [tk'] > [ṣ̌] (Dufour 2016, 404), instead of the expected *šutḳi*, which is attested with the marginal meaning 'to be irrigated' (JL, 262).

When someone wants to convince someone else to break an oath, the former may use this formula jokingly, as it is believed that the Bedouin take oaths lightly (al-Shahri 2000, 76, 245).

The word *gizˀmɛ́t* 'oath' is not found under the root √gzm (JL, 81–82). It is, however, found in MLZ (189), and in Rubin's supplement to JL (2014, 661) as "*gəzmɛ́t* (def. *ɛgzəmɛ́t*) 'swearing'." The term *fegʲˀrɔ́* 'bedouin'[8] is a plural *nisbah* adjective from *fɛ́gər* 'dawn, dawn-prayer, Nejd (in Dhofar)' (JL, 53). The semantic connection finds an explanation in that the Bedouin groups with whom Jibbali/Śḥərɛ̃́t speakers are in contact most often come from the Nejd, north of the Dhofar mountains.

(12)
e-gidrét ɔ lhes iyẽnˀ lɔ
The land has no share
ليس للارض قسمة اي حصة

This expresses idiomatically the concept that earth has no right to claim a share of food or drink, so victuals should not be wasted onto it (al-Shahri 2000, 76, 245).

The term *iyẽn* 'share' < √ʔmn is a variant of *yẽn* (JL, 3). Johnstone records this variant as typical of the eastern dialects of the language. This proverb corresponds to Mehri *arź hīs ḥaṭṭ lä* 'Die Erde hat keinen Anteil' (Sima 2005, 73).

---

[8] The speakers of Jibbali/Śḥərɛ̃́t use this term to refer to the Mahrah, and the singular *fegrí* ~ *fegʲrí* to indicate the Mehri language, alongside the terms derived from √mhr. The terms based on the root √fgr are perceived as a derogatory by the Mahrah (Watson p.c.).

(13)

e-ged yəbíʕan bə ḥanufəh

The valuable thing shows its own value

الانسان الخلوق يقيّم نفسه

The language of this proverb is admittedly a mixture of Jibbali/Śḥərɛ́t and Mehri (al-Shahri 2000, 76, 245), and indeed Sima records it in his collection of Mehri proverbs as *jīd yśōm ḥnäfh* (2005, 73–74).

Its meaning indicates that good things do not need to be advertised, as their worth shows itself. The term *ged* is Mehri for 'good' (ML, 128); cf. Jibbali/Śḥərɛ́t *raḥím* (JL, 210). The verb *yəbíʕan* is the Arabic verb 'to sell' treated here as a II-weak H2-stem in the 3.M.SG. of the imperfective. The term *ḥanuf* reflects the Mehri word for 'self' *ḥənōf* (ML, 283); cf. Jibbali/Śḥərɛ́t *nuf* (JL, 181). The Mehri term must not be confused with Jibbali/Śḥərɛ́t *ḥanuf* which strictly means 'to (one)self' (JL, 181). The [ə] vowel following *ḥanuf* 'self' represents the 3.M.SG. personal suffix *-əh* in Mehri (Watson 2012, 72–73, 77).

(14)

əxerᵊ kɔb sīr ʕar kɔb rīṣ́

The moving dog is better than the dog which is lying down

الكلب السيار خير من الكلب الرابض

This is said to encourage someone to act on a matter (al-Shahri 2000, 76, 246).

The participial form *sīr* < √*syr* 'moving' must be a Mehrism, as the root is very productive in Mehri, where it includes a verb meaning 'to go', as well as an array of additional meanings (ML,

355). Conversely, this root is significantly less productive in Jibbali/Śḥərέt (JL, 233). According to MLZ (466), the above-mentioned root does yield a verb meaning to 'to follow'; cf. proverb number **(82)**. Similarly to *sīr*, the form *riś* is a participle, recorded by JL (203) as *reź* 'lazy' < √*rbẓ*. The Mehri counterpart of this saying is *kōb sōyär xayr män kōb rōbäź* 'Ein Hund, der sich bewegt, ist besser als ein Hund, der nur daliegt' (Sima 2005, 74).

(15)

ε̄ xfet ar ε̄ xfet bə šɔ́fɔl

The one who can hide her pregnancy is the best at keeping secrets

لم تخفي الا من اخفت الحمل

This is said of someone who is good at keeping secrets (al-Shahri 2000, 77, 246).

As in entry number **(2)** above, the long vowel in the relativiser ε must be interpreted as relativiser + third-person singular of a perfective third-person H1-stem verb: **ε-εxfet*. This verbal form is recorded in JL (299) as *axfe* 'to keep hidden' < √*xfy*. The term *šɔ́fɔl* 'belly' exhibits some interesting traits: it seems to be realised as such only in the eastern dialects of the language, whereas in the central and western dialects it is pronounced *šɔ́fəl*. Moreover, according to JL (260), it is lexically feminine despite being grammatically masculine. It can, however, be used both as masculine and as feminine; cf. entry number **(37)** of this collection, and entry number **(12)** of the MLZ collection.

(16)

ε xarɔ́gʲ ġasᵊrē eḳiɔ́r k-ḥaṣaf

The one who dies at night can be buried in the morning

الذي يموت بالليل يقبر في الصباح

This is the second proverb of this collection analysed by Rubin (2014, 642) and means that everything must be done at the right time (al-Shahri 2000, 77, 246).

The term *gasˀre* 'at night' has a long final vowel here, which is recorded by neither by JL (89) nor by MLZ (667). The verbal form *eḳiɔ́r* is an imperfective 3.M.SG. of a passive Ga-stem < √kbr meaning 'to bury', hence, in this case, 'to be buried' (JL, 140). This proverb corresponds to Mehri *ḏ-mōt b-ḥalläyy, yaḳbōr k-ṣōbaḥ* 'Wer in der Nacht stirbt, wird am Morgen begraben' (Sima 2005, 74).

(17)

ɛ dirím gʲũlš yəs̃ḳɔ́ṣ̂a ʕālˀgʲán

The one whose camel is killed is only compensated by having a small camel

الذي يعقر جمله الكبير يُعَوَّض بجملٍ صغير

This proverb is used as a comment on the fact that what is given as compensation might not be commensurate with the loss (al-Shahri 2000, 77, 247).

The semantics of the verbs *dirím* and *yəs̃ḳɔ́ṣ̂a* are very specific to the local camel-raiding culture: the former < √drm 'to cut (a camel's) hocks, slaughter livestock (usually in a punitive raid); to hit someone hard', is a perfective third person of a Ga-stem passive (JL, 41). The latter < √ḳṣ́y 'to be paid, to receive blood money' is an imperfective 3.M.SG. of a Š1-stem (JL, 158). The expected definite article does not occur in the term *gʲũl-š* 'his camel', as often happens after a sonorant. The term *ʕālˀgʲán* < √ʕlg, recorded as *ʕalgɛn* '2–4 year old camel' in JL (12), is a diminutive form. It is noteworthy that the first vowel is long, contrary to the notation found in JL. MLZ (644) does not record this term. Cf. the Mehri proverb *ad-dirām bʿīrāh, yäšḳayź ʿaylūj* 'Der, dessen Kamelhengst getötet wurde, erhält als Entschädigung Kalb' (Sima 2005, 74).

(18)

e-diní ɔl ʕarṣ̂ ḏ āḥsar lɔ

The width of the earth is not like the width of a cloth belt

الدنيا ليست كعرض الإزار

This expression is used when someone does not know which way to turn, either physically or metaphorically (al-Shahri 2000, 77, 247).

The term *ʕarṣ̂*, whose lack of the expected definite article is likely due to the presence of the voiced pharyngeal fricative [ʕ], means 'width', which may lead one to suspect interference from Arabic, as only in MLZ (620) is the term recorded with the abovementioned meaning, along with other meanings related to weaning and meeting, which are recorded also in JL (15–16). Likewise, the term *āḥsar* < *a-maḥsar 'cloth belt' is recorded in MLZ (236), but not in JL.

(19)

e-défər xaṣ°m ɛ̄ nufš

The bad person is the enemy of himself

الانسان السيئ عدو نفسه

The meaning of this proverb is self-explanatory.

The genitive exponent ɛ and the definiteness marker ɛ preceding *nuf* 'self' coalesce, and are pronounced as a single long vowel *ɛ̄*. The Mehri counterpart of this proverb is *bnädäm ġamm xaṣm ḏa-ḥnäfh* 'Ein schlechter Mensch ist der Feind seiner selbst' (Sima 2005, 74–75).

(20)
e-défər əxer ʕãš mɛ̄l xɔh
The bad (person), a full mouth is better than him
السيء أفضل منه ملاء الفم

This is a reminder that it is expedient to accept any payment from a person who is in debt, as doing otherwise might lead to bitter consequences (al-Shahri 2000, 78, 248).

It is noteworthy that no genitive exponent can be found between the terms *mɛ̄l* 'fullness' (JL, 171) and *xɔh* (JL, 310), which could point to *mɛ̄l* being one of the few terms that can be used in the construct state, although it is not listed in Rubin (2014, 88). However, given the rarity of this term in the corpora, it is not possible to draw any conclusion in this respect. Alternatively, it is possible that the construct state was more widespread at the time when this proverb was coined, so that it came down the generations as it was, regardless of everyday language evolution. One must note, however, that the definite article, as has been pointed out above, may be omitted when following a sonorant. This proverb corresponds to Mehri *ġamm xayr mänh mlē ḏ-käff* '(Auch nur) eine Handvoll (von irgendetwas) ist besser als das Schlechte' (Sima 2005, 75), which translates as '(Even only) a handful (of anything) is better than the bad (person)', a translation that applies also to its Jibbali/Śḥərɛ̄t counterpart.

(21)

ɛd̠ilín ḥõl ẽžed iź ʕišyétʾ

So-and-so has taken the labour pains of the bird

فلان اخذ مخاض الحمامة البرية اي اناب عنها

This is a remark about someone who runs into trouble as a result of doing something, possibly unrequested, for someone else (al-Shahri 2000, 78, 248).

The verbal form *ḥõl* is a perfective third person of a Ga-stem < √*ḥml* meaning, among other things, 'to load; to take; to carry' (JL, 111). The plural form *ẽžed* < **e-mežed* 'labour pains' is not recorded, but, on the basis of similar CvCv́C forms—for example, *mɛrṭet/mirɛ́ṭ* 'instruction, message, parcel' (JL, 173)— must correspond to a singular **megdét*. Its being grammatically plural is shown by the subsequent use of the rather uncommon plural relativiser *iź* (Rubin 2014, 68) as a genitive exponent. The term *ʕišyétʾ* is from *ʕkb* 'pigeon' (JL, 11), with pre-pausal paragoge (Castagna 2018, 137). The term *ɛd̠ilín* 'so-and-so' (Rubin 2014, 64) corresponds to Arabic *fulān* 'id.', and functions as a proverbial affix, such as 'as the saying goes' (Norrick 2015, 24).

(22)

ɛd̠ilín e-nfaʕš beš i-míḥ

So-and-so's helpfulness[9] is wet

فلان عمله مبلول بالماء

This saying reminds the listener that some people's help is harmful. The semantic connection is explained by the fact that dry things are preserved, whereas wet things tend to decay (al-Shahri

---

[9] Al-Shahri (2000, 78) writes *hefulness*.

2000, 78, 248). The segment *e-nfaʕ-š* 'his help' contains the term *nfaʕ*, which is not recorded under the root √*nfʕ* by JL (181). MLZ (929), on the other hand, defines it as 'usefulness, help, aid' (النفع. المساعدة. العون).

The concept 'wet' is expressed here by means of periphrasis: *b-eš i-mîh* 'there is (the) water in it' or 'it has water'. Interestingly, the same periphrastic expression was used by a speaker of the insular (al-Ḥallānīya) dialect to express the same concept (Castagna 2018, 446). See also below, entry number **(33)**. Furthermore, although not formally comparable, the meaning of this proverb can be compared with that of the Mehri proverb *flän mänfaʕtäh bīs ḳaṣrōr* 'NN, in seinem Nutzen ist ein Körnchen Schmutz' (Sima 2005, 75).

(23)

ɛḏīlín ed-ešéḳɛ ṭer erᵊkíb

So-and-so has been given a drink whilst riding a beast of burden

فلان يسقي على ظهر الدابة

This refers to someone being helped unwillingly, so that the help this person is offered is of little use. The situation depicted by the proverb can be elucidated by the fact that drinking whilst riding a beast of burden is difficult, and most of the water will be spilt (al-Shahri 2000, 78, 249).

The verb *ešéḳɛ* < √*šky* 'to water, to give a drink', passive 3.M.SG. imperfective Ga-stem (JL, 262), is preceded by the prefix *(v)d-*, which, in combination with an imperfective verb, marks a circumstantial clause or indicates a progressive action (Rubin 2014, 158–61), so that the overall meaning of this expression is probably best translated as 'So-and-so is being given a drink whilst riding a beast of burden'.

(24)

ɛḏīlín ɔl ḳéləʕ be ʕiṇ dimʕɔ́tˀ lɔ
So-and-so didn't leave any tears in the eyes

فلان لم يُبقِ في العين دمعة

This expression is used to describe someone who has done something perfectly (al-Shahri 2000, 79, 249).

The third root consonant of the verb *ḳéləʕ*, a third-person perfective of a Ga-stem meaning 'to let, allow' (JL, 144), is a /ʕ/ which is desonorised to [ħ], as there is a long pause after it. The segment *be* is to be analysed as the preposition bə + the definite article preceding *ʕin* 'eye'. The final /n/ is desonorised/pre-aspirated in the latter term, as expected (Rubin 2014, 37).

(25)

ɛḏīlín ɔ kédəʕ b ɔ fédəʕ
He doesn't harm and he doesn't help

فلان لا فائدة منه ولا ضرر

This is used to describe someone who is completely neutral, or a good-for-nothing person (al-Shahri 2000, 79, 249).

The two terms *kédəʕ*, defined by MLZ (790) as 'to disturb' (يكدر), and *fédəʕ*, defined as 'relief, comfort' (MLZ, 691: الفرج), are both third-person perfectives of Ga-stems not recorded in JL. MLZ (790) records this proverb under the former entry as أَديليئن أَيكُدَعْ, and as أَذيلين أَفدع بو كَدَع under the latter (MLZ 691). Cf. also the Mehri proverb *flän lä-kdāʕ w-lä-nfāʕ* 'NN (macht) keinen Ärger, hat aber auch keinen Nutzen' (Sima 2005, 75).

(26)

ɛd̪īlín yəsxarɔ́ṭ ɛ̄sfɔ́r

So-and-so will argue even with the birds

فلان يشاتم الطيور

This expression describes a short-tempered person (al-Shahri 2000, 79, 249).

The verbal form *yəsxarɔ́ṭ* is an imperfective 3.M.SG. of a Š1-stem < √*xrṭ*, meaning 'to curse and swear at; to be able to be stripped of leaves' (JL, 305). The segment *ɛ̄sfɔ́r* 'the birds' has an initial long vowel as a result of the coalescence of the definite article and the first vowel of the term, which, contra JL (16), does not exhibit an initial /ʕ/ (< √*ʕsfr*). Conversely, MLZ (546) lists the term under the root √*sfr* and defines it as 'collective name for birds' (جمع عصفور. اسم جامع للطيور).[10] This expression formally corresponds to Mehri *flän yašxarṭan ʕasfēr* 'NN sucht eine Auseinandersetzung (sogar) mit den Vögeln' (Sima 2005, 75).

(27)

ɛd̪īlín axnīṭ meš šəʕil

So-and-so has taken all somebody else's energy

فلان أنهك او أُنهِكت قواه وصبره

This expression, whose meaning is self-explanatory, may either be used by the victim of such an action or by an observer (al-Shahri 2000, 79, 250).

The verb *axnīṭ*, a third-person perfective of a H1-stem meaning, among other things, 'to take out, take off', is listed in

---

[10] Compare Soqotri *isfero* 'oiseau' (LS, 70), which similarly lacks the etymological /ʕ/.

JL (303) as *axnít̞*, with a short vowel. Al-Shahri's (2000, 250) Arabic translation of this saying points out that the verb can be understood as an active as well as a passive form: أُنهِكت او أنهك. The nasal consonant [n] here neutralises the distinction between the active and passive vocalisations of the H1-stem verb in question (Rubin 2014, 42). The term *šəʕil* 'strength' is not recorded in the lexica. However, MLZ (803) records the verb *kaʕal* 'to hit something solid with strength' under the root √kʕl. The semantic connection is rather unproblematic, and given the high vocalic environment, a palatalisation /k/ > [š], as is well documented, seems likely (Bellem and Watson 2017, 627).

(28)

ɛd̪ilín eʕilīk̞ˤ leš ɔ́rrɔ́t
So-and-so has hung up the gall bladder against him
فلان علّقت ضده المرارة

This saying describes a forgetful person, on the basis of the folk belief that one can cause a person to forget something by hanging a gall bladder and speaking that person's name (al-Shahri 2000, 79, 250).

The verbal form *eʕilīk̞* is a third-person perfective of a passive H2-stem, meaning 'to hang (transitive)' (JL, 12), and is attested here with a long vowel. The term *ɔ́rrɔ́t* < *e-mɔrrɔ́t* 'gall bladder' is recorded as *mɛrrɔ́t* under the root √mrr (JL, 173).

(29)

ɛd̪ilín yərəġúm ɛ́ʕlɔ́k̞
So-and-so finds fault with gold
فلان يعيب دنانير الدهب

This describes a fussy person who finds fault with everything and everyone (al-Shahri 2000, 80, 250).

The verbal form *yərəġúm* is a 3.M.SG. imperfective of a Gb-stem meaning 'to criticise' (JL, 208). The peculiar vocalisation is due to allomorphy triggered by the guttural C^2, which results in /ə/ instead of /e/ (al-Kathiri and Dufour 2020, 187), and the sonorant C^3, resulting in /u/ instead of /ɔ/ (al-Kathiri and Dufour 2020, 183). The term *ʕɔlɔ́k̲* 'fine gold' (MLZ, 645: الذهب الخالص) is not recorded by JL. This is most certainly a plural form of a singular عولق = /ʕɔĺk̲/ ~ /ʕulk̲/, provided by al-Shahri in his commentary on this saying (al-Shahri 2000, 250).

(30)

ɛd̲ilín ɔ fek īdš berəkɔ́t ᵊ lɔ
He didn't rub the talisman
فلان لم يفرك يده بالبركة

This is said when bad people eventually get what they deserve (al-Shahri 2000, 80, 250).

Al-Shahri (2000, 80) translates 'he didn't rub the talisman' in English, and the same in Arabic (al-Shahri 2000, 250), and indeed, the verb *fek*, a third-person perfective of a G-stem deriving from the geminate root √fkk,[11] is listed with the meaning of 'to rub' in Morris et al. (2019, 79). However, this verb is reported to have the meaning 'to release' in both JL (55) and MLZ (714). As for the term *berəkɔ́t* 'talisman', it is not recorded as such by

---

[11] According to al-Kathiri and Dufour (2020, 186), "no opposition between Ga and Gb exists in practice with anisomorphic... roots, and we are simply faced with a G hyper-class."

any of the lexical sources. However, its morphology points to a diminutive form (Johnstone 1973) of *berekɛ́t* 'blessing' (JL, 28). Cf. the Mehri expression *flän fukk ḥidäh ab-bärkēt lä* 'NN hat seine Hand nicht mit Segen losgelassen' (Sima 2005, 75). In view of the presence of the term *īdš* 'his hand(s)', the proverb can be interpreted as 'so-and-so's hands didn't rub the talisman'.

(31)

ɛḏīlín ḍaʕarɔ́t īyēnš

His share has been spilt

فلان انسكبت وفقد حصته

This expression is used to describe the circumstances of someone who has come to be deprived of a source of wealth, affection, or security, e.g., an orphan (al-Shahri 2000, 80, 251).

The verbal form *ḍaʕarɔ́t* is a perfective 3.F.SG. of a Gb-stem meaning 'to spill, pour'. For the term *iyēn* 'share', which appears here with an initial long vowel due to the presence of the definite article, see entry number **(12)** above.

(32)

ɛḏīlín ḥa-yɔ́ḳrəm be-díni

So-and-so will swallow the earth

فلان سيبتلع الدنيا

This is used to describe greedy people (al-Shahri 2000, 80, 251).

The future marker *ḥa-*, which is currently less common than *a-* (Rubin 2012, 195), can be found in this proverb, attached to the subjunctive 3.M.SG. of a Ga-stem meaning 'to have trouble swallowing, make a noise swallowing' (JL, 149). This expression can be compared to Mehri *flän yḥōm ytēh dᵊnīyä* 'NN will die (ganze) Welt ausfessen' (Sima 2005, 76).

It is to be noted that the root √ḵrm in Soqotri means 'craving' (Naumkin et al. 2014, 591), which could be a slightly more appropriate meaning in this case. However, the second meaning listed by JL, 'make a noise swallowing', is not unfitting.

(33)

ɛd̠īlín ɔl ḵéləʕ l-ɛd̠īlín ɔl ṭirí b-ɔ ḵaʕʕun
He abused everything of mine (or his or hers), wet and dry

فلان لم يترك لفلان لا رطب ولا يأبس

This metaphor describes a terrible insult. The one who is left neither the wet nor the dry is the insulted person. According to al-Shahri (2000, 80, 251), living people are believed to be wet, whilst the dead are believed to be dry.

For the verbal form *ḵéləʕ*, see entry number **(24)**. The actual term for 'wet' *ṭirí* is used here, in the place of the periphrastic expression *b-eš i-mîḥ*; see above, entry number **(22)**. The Mehri counterpart of this expression is *flän l-ʿād ḵūlaʿ lä-flän l-ṯäryīt wa-l-ḵaś ʿayt* 'NN hat dem NN nichts übriggelassen, weder Feuchtes noch Trockenes' (Sima 2005, 76), whose meaning 'so-and-so has left nothing to so-and-so, neither wet nor dry' applies equally to its Jibbali/Śḥərɛ́t counterpart.

(34)

ɛd̠īlín əġasᵊré ṭer e-gédal
So-and-so spent the night on (his) foot

فلان ظل سهراناً على الموقد طوال الليل

This is a remark about someone who spends sleepless nights thinking about his troubles (al-Shahri 2000, 81, 251).

The verbal form *əġasˤré* is a perfective third person of a ᵠN1-stem deriving from the fourth-weak root √ġsry, meaning 'to spend the night, sleep the night (at)' (JL, 89). The term *gédal* is, etymologically speaking, a diminutive of *gedəl* 'foot' of the pattern *CēCéC* (JL, 71; MLZ, 180–81). The Mehri counterpart of this saying is *flän aġasrūh ashēr aś-śīwōṭ* 'NN ist die (ganze) Nacht wach geblieben beim Feuer' (Sima 2005, 76).

(35)

εḏīlín əl-fénɛ

This is the man of a face

فلان على نيّاته

This is said of a gullible person, as mentally sound people are believed to see both sides of a given situation, whilst a gullible person is believed to see only the face, i.e., one side (al-Shahri 2000, 81, 252). The term *fénɛ* means 'face' (JL, 59), but the preposition *l-* 'for, to' (Rubin 2014, 250) changes its meaning to 'before' (JL, 59). Therefore, in this case, the segment *əl-fénɛ* should probably be analysed as a propositional phrase made up of *əl* and *fénɛ*: i.e., 'to (one) face', meaning على نيّاته in Arabic, that is, *naïve, gullible, with good intentions*.

(36)

εḏīlín xiṭíṭˤ leš bə hum̥ bə śenḏér

He was given his share on a splinter of wood or (and) a seashell

فلان أُعطي بالمحّارة وشرخ الخشب

This means that when something was shared, the person to whom this proverb refers was given so small a share that it could fit on a seashell or on a splinter (al-Shahri 2000, 81, 252).

The verb *xiṭíṭ* is a third-person perfective of a passive G-stem (al-Kathiri and Dufour 2020, 195) whose active counterpart is *xeṭ* (*xeṭṭ* in the JL transcription) 'to write; to make signs on the ground; to point out a route' (JL, 308). The term *ḥuṃ* is translated as 'shell' in JL (109) and in MLZ (269: الفحم النباتي). The term *śɛnḏér* means 'big splinter of wood' (JL, 253). The overall meaning of this proverb is doubtful, as the English and Arabic translations are at variance with each other: whilst the Arabic translation would imply that both the 'splinter of wood' and the 'seashell' are in play, the English translation makes it clear that it is *either* the 'splinter of wood' *or* the 'seashell'. The recording offers little help, as the second *bə* might be either a preposition or a coordinating conjunction.

(37)
εḏīlín bə šɔ́fɔl trɔh
So-and-so has two stomachs
فلان بمعدتين

This expression is used to describe a person who is always worried about property or about people who are not within his or her sight (al-Shahri 2000, 81, 252). The use of the masculine numeral *trɔh* speaks to the fact that the term *šɔ́fɔl* can be either masculine or feminine (JL, 260). See also entry number **(15)** of this collection, and entry number **(12)** of the MLZ collection.

(38)

ɛḏīlín ɔ yəṭəféf b-ɔ yənúḏk̇

He doesn't float, he doesn't sink

فلان لا يطفو ولا يرسب

Similarly to entry number **(25)** of this collection, this proverb describes a good-for-nothing person (al-Shahri 2000, 82, 253). The verbal forms *yəṭəféf* and *yənúḏk̇* are, respectively, an imperfective 3.M.SG. of a G-stem deriving from a geminate root √ṭff meaning 'to float' (JL, 274), and an imperfective 3.M.SG. of a Ga-stem meaning 'to sink like a stone, go straight down into the water' (JL, 181).

(39)

ɛḏīlín ɔl gīlt heš b-ɔl t̠ɔ́b

He has false generosity and offends God

فلان لا كرامة له ولا ثواب

This proverb describes a person whose bad behaviour averts generosity in the world and a reward in the afterlife (al-Shahri 2000, 82, 253). The term *gīlt* is recorded as *gīlət* by JL (76) and means 'generosity; strength to endure', and the term *t̠ɔ́b* means 'good deed requited in heaven' (JL, 285). This expression can be compared to Mehri *flän lä-krōmät hēh w-lä-ṯwōb* 'NN hat keine Freigebigkeit und auch keine Dankbarkeit' (Sima 2005, 76): the German rendition can be translated as 'So-and-so has no generosity and no gratitude', which also fits the Jibbali/Śḥərɛ́t proverb.

(40)

ɛd̠ilín gerə beš e-núśub ɛ ṭṭɔ́dɔ

He has been affected by his mother's milk

فلان أثر عليه حليب الثدي

This is used to describe a person who is (over)zealous about his mother's requests.

However, this is not necessarily a criticism, as the duty of a son towards his mother and her family is an important tenet of the society of the Dhofar mountains (al-Shahri 2000, 82, 253). The verb *ger* < √grr is a perfective third person G-stem from a geminate root, and is recorded with the meaning 'to drag' in JL (77) and a similar meaning in MLZ (184: سحب). The term *ṭɔ́dɔ* is an unattested variant of the term recorded as *ṭɔ́dɛʾ* 'bosom, breast; nipple and breast' (JL, 283) and 'breast' (MLZ, 164: ثدي [المرأ]). Semantically, this saying may be interpreted actively as 'so-and-so, his mother's breast milk dragged him'.

(41)

ɛd̠ilín eḳaʕ leš šũš

His name found him

فلان طابق عليه اسمه او وافقه اسمه

This expression describes a person whose name and personality match each other, based on the folk belief that names become attached to people whose personality suits them (al-Shahri 2000, 82, 254).

The verbal class to which verbs like *eḳaʕ* < √wkʕ, a third-person perfective meaning 'to find' (JL, 290), belong is discussed in Rubin (2014, 109–10): he examines the cases of *edaʕ* 'to know'

(JL, 286) and *égaḥ* 'to enter' (JL, 288), and affirms that their having a *w as a first root consonant and a pharyngeal as a third root consonant obscures the differences between the Ga and Gb types. He further adds that *edaʕ* can be regarded as a Gb in Mehri, whereas *égaḥ* has no Mehri cognate. Therefore, it is likely that *eḳaʕ* is a Gb in Jibbali/Śḥərɛ́t too, and this is confirmed by al-Kathiri and Dufour (2020, 210). Cf. the Mehri proverb *flän hummäh aṭōbäḳ lēh* 'NN, sein Name paßt zu ihm' (Sima 2005, 76).

(42)

ɛḏīlín ɔl diní heš b-ɔ̄l axárt

He has nothing in this life and will have nothing in the hereafter

فلان ليس له دنيا ولا أخرة

This saying is similar in meaning to entry number **(39)** and describes a bad person who cannot expect any happiness or joy either in this world or in the hereafter (al-Shahri 2000, 83, 254).

JL (5) records *āxərt*, with a long vowel, but this is not confirmed by the present analysis. This is in all likelihood due to this term being used with a definite article in the vast majority of cases, and this usage being reflected in the JL data: *āxərt* < *a-axərt*. MLZ (93) does not record this term, despite recording the root √ʔxr.

(43)

ɛḏīlín bedərš šɔ́ʕɔt

The one who runs fastest arrives first

فلان سبقه العداؤون

Similarly to entry number **(4)**, this expression underlines the fact that those who waste time are certainly going to be outdone by more zealous people (al-Shahri 2000, 83, 254).

The perfective third-person Gb-stem verb *bédər* 'to outrun' (JL, 23) agrees with *šɔ́ʕɔt* 'runner', which is not recorded by JL, and is only recorded in its singular form by MLZ (478): ‏شعأً: الركض,‏ ‏الجري.‏[12] Despite its being morphologically a feminine singular noun, it is treated as a plural. Furthermore, the Arabic translation of the proverb employs the masculine plural noun ‏العداؤون‏ (al-Shahri 2000, 254). Compare the singular form ‏عداء‏ 'runner, racer' (Wehr and Cowan 1976, 599).

(44)

ɛd̠ilín məḵˤré ʕar ĩt

That person should be hidden from death

‏فلان يستحق بان يُخفي عن الموت‏

This expression may be used both to describe a very good person who is universally respected and cherished, and when someone recovers from an illness, or emerges unscathed from a dangerous situation (al-Shahri 2000, 83, 254).

The passive participle *məḵˤré* 'hidden' (MLZ, 744), is not recorded in JL (150), although it does record the verbs and other terms connected to the root √ḵry. The term *ĩt* comes from *e-mit* 'death' (JL, 176). This participial form is used here to express deontic modality.

---

[12] However, the term *šɔ́ʕɔt* could also be the feminine of an active participle.

(45)

ɛd̠īlín ɔl ṭḳīʕ mən šum ɛd gʲɔ́fɔ lɔ

No-one cares about him the smallest bit, not even the distance between the shadow and the sun

فلان لا احد يهتم به بقدر المسافة بين الشمس والظل

This describes an unimportant and neglected person.

The semantic connection finds an explanation in the folk belief that there is a small distance between the sunlight and the shadow. Therefore, this small distance is treated here as a metaphor for belittlement (al-Shahri 2000, 83, 255). The verb *ṭḳīʕ*,[13] a third-person perfective, must be the passive counterpart of the active H1-stem *eṭkaʕ* 'to look' (JL, 276). It is noteworthy that here, as well as in other cases which will be discussed in the conclusions below, a long vowel *ī* appears in the vocalism of passive verbs. The term *gʲɔ́fɔ* stands for *gɔ́fɛʔ* 'shadow' (JL, 72) and, similarly to the term *ṭɔ́dɔ* 'breast' in entry **(40)** above, exhibits an unexpected final [ɔ]. Moreover, it must be pointed out that al-Shahri renders this sound with ا in both cases.

(46)

ɛd̠īlín ɔl nuź b-ɔl réḳʕat

The dye and the quality of the cloth are both bad

فلان ليس كالثوب ذو نيل كافٍ أو متانة

This proverb applies to someone who is both of displeasing appearance and of bad manners (al-Shahri 2000, 84, 255). The terms *nuź* and *réḳʕat* mean, respectively, 'indigo' (JL, 200) and

---

[13] For *eṭkīʕ*, with vowel loss due to the phonological process described by al-Kathiri and Dufour (2020, 183).

'patch, rag' (JL, 212). Therefore, the literal meaning of this expression is 'so-and-so is neither indigo nor a rag (patch)'.

(47)

ɛd̪ilín kse ṣ́ɛd məšxerṭɔ́t

He has found an easy way to strip the leaves from the Christ's-thorn tree

فلان وجد سدرة سهلة الخرط

This is used to describe someone who took advantage of someone else's weakness or gullibility (al-Shahri 2000, 84, 255).

The verbal form *kse* is a perfective third person of a Ga-stem meaning 'to find' (JL, 135).[14] The term *ṣ́ɛd* denotes *Ziziphus spina-christi* (Miller and Morris 1988, 242), or Christ-thorn tree, whose fruits are edible. The feminine participial form *məšxerṭɔ́t* 'stripped of leaves', deriving from a Š1-stem, is not recorded elsewhere. Notwithstanding al-Shahri's English translation, the literal meaning of this expression seems to be 'so-and-so found a Christ-thorn tree stripped of its leaves'. The image of a Christ-thorn tree without leaves is used metaphorically to describe a mild and harmless person in Soqotra. The image itself can be traced back to the Qur'an (56.28).

(48)

ɛd̪ilín b-ɛd̪ilín lhes ē-ṭof bə-ḥabbərrédi

So-and-so and So-and-so is like 'Toph' and 'Habaradi'

فلان وفلان كنبات الطوف ونبات الحبرّادي

---

[14] According to al-Kathiri and Dufour (2020, 203), this verb is typical of the central dialects of Jibbali/Śḥərɛ̄t.

The two plants mentioned in this proverb, namely *ṭof* 'Aloe dhufariensis' (Miller and Morris 1988, 182) and *ḥabbərrédi* 'Kleinia saginata' (Miller and Morris 1988, 110), are very different from each other, and this expression is used to describe two very different individuals (al-Shahri 2000, 84,256). The definite article preceding *ṭof* is realised as a long vowel (see also the following proverb). The term *ḥabbərrédi* is recorded by Miller and Morris with /h/, but al-Shahri pronounces and transcribes /ḥ/ instead. Al-Shahri's pronunciation seems to be confirmed by MLZ's (214) version of this expression: حبرادي بيطُف.

(49)

ɛḏīlín lhes ē-ṭiḳ ē-daʕán

He is like a fig tree in the middle of a barren plain

مثل التينة الفريدة في الارض الجرداء[15]فلا

This expression is used to describe a person who is more widely known than others, in spite of not being any better (or worse) than others (al-Shahri 2000, 84, 256).

Similarly to entry number **(48)** above, there occurs an unexpected long vowel [eː] in place of the definite article's short vowel. This might lead one to postulate a vowel after the preposition, i.e., *lhes ɛ*, perhaps through analogical levelling after the pattern of compound prepositions such as *ḥaṣ-ɛ* or *ḥaḳt-ɛ* (Rubin 2014, 361–63, 371–72).

---

[15] فلا for فلان due to mistyping.

(50)

ɛḏīlín ɔl d-ḥɔb b-ɔl d-rɔ́kɔl

Not for milking, not for owning

فلان لا للحلب ولا للكسب

This is said, similarly to entries **(25)** and **(38)**, of a good-for-nothing person (al-Shahri 2000, 84, 256).

The *d-* prefix in this case is an allomorph of the preposition *ɛd* 'up to, till, until' (Rubin 2014, 228–30), which lacks the initial vowel due to the phonological process described in the commentary of entry number **(45)** above. The term *ḥɔb* is a verbal noun meaning '(one) milking' (JL, 109). The term *rɔ́kɔl* is not recorded in JL, whereas MLZ (391) defines it as 'cow pen' (مربض الابقار). It is worth noting that the [ɔ] vowel in the unstressed syllable of the term in question, which occurs instead of the expected [ə], may be due to the same phenomenon described above in entries **(40)** and **(45)**. In view of the terms used, this proverb would be best translated as 'so-and-so is neither for milking nor for the cow pen'.

(51)

ɛḏīlín ber feṣġ ɛd ś́ɔ́ṭ

So-and-so has spat into the fire

فلان قد بصق في النار

This is used to describe a person who talks too much and, for this reason, cannot be believed, on the basis of the folk belief that a person who spits into the fire becomes a liar (al-Shahri 2000, 85, 141, 256, 332).

The verbal form *feṣġ* is a perfective third person of a Ga-stem meaning 'to spit' (JL, 64). The use of the auxiliary verb *ber* conveys, in this case, the meaning of 'just' or 'already' (Rubin 2014, 165). The preposition *ɛd* 'until' is used here in place of *ʕak* 'in'.

(52)

ɛḏīlín axníṭ e-līnit əl ḥārɔ́t
He had consumed all the white and black
فلان أخرج السواد على البياض

This is an expression of reproach towards someone who has taken advantage of another person. The white and black should be regarded as metaphors for fat and meat, respectively (al-Shahri 2000, 85, 257).

The verbal form *axníṭ* is a perfective third person of a H1-stem meaning 'to take out' (JL, 303). It appears here in the active voice with the expected short [i], in contrast with its passive counterpart in entry number **(27)**, which has a long [iː].

The term *ḥārɔ́t* 'black (F.SG.)' is perceived as [ħaeˈrɔt] in this and another recording,[16] which may be due to the articulatory transitional effect from [ħ] to [r]. This occurs also in the speech of an aged speaker of the Hallaniyah dialect (Castagna 2018, 447). The phenomenon described by Rubin (2014, 41), whereby /a/ is realised as [aj] after /ʕ/ and /ġ/, may be of some relevance, although the author does not mention its occurrence after /ḥ/.

The English translation is at variance with the Arabic translation, which, by contrast, literally means 'So-and-so took out the whiteness upon the blackness'.

---

[16] See proverb **(43)** of the MLZ collection.

(53)

ɛd̠ilín ɔl šɛn b-ɔl šokum

So-and-so is not with us and not with you

فلان لا معنا ولا معكم

This expression describes a braggart, whose actions are not useful to anybody (al-Shahri 2000, 85, 257). The preposition *k-* 'with' appears here in the form of an allomorph, or mono-consonantal base (Rubin 2014, 267), used with personal suffixes. The Mehri counterpart of this expression is *flän l-šän wa-l-šīkäm* 'NN ist weder auf unserer noch auf eurer Seite' (Sima 2005, 77).

(54)

ɛd̠ilín ɔl ɛ́gʲeh b-ɔl ḳifɛ́

So-and-so has no front and no back

فلان لا وجه ولا قفا

This is a remark made about a person of loose morals who shows no regret whatsoever (al-Shahri 2000, 85, 257).

This is the third proverb of this collection analysed by Rubin (2014, 643). The term *ɛ́gʲeh* 'face' (JL, 288) stems from the root √*wgh*, from which Arabic وجه stems too, and in view of the existence of the native term *kɛrfef* (JL, 134), the former may be suspected to be an ancient and/or phonetically well-accommodated Arabic borrowing. Compare the Mehri expression *flän l-bēh l-wajh w-lä-ḳfē* 'NN hat weder ein Gesicht noch einen Rücken' (Sima 2005, 77).

(55)

ɛd̠īlín taʕśéśenᵊ beš yurš͂ɔ́b

A beast of burden can carry him

فلان تنهض به الجمال

This expression, similarly to entries **(35)** and **(47)**, alludes to someone's gullibility (al-Shahri 2000, 85, 258).

The H1-stem verb *taʕśéśen* 'to rouse' (JL, 17) appears here in the 3.F.PL. of the imperfective. The term *yurš͂ɔ́b*, which looks deceptively like a verbal form, is actually a plural whose singular is *ɛrkíb* 'riding-camel' (JL, 211). The initial [ju] glide in this term is due to the conjunct effect of the /š͂/ lip-rounding and the regular retroflexion of /r/ before a coronal, so that the phonemic representation of this term should rather be /ɛrš͂ɔ́b/. This saying corresponds to Mehri *flän taʿśūśan bēh rīkōb* 'Auf NN sitzen die Reittiere auf' (Sima 2005, 77). A more faithful English rendition of this expression is 'So-and-so is carried by camels'.

(56)

ɛd̠īlín aġᵊmíd ɔ́ʕź ɔ yəš͂ɔ́š ḥakᵊ lɔ

So-and-so owes God nothing

لقد أمسى فلان وليس الله حق عليه

This is a comment made to praise people who work hard (al-Shahri 2000, 86, 258).

The verb *aġᵊmíd*, a perfective third person of a H1-stem, normally means 'to be, appear in the evening; to sheath' (JL, 86).

The term ɔʕẓ́ 'God' (JL, 22) is one whose etymology is not immediately transparent. Its Mehreyyet[17] cognate bēlī comes from the root √bʕl and is often used is its definite form a-bēlī (Watson 2012, 259), and the processes underlying the Jibbali/Śḥərέt form can be summarised thus: *e-baʕli > *e-bɔʕli > *ɔʕli > *ɔʕẓ́i > ɔʕẓ́. The verb yəšɔ́š < √šyb 'bring water from afar' (JL, 265; MLZ, 486: جلب الماء من بعيد) is an imperfective 3.M.SG. of a Ga-stem with a 3.M.SG. personal suffix attached. Its final root consonant /b/ is elided between the preceding vowel and the vowel of the above-mentioned suffix (Rubin 2014, 28–29). The use of this verb to mean 'have a right' is puzzling. Overall, the interpretation of this proverb vis-à-vis its literal meaning is unclear, and the English translation provided by al-Shahri undoubtedly makes it more difficult to interpret it. However, al-Shahri's Arabic translation لقد أمسى فلان وليس الله حق عليه might be of some guidance here, in that it literally means 'so-and-so has become thus (at night), and God does not have any right over him', implying that God has tried the poor fellow in question so much during the day that, once he has made it to sunset, even God has no right to mistreat him further.

(57)

εdīlín ɔl edaʕ ɔl iné εbḥer b-ɔl iné εṣ̌her
So-and-so doesn't know who is on the sea and who is on the land
لم يعلم فلان بمن سلك طريق البحر او طريق البر

---

[17] This is the native glottonym that designates the variety of Mehri spoken in the Sultanate of Oman, and is perceived as more correct than *Omani Mehri* by the speakers.

This is the fourth proverb analysed by Rubin (2014, 643) and describes a person who does not pay attention to the surrounding events (al-Shahri 2000, 86, 258). Both ɛbḥer and ɛśḥer are perfective third-person H1-stem denominative verbs meaning 'to go by sea' and 'to go to the mountains' respectively. JL does not record them, whilst they can be found in MLZ (114, 504) as ذهب باتجاه and صعد \ توجه إلى الجبل. The proverb is also recorded by MLZ (114), as اذيلين ألدع إنه ابحر بل ناشحئر. Cf. also Mehri *flän l-wīdaʿ ḥābū häśän abḥayräm wa-l-häśän aśḥayräm* 'NN weiß weder was die Leute am Meer noch was (die Leute) in den Bergen machen' (Sima 2005, 77).

(58)

ɛd̠īlín ɔl s̃ərᵊkéb b-ɔl s̃ənʕíś

He cannot ride and cannot be carried

فلان لم يستحمل الركوب على الدابة ولا على النعش

This proverb describes someone who turns down every kind of advice and help (al-Shahri 2000, 86, 259).

The two verbs in this proverb are both perfective third-person forms of Š1-stems. The first form, *s̃ərᵊkéb*, is reported to mean 'to be ridden' in JL (211), with a similar meaning in MLZ (393: رُكِبَ). However, al-Shahri's Arabic translation of this verb as لم يستحمل الركوب على الدابة 'he can't bear riding on the mount' implies that the subject is unable or unwilling to ride, rather than not ridden. The second verb, *s̃ənʕíś*, is recorded by JL (178) as '(patient, corpse) to be carried on a stretcher, bier', which explains the Arabic translation ولا على النعش '…nor on a coffin'. The literal meaning of the proverb may therefore be given as 'so-and-so can ride neither a beast nor a bier'. MLZ (393) records this proverb as أذيلين أيشركب بيشعُتش. The last vowel in *s̃ənʕíś* is [i], where one would expect [e]: this may be due to the raising effect of the nasal [n] taking place through the intervening [ʕ]. This proverb corresponds to Mehri *flän l-šärkūb wa-l-šänʕūś* 'NN (kann) man weder reiten lassen noch auf der Totenbahre trage' (Sima 2005, 77–78), which translates to 'So-and-so (can) neither be ridden nor carried on a bier', a translation that also applies to the Jibbali/Śḥərɛ̄t proverb.

(59)

ɛ-ḏelɛ́ ibrérən

The early morning makes everything clear

بعد طلوع الشمس كل شي يُبان

This is said by someone who is accused of a misdeed but is actually innocent, and is also used when a disturbance occurs at night, to suggest that it is more convenient to wait until morning to look into it (al-Shahri 2000, 86, 259).

The term *ḏelɛ́* meaning 'early morning' seems to be a variant of *ḏelɛ́b* (JL, 46), which carries the same meaning. That *ḏelɛ́* is a full-status lexeme, and not a pre-pausal realisation of *ḏelɛ́b*, is proven by the fact that (1) the term is transcribed as ذيلاء by al-Shahri (2000, 259) and (2) Johnstone lists this term in the bilingual Mehri-Jibbali wordlist at the end of the *Mehri Lexicon* (ML, 560). The verb *ibrérən* is clearly a H2-stem, but neither JL (27) nor MLZ (123–24) lists it under the corresponding root √brr.

(60)

ɛḏīlín ᵊrkɔt a-ḏánum e-ḳéṣ̂ər

So-and-so trod on the lion's tail

فلان دعس او داس على ذيل الاسد

This is used as a warning that one should not look for trouble by provoking the anger of someone stronger than oneself (al-Shahri 2000, 86, 259).

The verbal form rkɔt is a perfective third person of a Ga-stem < √rkt meaning 'to step, to tread upon, put a foot on the ground' (JL, 211). The term *ḏánum* is unexpected for *ḏunub* 'tail' (JL, 47) and might be a characteristic of the speaker's dialect. It must be noted that this term is subject to a good deal of variation among dialects: for example, it is often, but not invariably, realised as *ḏunúf* by insular speakers (Castagna 2018, 445), although in the case of the dialect of al-Ḥallanīyah, this may be viewed as part of a wider sound change /b/ > [f] in certain phonotactic environments (Castagna 2018, 116–18). At any rate, al-Shahri utters *ḏanum* but transcribes ذونوب. Cf. Mehri *axāh hēt rkätk aṭ-ṭār ḏnōb ḏ-kayźar* 'Als ob du auf den Schwanz des Leoparden getreten wärst' (Sima 2005, 78). The use of 'lion' instead of 'leopard' in al-Shahri's English translation is arbitrary.

(61)
εḏīlín e-nṭəfɔ́tš ε təġrér
His shins are full
فلان نخاع عظمه ملان

This is used to describe a person who is always eager to help (al-Shahri 2000, 87, 260).

The term *e-nṭəfɔ́tš*, a definite form of a feminine noun with a personal suffix attached, is found in JL (181) as *nəḏfɔ́t* 'leg-bone of a slaughtered animal'. Rather curiously, the meaning of the verb *təġrér*, an imperfective 3.F.SG of a G-stem < √ġrr, is 'to deceive, to cheat', according to lexicographic sources (JL, 87; MLZ,

663: غش, دلس) as well as native speakers (p.c.). Al-Shahri's Arabic translation, which can be interpreted as 'So-and-so the marrow of his bone is full' is not helpful.

(62)

ɛd̲ilín yɔġɔtyɔ́t̲ mən ĩdét

So-and-so even gets angry with the breeze

فلان يغضب حتى من النسيم

This saying describes, similarly to entry number **(26)**, a short-tempered person (al-Shahri 2000, 87, 260).

The verbal form *yɔġɔtyɔ́t̲* is an imperfective 3.M.SG. of a T1-stem < √ġyt̲ meaning 'to anger' (JL, 91; MLZ, 684: إغتاظ). Given that Arabic has a Gt-stem (measure VIII) with the same meaning, this could be an Arabic borrowing, and the use of the preposition *mən* reinforces this hypothesis (Wehr and Cowan 1976, 691). The term *ĩdét* < *e-midét means 'south wind' (JL, 169). This saying is similar in meaning to Mehri *flän yaġt̲ᵃyūt̲ män (t̲ār) ḳāʿ* 'NN wird schon zornig (, wenn er nur) auf dem Erdboden (steht)' (Sima 2005, 78), despite some lexical differences.

(63)

ɛd̲ilín yaġér l-e-naʕrír

When he hears a cry of fear he joins it

فلان يتحرك لهتاف البقر

This is used to describe a person who is overly curious (al-Shahri 2000, 87, 260).

The verbal form *yaġér* is an imperfective 3.M.SG. of a Ga-stem < √ġbr meaning 'to meet' (JL, 82). The term *naʕrír* 'wailing' is not recorded by JL. It is, however, recorded in MLZ (923:

(النحيب [في البكاء]). Overall, the literal meaning of this expression can be more faithfully rendered as 'So-and-so joins the wailing'.

(64)

ɛd̠īlín bɛr bēba (ber mēma)

So-and-so is the son of his father (or mother)

فلان ابن ابيه او ابن امه اي (الولد سر ابيه او سر امه)

This describes the commonalities between a person and his parents (al-Shahri 2000, 87, 260). The term *bɛr* 'son' (JL, 28) is one of the terms that can head a construct chain (Rubin 2014, 88). The terms *bēba* and *mēma,* apparently diminutives formed after the *CēCéC* pattern (Johnstone 1973), are not listed in the written sources used in this study. However, they are reminiscent of Arabic بابا and ماما, and are widely used in Soqotri (Morris et al. 2019, 88). Cf. Mehri *flän bär ḥībäh aw bär ḥāmēh* 'NN ist (wahrlich) der Sohn seines Vaters (oder: der Sohn seiner Mutter)' (Sima 2005, 78).

(65)

ɛd̠īlín ʕɔd ɔ ṭē śe mən níśi íź xɔrf lɔ

So-and-so has not yet smelled the first days of the monsoon yet

فلان لم يكن قد شم شيئاً من أيام بدايات الخريف

This is said of someone who is accustomed to an easy life and does not know hardship (al-Shahri 2000, 87, 261).

The use of *ʕɔd* instead of *d-ʕɔd* to convey something that has not happened yet is rather unexpected (Rubin 2014, 168–71). The verbal form *ṭē* is a perfective third person of a G-stem <

√ṭwy meaning 'to smell' (JL, 50).[18] The term níśi is the name of a star which can be observed at the beginning of the monsoon season (MLZ, 915) and is not recorded in JL. However, it is worth pointing out that the verbs listed in JL (195) under the root √nsv are related to the transhumance, which may be a viable semantic connection to the beginning of the monsoon. Indeed, it is in the wider sense of 'beginning' that this term is used here, as the Arabic translation أيام بدايات الخريف 'days at the beginning of the monsoon' would suggest (al-Shahri 2000, 261). The use of the plural relativiser iẑ is to be noted.

(66)

ɛd̠ílín lhes śiréft

So-and-so is like a glow-worm

فلان مثل الدودة اللزجة المضيئة

This is a comment about a nosy person whom it is difficult to get rid of (al-Shahri 2000, 88, 261).

The semantic connection is explained by the term śiréft, meaning a sticky substance produced by a glow-worm (MLZ, 512). This term is not recorded under the root √śrf in JL (254).

(67)

ɛd̠ílín ɔl məfkḗkᵊ beš ĩkḷétᵊ lɔ

So-and-so is not rubbed with roasted millet

فلان لم تُفرك به الذرة المقلية عند صغره

---

[18] Al-Kathiri and Dufour (2020, 195) state that the difference between Ga and Gb stems is obfuscated in doubly weak roots. However, they indicate that this verb exhibits some characteristics of a Ga-stem.

This is yet another proverb that, similarly to entries **(28)**, **(38)**, and **(50)**, describes people who lack cleverness, on the basis of a folk belief according to which the mental faculties of an individual will be enhanced if he or she is rubbed with roasted millet as an infant (al-Shahri 2000, 88, 261).

The participial form *məfkẽk* < √*fkk* means 'rubbed'; cf. *fekk* 'to rub' (Morris et al. 2019, 79). The long vowel is unexpected and might be due to a prosodic phenomenon. The term *ĩḳlɛ́t* < **e-məkəlɛ́t* is recorded with the meaning of 'coffee-roaster, frying pan' in JL (146). However, the meaning 'roast dhurah' is found in Rubin (2014, 665).

(68)

ɛd̠īlín mítəl ɔ́-gʲor ɛ ṭáḥan ẽkik

So-and-so became like a slave who ground a ton of grain

فلان كالعبد الذي طحن المكيك

This saying applies to those who work properly at the beginning of a task, but become less accurate towards the end of it. It is a reference to a local legend according to which a slave started to grind grains properly, but became so inaccurate towards the end of his task that he trapped his testicles in the roller (al-Shahri 2000, 88, 262).

The Gb-stem verb *mítəl*, which appears here as a perfective third person, means 'to be like someone (but oftenest in curses)' (JL, 176). The verbal form *ṭáḥan* is a perfective third person of a Gb-stem meaning 'to mill, grind' (JL, 276). The term *ẽkík* < **e-mekík* 'measure of food'[19] (JL, 170) may be interpreted as 'grain'

---

[19] To be precise, a mass measure (Watson, p.c.).

here. The use of 'a ton' in the English translation of the proverb is arbitrary, and does not reflect the Jibbali/Śḥərɛ́t and Arabic text.

(69)

ɛd̠ɪ́lɪ́n ɔ yəḥḗl ɔ śɛdˀ b-ɔ maʕtḗr

He cannot carry the panniers or even the smaller load in between them

فلان لا يتحمل حمولة كاملة ولا جزءاً منها

This proverb adds to the series of remarks about useless individuals, which includes entries **(28)**, **(38)**, **(50)**, and **(67)** (al-Shahri 2000, 88, 262). The verbal form *yəḥḗl* is an imperfective 3.M.SG. of a Ga-stem meaning 'to load; to take; to carry' (JL, 111). The terms *śɛd* and *maʕtḗr* indicate two different units of measurement, which are not recorded in the sources. This expression bears some similarities to the Mehri expression *la-ḥmōlät wa-l-maʕtᵃbīr* '(NN trägt) weder die (ganze) Last noch einen Teil davon' (Sima 2005, 78).

(70)

ɛd̠ɪ́lɪ́n ḳélə́ʕ tun ḥagʲᵊlɔ́

So-and-so left us in the open

فلان تركنا وحدنا في العراء

This is a comment made when someone beloved and respected is temporarily or permanently absent from a community (al-Shahri 2000, 89, 262).

The verbal form *ḳélə́ʕ* is a third-person perfective of a Ga-stem meaning 'to let, allow' (JL, 144). The term *ḥagʲᵊlɔ́* 'in the open' is a masculine plural *nisbah* adjective with adverbial force, which is not recorded in the lexica. However, the corresponding root √ḥgl pertains to the pasturing of animals (JL, 106; MLZ, 222), which is an outdoor activity *par excellence*. Therefore, the existence of a *nisbah* adjective **ḥagⁱᵊlí* (and its plural counterpart *ḥagⁱᵊlɔ́*) related to this activity seems far from unlikely. Despite a marked lexical divergence, this expression corresponds in meaning to Mehri *flän šūtōmän m-baʿdäh* 'NN, wir sind nach seinem Weggehen Waisen geworden' (Sima 2005, 78–79).

(71)

ɛd̠ilín xɔlɔ́ṭ e-ṭít l-e-rīyet
So-and-so mixes the thirsty with those who have drunk their fill

فلان خلط بين الظمأى والشاربة

This proverb describes someone who is not able to tell good from evil (al-Shahri 2000, 89, 263).

The verbal form *xɔlɔ́ṭ* is a perfective third person of a Ga-stem meaning 'to mix' (JL, 300). The term *ṭít*, meaning 'thirsty (a cow, for example). This cannot be used for a human being' (MLZ, 601: عطشى [البقرة مثلا] ولا تستخدم مع الانسان) is not recorded by JL (49), although it does record the root √ṭmy. Similarly, the term *riyet* 'quenched' is not listed under the root √rwy in JL (218), but appears in MLZ (361) under the root √rby.[20] This is etymologically controversial, as evidence from other Semitic languages suggests that the above term should be derived from √rwy; cf. the meanings connected to 'drinking' under Arabic روى (Wehr and Cowan 1976, 369) and Gəʕəz ሮየ (Leslau 2006, 478), as well as

---

[20] This term is the feminine form of رَيّ. It is recorded as رِيُتْ, which would suggest *riyɔ́t* rather than *riyet*.

the cognate terms containing a /w/ as a second root consonant in Mehri (ML, 334).

(72)

ɛdĩlín ɔ nfaʕ b-ɔ s̃faʕ

He is neither useful for work nor for playing

فلان لا نفع منه ولا شفع

This is yet another remark about useless people (al-Shahri 2000, 89, 263). Cf. entries **(28)**, **(38)**, **(50)**, **(67)**, and **(69)**.

The terms *nfaʕ* and *s̃faʕ* are problematic in that they could be either H1-stem verbs (with initial vowel loss, as described in entry **(45)** above), or nouns deriving from the roots √*nfʕ* (JL, 181; MLZ, 929) and √*s̃fʕ*, an Arabic borrowing, *s̃faʕ* < شفع 'to mediate, use one's good offices, put in a good word, intercede, intervene, plead' (Wehr and Cowan 1976, 478), with /s̃/ for Arabic <ش>, as is common in Arabic loanwords; cf. *s̃ɛ́hi* 'tea' < south Arabian Arabic dialects *šahi* (JL, 265). Compare Mehri *lä-šfāʕ w-lä-nfāʕ* '(NN bringt) weder Hilfe noch Nutzen' (Sima 2005, 79), whose meaning 'So-and-so, no help and no benefit' better renders the Jibbali/S̃ḥərɛ́t expression.

(73)

ɛdĩlín e-dɔrs̃ mən s̃ᵊbɔ́ts̃

So-and-so, his blood is from his gums

فلان دمه من لثّته

This metaphor describes someone who causes trouble for relatives (al-Shahri 2000, 89, 263).

The term *s̃bɔ́t* 'gums' is recorded with a short vowel in JL (260). Interestingly, MLZ (469) lists this term with a long vowel, as pronounced by al-Shahri, but with the totally different meaning of 'skin that surrounds fingernails' (الجلد المحيط بالأظافر).

(74)

ɛ ḏirəfɔ́t təḥkék ḥanúfs

He who feels the itch should scratch it himself

من احست بالحكة عليها بأن تحك لنفسها

This saying underlines the importance of dealing with one's own problems (al-Shahri 2000, 89, 264).

The verbal form *ḏirəfɔ́t* (with a long vowel) is a perfective 3.F.SG. of a Gb-stem meaning 'to itch, be itchy' (JL, 47). The following verbal form *təḥkék* is an imperfective 3.F.SG. of a H1-stem reported to mean 'to plane, level, smoothe' (JL, 107). Interestingly, MLZ does not record either this form or the T1-stem recorded by JL (107) with the meaning 'to scratch'. This is one of the few items in this collection in which the subject is feminine, although al-Shahri's English translation has the pronoun 'he' (al-Shahri 2000, 89). However, the Arabic translation uses the feminine gender. This saying can be compared to Mehri *ḏärfōt taḥt*ᵃ*kūk ḥnäfs* 'Das Jucken kratzt sich selbst' (Sima 2005, 79).

(75)

e-rɛš delíl b ēṣifirét

The head shows the skill of the hairdresser

الرأس يدل على شخصية ومهارة الضافرة

This means that actions reveal the personality of the person who acts (al-Shahri 2000, 89, 264).

The term *delíl* means 'guide' (JL, 38). The long vowel in the segment *ēṣifirét* is due to the coalescence of the vowel in the preceding preposition *bə* and the definite article: **bə-e-ṣifirét*. This noun is recorded by JL (324) as 'plait, tress of hair'. However, MLZ (568) records it as 'a woman who braids the hair' (المرأة التي تقوم بضفر الشعر), which, *vis-à-vis* the Arabic rendition of this proverb, looks like a semantically more fitting interpretation.

(76)

érxe i-nītk b-ɔ teṣˤm e-déhər

Instead of fasting for your whole life, be happy

إن تكن واسع الصدر صافي النية أفضل من صيامك الدهر كله

This is a piece of advice to a pious but unlucky person to stop fasting to please God and be happy (al-Shahri 2000, 90, 264).

The first verbal form is an imperative of a H1-stem meaning 'to slacken; to let go (of a rope)' (JL, 218), whilst the second one, *teṣˤm*, is a subjunctive 3.M.SG. of a G-stem deriving from a hollow root √ṣwm 'to fast' (JL, 243) and is part of a negative imperative. The term *nīt* 'intention, determination' (MLZ, 945: النية, القصد, العزم) is not listed in JL. In view of the above, the expression is probably best translated as 'let go of your intention and don't fast forever!'.

(77)

ɛrṣ xalέ yəté kelέ ɛ-brέš

The area is deserted, the wolf eats his son

الارض مهجورة لا قوت بها ياكل الذئب ولده

This saying describes a place which is devoid of any form of life (al-Shahri 2000, 90, 265).

The verbal form is an imperfective 3.M.SG. of a G-stem deriving from the doubly weak root √twy meaning 'to eat' (JL, 273). The term *kelέ*, which al-Shahri translates as 'wolf' and ذئب (al-

Shahri 2000, 90), is unattested. Interestingly, this term follows the same *CeCɛ* pattern as *ḏelɛ́* 'early morning' (see also entry **(59)** of this collection), and shares with the latter the same apparent loss of /b/ as third root consonant, as well as semantics that match those of the /b/-final variant. This proverb is formally comparable with Mehri *arẓ xlī kawb ytäyw ḥabrēh* 'Wenn das Land öd ist, frißt der Hund sein Junges' (Sima 2005, 79).

(78)

ɛzd ãġ°tḗš ġḗš

Let the quick-tempered person become worse

زيد الأحمق حماقة

This saying describes someone who is always in a bad mood (al-Shahri 2000, 90, 265).

The verbal form *ɛzd* is an imperative of a H1-stem listed in JL (321) as *ezed*. Both the participial form *ãġ°tḗš* < *a-maġtḗš* 'cross, frowning' and *ġḗš* 'trouble; unpleasant thing, person' derive from the root √*ġyš* (JL, 92). However, *ãġ°tḗš* is rendered in Arabic with الأحمق 'dumb, stupid, silly, foolish, fatuous; fool, simpleton, imbecile' (Wehr and Cowan 1976, 206), which provides an indication as to the meaning of this proverb.

This proverb is recorded by MLZ (683) as أزد آغتآبش غابش. Also, cf. Mehri *azyäd mša'mi 'amūt* 'Vermehre dem Zornigen noch den Zorn' (Sima 2005, 79), notwithstanding the lexical divergences.

(79)

ē šeš lob ɔ yətiɔ̄k° lɔ

He who has the word no, is safe

من يمتلك كلمة لا, لا تعيه الحيلة

This stresses the importance of saying 'no' when it is wise to do so (al-Shahri 2000, 90, 265). The term *lob* expresses anaphoric negation (i.e., 'no!') in Jibbali/Śḥərέt (JL, 166). Al-Shahri's Arabic translation of the verbal form *yəṭiɔ́k* لا تعيه الحيلة 'is not affected by cunning', an imperfective 3.M.SG. of a Gb-stem < √ṭwk̲, is at variance with the meanings listed by JL (281) for this verb, namely 'to be given a liability, be stuck with (**b-**) someone; to be at one's wit's end, unable to cope'. This form is not recorded by MLZ (595) under √ṭwk̲, but semantically related terms can be found under √ṭbk̲ (MLZ, 595, 576). With regard to this expression, one of the meanings listed by JL, 'to be unable to cope', seems the most fitting one.

(80)

ɛ šəʕíd ɔ ṭilím

He who has been promised something can expect that the promise will be kept

من وُعِد لم يُظلم

This is used as a remark on unpaid debts (al-Shahri 2000, 90, 266).

Al-Shahri in the first instance utters *šəʕéd*, the active voice of a perfective third person of a Š2-stem,[21] and then in the second instance uses its passive counterpart *šəʕíd*, probably due to a slip. The use of a passive Š-stem is remarkable. However, given the

---

[21] The I-weak root √wʕd, from which this verb is derived, and the fact that only one Š-stem is recorded by JL, make the distinction between Š1 and Š2 difficult to determine. However, MLZ (978) records شعد and شعيد. The second form, corresponding to a Š2, seems to match *šəʕéd*.

basically active meaning of *šəʕed* 'to arrange a meeting, to swear, vow to do something' (JL, 286), the use of its passive counterpart to convey the sense of 'being promised something' has a strong semantic motivation. The second verbal form is the passive perfective third person of a Ga-stem meaning 'to oppress, be unjust' (JL, 49).

(81)

ɛ̄ šeš a-ġēg yəduren̄

He who has strong men at his back can show off in the arena

من معه قوة الرجال يصول ويجول في الميدان

According to folk history, this sentence was uttered by a tribal leader who, at a tribal gathering, was marginalised by other tribal leaders on account of the small size of his tribe. He then ordered his people to have as many children as possible, so that twenty years later he attended another such gathering backed by a sizeable force of men. At present, it is used when a person in trouble is helped by family and friends (al-Shahri 2000, 91, 266).

The relativiser ɛ is realised as a long vowel here, as it is in entry **(79)** above. The verbal form *yəduren̄* is an imperfective 3.M.SG. of a H2-stem deriving from a hollow root √*dwr* meaning 'to return' (JL, 43; MLZ, 344: عاد, آب, رجع). The semantics of this verb in this context are unclear. The stress falling on the *-(v)n* suffix of the imperfective is likely due to topicalisation, as described by Dufour (2016, 36).

(82)

śom l-e-ššefḳ b-ɔl (t)serᵊš lɔ

Sell to the bridegroom but do not accompany him

بع على العريس ولا ترافقه

This proverb comments on the fact that, given the physical and mental strain entailed by a wedding, one can profit by selling overpriced goods to a bridegroom, who is too tired to bargain. Conversely, those who choose to stand by the bridegroom as he organises his wedding will share the strain (al-Shahri 2000, 91, 267).

The verbal form *śom* is an imperative of a G-stem meaning 'to sell' (JL, 244).[22] The term *šefḳ* 'bridegroom' (MLZ, 480: العريس; see also entry **(115)** in this collection) is not recorded in JL, although JL (260) does record the root √*šfḳ* as covering verbs and other terms related to marriage and weddings. The lack of a t-prefix in the subjunctive 2.M.SG. verb *(t)serᵊš* 'accompany' (MLZ, 466: رافق وواكب) may only be explained if it belongs to the H2-stem class (Rubin 2014, 146; Testen 1992). The corresponding Mehri proverb is *śōm k-hīfäk w-lä-šsäyräh lä* 'Verkauf (etwas) an den Brautwerber, aber geh nicht mit ihm mit' (Sima 2005, 79–80).

(83)

iź šéḵum b-iź gʲũś fáxrɛ e-yɔ iṣɔ́ḥ

Those who leave early in the morning, while it is still dark, and those who leave a little before them, will arrive together in the morning

الذين غادروا في منتصف الليل او اخره جميعهم يصلون صباحاً معاً

This means that those who start something earlier will not necessarily finish earlier (al-Shahri 2000, 91, 267).

---

[22] This form is from the hollow root √*ś?m*, which has no distinction between Ga and Gb (al-Kathiri and Dufour 2020, 210).

The verbal form *gʲũś*, a perfective third person of a H2-stem meaning 'to go late at night' (MLZ, 208: سار \ ذهب \ غادر في اخر الليل \ الصباح الباكر) is not recorded by JL.[23] Additionally, MLZ lists it under the root √gwś, but al-Shahri pronounces it with a clearly audible nasalised vowel, which would point to the root actually being √gmś; see also entry number **(89)** below. Compare the Mehri proverb *ḏä-syōräm fäḵḥ ḏ-ʿāṣar (ḏ-ḥalläyy) yäṣabham käll faxrä* 'Die um Mitternacht (oder: am Ende der Nacht) (los)gehen, werden am Morgen alle zusammen sein' (Sima 2005, 80). Curiously, the actions described by the original Jibbali/Śḥərέt version of the expression and its Arabic translation are provided in reverse order in the English translation.

(84)

ɛ̄ ṣɔ̄r šeš ɔ́ʕz

God is with the one who has patience

إن الله مع الصابرين

This is a remark about those who eventually get what they wanted, after a long wait (al-Shahri 2000, 91, 267).

The relativiser *ɛ* is realised as a long vowel here, as in entries **(79)** and **(81)** above. The verbal form *ṣɔ̄r* is a perfective third-person Ga-stem meaning 'to be patient' < √ṣbr (JL, 235). This proverb is also recorded by al-Maʿshani (2017, 84). Cf. Mehri *käll ḏ-ṣbōr bäli šēh* 'Jeder der geduldig ist, mit dem ist Gott' (Sima 2005, 80).

---

[23] The initial vowel is lost because of the preceding sonorant (al-Kathiri and Dufour 2020, 183).

(85)

e-ṭerd yɔlḥɔ́ḳ her ɔl kun ṭerdᵊ lɛš

Only the skillful pursuer can catch his quarry

الباحث عن ماله المسروق يستطيع اللحق به بسرعة الا إذا كان كسولاً

This is used to underline the importance of catching an animal thief immediately. It is also used ironically if the animal cannot be retrieved before it is eaten by the thief (al-Shahri 2000, 92, 268).

The term *ṭerd* 'pursuer' (MLZ, 580: الذي يلاحق لصوص الماشية 'The one who tracks down cattle thieves') is not recorded in JL, although the terms listed under the root √ṭrd are semantically related to this term (JL, 279–80). The vowel [ɛ] in the suffix attached to the preposition *l-* is unexpected (Rubin 2014, 268). The verbal form *yɔlḥɔ́ḳ* is a subjunctive 3.M.SG. of a Gb-stem meaning 'to catch up with, overtake, run after' (JL, 163) and is used here with optative force.

The literal meaning of this expression is problematic: notwithstanding the Arabic and English renditions, the Jibbali/Śḥərε̄t texts seems to mean 'the pursuer will catch if there is no other pursuer against him'.

(86)

a-ʕaḳar ṣerb

The youth is spring (the season)

النمو والفتوة هي الربيع

This is said of a person whose appearance and/or circumstances improved with age (al-Shahri 2000, 92, 268).

The term ʕaḵar is reported to mean 'size' (JL, 11) and, additionally, 'growth' (MLZ, 639–40: الكِبَر. الطول. النمو), with the latter meaning probably to be interpreted here as 'age of growth' and, therefore, 'youth'. The term ṣerb means 'autumn (the period from October to December after the monsoon rains)' (JL, 241).

(87)

ə-ʕáśər ɛ-raḥím əxer ar a-ġa e-défər

A good friend is better than a bad brother

الصديق الجيد خير من الشقيق السيئ

This self-explanatory proverb stems from the awareness that friends are often closer than one's own relatives (al-Shahri 2000, 92, 268). The term ʕáśər means 'husband; close friend' (JL, 17). The adjective raḥím has the peculiar meaning 'beautiful, good' (JL, 210; MLZ, 368: حسن) *vis á vis* its Arabic cognate raḥīm 'merciful, compassionate' (Wehr and Cowan 1976, 332).

(88)

aʕʕər e-défər bə-tbaʕ ser śɛfš

Send an incapable man and follow him

أرسل الأحمق واقتفي أثره

This is said upon someone's failure to carry out a task (al-Shahri 2000, 92, 268).

The imperative aʕʕər stems from a H1-stem verb < √ʕrr meaning 'to send, send for' (JL, 14). The term śɛf is used here in its original meaning 'trace, track' (JL, 246). However, it underwent a process of grammaticalisation in Mehri and Jibbali/Śḥərɛ̄t into a discourse particle meaning 'it turned out'. This process is discussed in Watson and al-Mahri (2017, 95–96).

(89)

ɔ̃l ɛ̃-yɔ mugʲũś

You can own something belonging to another for only a few hours

مال الناس يبقى معك صبحية او برهة فقط

This is a comment made upon re-gaining possession of something that had been lent sooner than the borrower expected (al-Shahri 2000, 92, 269).

The H2-stem participial form *mugʲũś* 'gone at late night' is unrecorded (MLZ, 208) and, similarly to the form of the same verb used in entry number **(83)** above, it is pronounced with a nasalised consonant, which would argue for a √*gmś* root, despite its being listed under √*gwś* (MLZ, 208).

(90)

ãʕtilím míbdi

The learner over-exaggerates

الحديث الخبرة كثيرالمبالغة

This is a comment made about someone who, in new circumstances, claims to know how to act despite actually not knowing (al-Shahri 2000, 93, 269).

This proverb is made up of two participial forms: *ãʕtilím* < **e-maʕtilím* 'educated' from the root √*ʕlm* (JL, 13), which is better translated as 'learner' in this case; and *míbdi*, which seems to convey the sense of 'exaggerated' (كثير المبالغة), and is, in all likelihood, connected to √*bdy* 'lying' (JL, 23; MLZ, 119–20), but is hitherto unrecorded.

This proverb is also recorded by MLZ (119) as أَعْتِلِمْ مِبّدي.

2. Proverbs and Linguistic Analysis

(91)

ɔ̇̃ɫ yəślél āʕlš

The property lifts its owner

المال يحمل ويرفع صاحبه

This can be used either as an encouragement to be financially independent, or as a comment about someone who, in spite of not being liked by most members of a community, is wealthy (al-Shahri 2000, 93, 269).

The verbal form is an imperfective 3.M.SG. of a G-stem meaning 'lift up off the ground' (JL, 252). Unlike in entry number **(89)** above, the devoicing/pre-aspiration of /l/ is clearly audible here. The segment āʕlš is from *a-baʕl-š. This expression corresponds to Mehri *mōl yrōfaʕ baʕläh* 'Besitz erhebt seinen Besitzer' (Sima 2005, 80).

(92)

a-ġarɔ́ ə-gīd yəṭabri

The good speech breaks me down

الكلام الجيد يُحد ويُهدئ من غضبي

This is used when someone tries to convince another person by means of heated arguments at first, and then calms down and uses more relaxed and friendly manners (al-Shahri 2000, 93, 270).

This saying features a mixed Mehri–Jibbali/Śḥərḗt language, although, as al-Shahri explains in the Arabic commentary, هذا المثل مخلوط المهرية الشحرية إلا انه يميل الى المهرية اكثر من الشحرية مع العلم بان اللغتين متقاربان جداً 'This proverb is a mixture of the Mehri and Shehri languages, but it tends to Mehri more than to Shehri, notwithstanding the close kinship of the two languages'. The verb *yəṭabri* 'breaks me', for example, is the normal form for 'it breaks me' in Mehri, with a 1.C.SG. personal suffix attached. That said, the Mehri version of this proverb, *ġrō jīd yṯōbär ḥaysi* 'Eine gute Rede bricht meinen Zorn' (Sima 2005, 80), features the additional segment *ḥaysi* 'my anger'.

(93)

ɔ ġɔlɔ́b l-ōlš ɔ́ leš miṯɔ́rə lɔ

You cannot blame a person for keeping his own property

من لم التهاون في ماله لا لوم عليه

This proverb is used when a person complains about not being able to obtain something for free (al-Shahri 2000, 93, 270).

In utterance-initial position, ɔ represents the relativiser ɛ having been influenced by the leftmost vowel of the following segment, as expected in the presence of an intervening guttural (JL, xxix–xxx). The verbal form *ġɔlɔ́b* is a perfective third person of a Ga-stem meaning 'to refuse' (JL, 85). The vowel in the pronominal suffix attached to the preposition *l-* is [e], unlike in entry number **(85)** above, which has [ɛ]. The term *miṯɔ́r*, which appears here with the meaning 'blame', is not recorded in the lexical sources used in this study. In light of the above, the literal meaning of this expression is 'he who doesn't refuse his wealth, there is no blame on him'.

(94)

ɛ aġad yəkɔ́ṣ ḥɔ́gət fɛlɔ́ yəs̃eṣɔ́fɔ

He who travels about will gain wealth or knowledge

من سعى يكسب مالاً او معلومة

This is used either to encourage lazy people to seek adventure, or as a comment about those who have attained something valuable as a result of travelling (al-Shahri 2000, 94, 270).

The imperfective 3.M.SG. of a Ga-stem verb *yɔkɔ́ś* < √kśy is recorded in JL (158) as 'to pay; to pay blood-money', which, given the general meaning of the proverb, would not make sense. However, if we view this verb as an Arabic loan, we can find the meaning 'to fulfil', associated with the expression قضي الحاجة (Wehr and Cowan 1976, 212), which is consistent with both the English and the Arabic translation of this proverb. The final vowel in the verb *yɔśeṣɔ́fɔ*, an imperfective 3.M.SG. of a Š1-stem < √ṣfv meaning 'to gather news, find out' (JL, 237), is transcribed by al-Shahri (2000, 270) as إ, which normally indicates [ɛ]. It therefore exhibits the same phenomenon found in entries **(40)** and **(45)** above, where the term *t̪ɔ́dɛ* 'breast' is realised as *t̪ɔ́dɔ*, and the term *gɔ́fɛ* 'shadow' is realised as *gɔ́fɔ*. The Mehri counterpart of this saying is *ḏ-yäsyūr, ykayẑ ḥōjät w-lī yäṣṣayf* 'Wer (aus dem Haus) geht, erledigt wichtige Dinge und eignet sich Wissen an' (Sima 2005, 80–81)

(95)
ɛ-ferdɔ́t tfɔ́rd ɛd ēmítés
When an animal is frightened it takes flight and re-joins its herd
الجافلة تهرب الى أمهاتها

This sentence is uttered to comment on the faithfulness of certain people towards their families and tribes, so that they will always remember home regardless of how far they travel, and will not let hard feelings come between them and their loved ones (al-Shahri 2000, 94, 270).

The verbal form *tfɔ́rd* is an imperfective 3.F.SG. of a Ga-stem meaning 'to stampede, panic' (JL, 59) and, as is the case with entry number **(21)** of the MLZ collection, it is realised with a long vowel. The segment *ēmítέs* 'her mothers' is the result of the plural *εmə́tə* 'mothers' (JL, 3) with a definite article *ε* and a postposed 3.F.SG. personal suffix attached. Compare the Mehri expression *ḏ-färdōt tfōräd taḥwēl ḥāmutyäs* '(Das Kälbchen,) das Angst bekommt, läuft vor Angst zu seinen Müttern' (Sima 2005, 81). In light of the original text, its Arabic translation, and its Mehri counterpart, this expression can be more faithfully rendered in English as 'the frightened animal runs to its mothers in fear'.

(96)
e-ffudún ɔ ṭ-ṭɔ́rəs ar e-ġits
A stone only break his sister
لا تكسر الحجارة إلا اختها

This means that stubborn people can only be made to see reason by someone more stubborn than them (al-Shahri 2000, 94, 271).

As in entry number **(40)**, it is possible to observe here a term whose initial sound is a voiceless non-glottalic consonant with a definite marker: *e-ffudún*. The 3.F.SG. prefix of the imperfective Ga verbal form *ṭṭɔ́rəs* < *tṭɔ́rəs*, meaning 'to break' (JL, 282) shows the effects of regressive assimilation. There is a 3.F.SG. personal suffix *-s* attached to it, referring to *fudún* 'rock' (JL, 51), which must, at least in this case, be regarded as lexically feminine. The corresponding Mehri expression is *ṣōwar aṭṭᵃḵūḵas är ġits* 'Ein Stein zerschlägt nur seine Schwester' (Sima 2005, 81), also recorded by ML (368) as a *ṣāwar, ṭəbrīs ār aġās* 'only a stone can break a stone'.[24]

(97)

e-ḳiśɛ́t śirík b īźirún

The wolf is the partner of the goat-herder

الدئب شريك برعاة الغنم

This is a remark about the clever taking advantage of the simple (al-Shahri 2000, 94, 271). It uses the terms *ḳiśɛ́t* 'wolf' (JL, 153; MLZ, 748: ذئب), and *iźirún* 'shepherd' (JL, 4; MLZ, 830: رعاة الغنم).

(98)

ɛ ḳizáʕ! ɛ ḳizáʕ! ɔl ʕáśər heš b-ɔ̄l beṭáḥ

You, Kieza, wake up. You have no husband and no baydhah

يا قيزاع يا قيزاع لا زوج عندك ولا بيظح

This is used to joke about daydreamers and is based on a folk tale in which a woman named Ḳizaʕ had been talking in her sleep about getting married whilst she was out in the wild with other women in order to harvest the *beṭaḥ* plant (al-Shahri 2000, 95, 271).

The vocative particle ɛ (JL, 1) receives a prominent stress within the utterance. The feminine personal name Ḳizaʕ seems not to be recorded elsewhere; however, cf. Arabic قزعة 'wind-driven, tattered clouds, scud; tuft of hair' (Wehr and Cowan 1976, 761), and see also Castagna (2022b). The plant name *beṭaḥ* corresponds to *Gladiolus ukambanensis* (Miller and Morris 1988, 150), a plant whose corms are traditionally eaten.

---

[24] Literally 'the stone, only its brother breaks it'.

(99)

e-ḳiśśét tṩsɔrḥ

The lone cow is always in danger

الحيوان الذي يرعى منفرجاً يتعرض للخطر

This saying is a reminder that there is no safety in being alone (al-Shahri 2000, 95, 272).

The term *ḳiśśét* is an etymological cognate with *ḳiśét* 'wolf' (see entry number **(97)** above). Al-Shahri's Arabic translation الحيوان 'the animal', however, suggests this is the most fitting meaning in this case. The verbal form *tṩsɔrḥ* is an imperfective 3.F.SG. of a Š1-stem meaning 'to be in danger' and is not recorded in the lexical sources used in this study.

(100)

ɛ ḳéṣər Ɛrgʲɛ́f! ed tak tak l-enúfk (l-enúf) b-ed ḳéləʕk ḳéləʕk ḥanúf

You, the lion of Arjaff, if you save something, you save it for yourself. If you eat everything, you will be the loser

يا اسد منطقة ارجاف إن أسرفت أسرفت على نفسك وإن وفرت وفرت لنفسك

This is a remark about someone who tends to be a spendthrift (al-Shahri 2000, 95, 272). According to al-Shahri, *Ɛrgʲɛ́f* is a place where the Arabian leopard used to live. A place named *Arjef* can be found today in eastern Dhofar at 17°56'35.7"N 55°04'36.0"E.[25] The meaning of *ed* in this case seems to be that of 'if', normally *əḏə* (Rubin 2014, 349). Alternatively, this might be an allomorph of the preposition *ɛd* (Rubin 2014, 365–66). The segment *ḥanúf* 'for (your)self' is made up of the preposition *hɛr* 'to, for' and the

---

[25] No Jibbali/Śḥərɛ́t speakers currently live in the area.

reflexive pronoun *ɛnúf* (Rubin 2014, 64). The verbal forms *tak* and *ḳəlaʕk* are, respectively, a perfective 2.M.SG. of a G-stem < √*twy* 'to eat' (JL, 273) and a perfective 2.M.SG. of a Ga-stem meaning 'to let, allow' (JL, 144), which is understood to have the meaning of 'eat' here. The Arabic rendition of this saying employs the form IV verb أسرف 'to waste, squander, dissipate, spend lavishly' (Wehr and Cowan 1976, 408), and the form II verb وفر 'to save' (Wehr and Cowan 1978, 1083).

(101)

ɛ k-e-défər iṣɔ́ḥ défər
The one who accompanies the bad becomes bad

من عاشر السيئ يكون سيئاً مثله

This proverb is used as a warning of the consequences of being with people of ill repute (al-Shahri 2000, 95, 262).

The H1-stem verb *iṣɔ́ḥ* is used here in the sense of 'becoming' (JL, 234), in a parallel fashion to its Arabic cognate, the causative verb *aṣbaḥa* 'to become' (Wehr and Cowan 1976, 500), which likewise exhibits a connection to the semantic field of 'morning'. Although √*ṣbḥ* is not the native Modern South Arabian root for 'morning', one should not rule out a parallel development *a priori*, as this would offer a satisfactory explanation for the use of the verb in the sense of 'becoming' here. In Mehri, the expression *ḥayr yäsyūr k-ḥayr yäšḥäyl źraṯyäh* 'Der Esel geht (nur) mit dem Esel, der seinen Kot liebt' (Sima 2005, 81) is similar in meaning, despite the profound lexical divergences.

A variant of this expression is *her aġad-ək kə-raḥím tken raḥím / her aġad-ək kə-misérʳd tken misérʳd* 'if you go with the good, you will good. If you go with the evil, you will be evil'.

This comes from an elderly speaker from al-Ḥallānīya (Kuria Muria; Castagna 2018, 415).

(102)

ɔl bke tɔ ar sudḳi b-ɔl ṣ́hek tɔ ar ḥaṣᵊmi (xaṣᵊmi)

He who makes me cry is a friend, and he who makes me laugh is an enemy

لم يبكني إلا من صدق معي ولم يضحكني إلا عدوي

This may be said upon making an unpleasant, but necessary, negative remark, or upon being flattered (al-Shahri 2000, 96, 273).

Al-Shahri utters a [ħ] instead of a [x] in the first repetition of the term *xaṣᵊm* (JL, 306). A similar and more systematic phenomenon has been documented in the dialect of al-Ḥallānīyah in the vicinity of low vowels (Castagna 2018, 126–27). The verbal forms are imperfective third-person forms of two H1-stems meaning, respectively, 'to cause to weep' (JL, 25) and 'to make laugh' (JL, 325). The similarities to Mehri *raḥmät Allah lä-ḏ-bäkyīni, w-naʕlat Allah lä-ḏ-źaḥkīni* 'Die Gnade Gottes für den, der mich beweint, und der Fluch Gottes für den, der mich verlacht' (Sima 2005, 81) are hard to miss.

(103)

ɔl aʕtɔ́dɔ b-ɔl ṭólum

He is not aggressive nor unjust

لم يعتدي ولم يظلم

This is said when a son behaves like his father (al-Shahri 2000, 96, 273).

The verbal form əʕtɔ́dɔ, a perfective third person of a T2-stem < √ʕdw, is listed in JL (7) as a'tede 'to attack', and as 'assault' < √ʕdy in MLZ (614: اَعتُدى). The verb ṭólum is a perfective third-person form of a Ga-stem meaning 'to oppress, be unjust' (JL, 49).

(104)

ɔl ɛléd b-ɔ teléd

So-and-so, no sons, no daughters

لا اولاد ذكور ولا اُناث

This can be either a comment about someone who has not wanted to get married, or a sympathetic remark about someone who, in spite of being married, does not have children (al-Shahri 2000, 96, 273).

The term teléd, not recorded by JL, is listed in MLZ (156) with the meaning 'issue, posterity, legacy' (العقب \ الذرية. التركة). MLZ records this proverb within the same entry, giving a slightly different Arabic translation: فلان ليس له ولد وعقب 'so-and-so has neither a son nor a legacy'. This expression is recorded as أذيلين أل ألد بو تلد by MLZ (156). The nearly identical counterpart of this expression in Mehri is lä-wlēd w-lä-tlēd '(Er hat) keine Kinder und (seine Frau) wird auch keine mehr zur Welt bringen' (Sima 2005, 82).

(105)

ɔl te he ɛ bə Məṣ°nín lɔ tte ʕar hɛt ɛ b e-Foruš

I didn't eat here in Massneen, how can you eat in Foroush?

انا الذي في مصنين لم أكل فكيف تأكل انت الذي في فوروش؟

This saying is uttered when someone cannot have something that someone else can have easily, and stems from a folk tale of two jinns, living in separate caves named *Məṣnín* and *Foruš̃* near Wadi Darbat. When the jinn in *Foruš̃* asked if there was anything to eat, the jinn in *Məṣnín* replied with this sentence (al-Shahri 2000, 96, 274).

The place-name *Məṣnín* is also recorded by MLZ (872). The use of *ʕar* 'only, except' with the meaning of 'how come' is idiomatic. Both verbal forms are derived from the Ga-stem < √*twy* 'to eat' (JL, 273): the first one behaves as an imperfective 1.C.SG., although it lacks the expected prefix (al-Kathiri and Dufour 2020, 215).[26]

(106)
ɔl te dúgʲur lɔ ɛštéḳə ʕar e-míhɛ́š
I don't eat the beans but I drink their water
لا اكل الفاصوليا وإنما أشرب ماءها؟

This is used when someone claims not to be doing something whilst doing something very similar to what he claims not to be doing (al-Shahri 2000, 96, 274).

The intonation of the speaker, as well as the Arabic translation, make it clear that this is a question. The imperfective 1.C.SG. of the G-stem < √*twy*, as in the preceding entry, lacks the corresponding prefix. The second verbal form *ɛštéḳə* is an imperfective 1.C.SG. of a T1-stem < √*šḳy* meaning 'to drink' (JL,

---

[26] This prefix is a short vowel, so that the preceding negation *ɔl* might have a role in neutralising it.

262).²⁷ The segment *e-mîhéš* 'its water' indicates broth rather than water, as shown by a similar expression in Mehri involving meat instead of beans: *atäyw tiwyäs lä är mräkas* 'Ich esse nicht ihr Fleisch sondern (trinke) nur ihre Brühe' (Sima 2005, 82).

(107)

ɔl ṭirɔ́t b-ɔ́l ġizyũt
It has not been fractured and has not been sprained

لم تنكسر ولم تنفك

This proverb is used in two ways: either as a comment about an action which, although frowned upon, has not caused any trouble, or about a problem whose solutions are all likely to have the same outcome (al-Shahri 2000, 97, 274).

The first verbal form *ṭirɔ́t* is a perfective 3.F.SG. of a passive Ga-stem < √*ṭbr* meaning 'to break' (JL, 282). The second verbal form is a perfective 3.F.SG. of a Gb-stem *ġizyũt* meaning 'to get a sprained joint' < √*ġzm* (JL, 92). Compare the Mehri expression *l-ṭäbrōt wa-l-ġazmōt* 'Es ist weder gebrochen noch verstaucht' (Sima 2005, 82).

(108)

ɔl gʲíbər níḳi b-ɔl ḥ-mu əntwáh
The genitals were not clean and the water was not saved

لا الفرج تنظف ولا الماء توفر

This is used when a big effort is made in vain. Additionally, it may be used as a comment about unsuccessful backbiting (al-Shahri 2000, 97, 275).

---

²⁷ For a commentary on this verb, see entry number **(4)** of this collection.

Like entry number **(13)** of this collection, the language used is strongly influenced by Mehri: *gī́bər* is 'vulva' in Mehri (ML, 113); compare Jibbali/Śḥərɛ́t *ẓyɛb* (JL, 69). The Mehri term *mu(h)* 'water' (ML, 274) is used in conjunction with the Mehri definiteness marker *ḥ-* (Watson 2012, 63–64). The verb *əntwah* 'to be plentiful', in the T-stem, rendered in Arabic as وفر 'to abound' (Wehr and Cowan 1976, 1083), is not recorded in the lexical sources used in this study. However, the presence of a [w] points to a non-native term (Rubin 2014, 33–35). Additionally, compare the Mehri verb *nəwo* '(rain-clouds) to pile up' < √nwʔ (ML, 305). Rather unexpectedly, Sima does not record any corresponding proverb in Mehri.

(109)

ɔl ḥaré ʕar ɛ ɛgdéb b-ɔl beké ʕar ɛ taʕáb

Only those in need ask for help, and only those in pain will cry

لم يطلب إلا من أعدم ولم يبكِ إلا من تألّم

This saying is used to reproach those who declare that someone apparently in need is, in fact, lying (al-Shahri 2000, 97, 275).

According to Rubin (2012), the Ga-stem verb *ḥaré* 'to beg' (JL, 115), which appears here in the perfective third-person form, is the source of the future markers *dḥa-*, *ḥa-*, and *a-*. The verbal form *ɛgdéb* is a perfective third person of a H1-stem meaning 'to become poor and hungry' (JL, 70). The third verbal form *beké* is a perfective third person of a Ga-stem meaning 'to weep' (JL, 25). Finally, the fourth verbal form is a perfective third person of a Gb-stem meaning 'to be weary' (JL, 269).

2. Proverbs and Linguistic Analysis

(110)

ɔl rɛš b-ɔl gʲɔd

Neither head nor the skin

لا رأس ولا جلد

This is used as a comment about an unsuccessful search (al-Shahri 2000, 97, 275). The Mehri counterpart of this expression is *la-hrēh wa-l-jōd* 'Weder Kopf noch Haut' (Sima 2005, 82).

(111)

ɔl Səʕad b-ɔl Masʕúd əxér

Neither Sa'ad nor Masa'oud is better

لا سعد ولا مسعود افضل

This saying is used when having to choose between two things that are equally unappealing (al-Shahri 2000, 98, 276). *Səʕad* and *Masʕúd* are two personal names of Arabic origin.

(112)

ɔl śerᵊġét b-ɔ̄l farḥát

I'm not attracted by him (or her), and I don't even like him (or her)

لا ميل ولا رغبة

This saying is used as a description of someone who is deemed not to be attractive in any way, either physically or in terms of personality (al-Shahri 2000, 98, 276). The two nouns appearing in this expression, *śerᵊġét* and *ferḥát*, mean, respectively, 'physical desire' (JL, 255) and 'happiness' (JL, 60). However, MLZ (695) renders the latter as رغبة, 'desire', which seems more fitting in this context. Therefore, the overall meaning can be understood as '(I feel) no (physical) desire and no longing (for so-and-so)'. Compare Mehri *flān l-śärġāt wa-l-färḥāt* 'NN—weder Leidenschaft noch Freude' (Sima 2005, 82). See also entry **(176)** of this collection.

(113)

ɔl ś̃ᵊnít b-ɔ̄l xɔ̄r

He has neither a good appearance nor hidden qualities

لا مظهر حسن ولا خفايا حسنة

The meaning of this proverb is similar to that of proverb number **(112)** above, although no physical attraction is necessarily implied in this case (al-Shahri 2000, 98,276).

The term *ś̃ᵊnít* means 'sight' (JL, 253) and *xɔ̄r* means 'analysis of the human being, his noble qualities (opposite of evident)' (MLZ, 313: [مخير الانسان \ صفاته النبيلة [عكس المظهر).[28]

(114)

ɔl s̃ɔrɔ́ken ṭēl ʕar her nənḥáǵ

We only made the music for dancing

لم نطبل إلا من اجل ان نرقص

This is often said when someone asks why a certain event is taking place, and the reason is rather obvious (al-Shahri 2000, 98, 276).

The verbal form *s̃ɔrɔ́ken* is a perfective 1.C.PL. of a Ga-stem meaning 'to make' (JL, 267). The vowel between C^1 and C^2 is normally [e], but here it assimilates to the stressed vowel in an

---

[28] This term is not recorded by JL.

assimilatory process typical of the eastern dialects of the language.[29] The second verbal form *nənḥáǵ* is an imperfective 1.C.PL. of a Ga-stem meaning 'to dance' (JL, 186; al-Kathiri and Dufour 2020, 202). The term *ṭɛ̄l* < √*ṭbl* 'drum' (JL, 274) is used synecdochally here for 'music'.

(115)

e-lšín ɛ̄-ššefḳ

The tongue of a suitor

لسان الخاطب

This remark is used when someone's actions, performance or general behaviour does not live up to one's expectations (al-Shahri 2000, 98, 277).

The term *šefḳ* 'bridegroom' (MLZ, 480: العريس) is used here idiomatically for 'someone whose words are persuasive' and is translated as 'suitor' in English (al-Shahri 2000, 98), and خاتب in Arabic (al-Shahri, 277). This expression formally corresponds to Mehri *lšän ḏ-hīfaḳ* '(Er hat) die Zunge eines Brautwerbers' (Sima 2005, 83).

(116)

ɔl meʕʕádəd śɛ́fɛ b-ɔ̄l teṯ śəbrɔ́t

Don't delay marrying a beautiful woman, and don't delay using the freshly grown grass

لا تأجيل للأرض الخصبة ولا للمرأة الجميلة

This is used to convince someone to act on a matter sooner rather than later (al-Shahri 2000, 99, 277).

---

[29] See Introduction, p. 20. See also entry number **(5)** of the MLZ collection.

The participial form *meʃʕádəd* 'late' is linked to a Š1-stem verb *šaʕded* derived from the root √ʕdd, meaning 'to put something aside temporarily' (JL, 6), and hence 'to procrastinate'. JL does not record a participial form for this verb. However, MLZ (612) does: مذخور \ مؤخر لوقت الحاجة \ الشدة. It is noteworthy that this participial form is used as a predicate.

The term *ɕ́ɛ́fɛ* means 'untouched, uncropped grass' (JL, 246). The F.SG. adjective *ṣ́əbrɔ́t* 'perfect' is not recorded in JL. However, MLZ (499) records it with the meaning 'perfection' (الاتقان).

(117)
ɔl ʕara b-ɔ šidád
There is no guard and no door
لا حراس ولا باب موصد

This saying may be used in three different circumstances: (1) when there is nothing to be afraid of, (2) when one is not afraid of someone else's threats, or (3) as a comment on property being left unguarded at the mercy of thieves (al-Shahri 2000, 99, 277).

The term *ʕara* 'vigil, sleeplessness' (MLZ, 623: السهر, السهاد) is not recorded by JL. The term *šidád* is translated as 'door' in English (al-Shahri 2000, 99), and باب موصد in Arabic (al-Shahri, 277). However, MLZ (474) has سد 'obstruction' (Wehr and Cowan 1976, 403), to which *šidad* seems to be etymologically related.

(118)
ɔl kɔb b-ɔl ḳiṣ́əʕét
No dogs, no rats
لاذئاب ولا قوارض ولا...

This is said in response to enquiries about one's situation and means that everything is basically fine (al-Shahri 2000, 99, 278).

The term ḳiṣ̂əʕet 'rats/rodents' is not recorded as such by JL or MLZ. However, both publications do list verbs and nouns within the semantic field of 'biting' (JL, 157; MLZ, 755: قرض). The final ولا 'nor' in the Arabic translation of this proverb implies that other items may be (optionally?) attached to this proverb.

(119)

ɔl mušúr b-ɔl aḳʕát

No sardines food and no winter winds

لا علف للحيوان ولا رياح الشتاء

This is used when a person refuses to lend any kind of help (al-Shahri 2000, 100, 278).

The term *mušur*, not listed in JL, is translated as 'livestock fodder' by MLZ (868: علف الماشية). The term *aḳʕát* is from √kʕw 'strong, cold, rainless wind' (JL, 140; Morris et al. 2019, 76). Since sardines are indeed used as animal fodder in Dhofar during the dry season, and the fresh winter grass is similarly used to feed livestock, al-Shahri's translation makes sense.

(120)

ɔl mɔ́lɔkᵊ li i-defər ar bə xɔš

The bad person cannot conquer me except by his mouth

لم يهزمني السيئ البذي إلا بفمه (لسانه)

This is said when giving up an argument with someone evil (al-Shahri 2000, 100, 279). The corresponding expression in Mehri is *mlōk lī bḏi är bä-lšänäh* 'Der Böse beherrscht mich nur durch seine Zunge' (Sima 2005, 83). The verbal form *mɔlɔk* is a perfective third person of a Ga-stem meaning 'to own' (JL, 171).

(121)

ɔl yəṣáf e-ḏēh / ɔ léṣəf e-ḏēh
Even the very best person is not safe from misfortune
لم ولن يسلم الانسان الطيب الجميل

This is said when a person who is generally successful falls into misfortune (al-Shahri 2000, 100, 279).

The interpretation of this proverb is problematic in view of some degree of ambiguity in the recording which could not be clarified through either the translations provided or the transcription given by al-Shahri. Consequently, the utterance may be segmented in two different ways. The verbal forms *yəṣáf* and *léṣəf* are, respectively, an imperfective and a subjunctive 3.M.SG. of a Gb-stem deriving from √*wṣf* and meaning 'to survive trials' (JL, 293). The term *ḏēh* 'misfortune' < √*ḏbh* is not listed in JL. MLZ (349) records a H1-stem verb under the above-mentioned root, meaning 'to distort, to seek/try to distort something' (شوه, سعى \ حاول تشويه الشيء), so this is likely to be a nominal form derived from this root.

(122)

ɔl edəʕ de bə de b-ɔl bə e-tek a ḥéfəl
No one knows anything about anyone, nor about the ripe figs
لم يعلم احد بأحد ولا بالتينة ذات الثمار الناضجة

This is used to comment about one's inability to give help, or to suggest that someone is under the wrong impression about someone (al-Shahri 2000, 100, 279).

The verbal form *edəʕ* is a perfective third person of a Gb-stem meaning 'to know' (JL, 286).[30]

The relativiser is realised as [a], probably because of the contiguity of a pharyngeal consonant.

The term *teḳ* means 'wild fig' (JL, 282).

The term *ḥéfəl* is not recorded as such by the lexical sources used in this study. However, the root √ḥfl is listed both by JL (104–5) and MLZ (249–50), and the terms listed fall within the semantic field of fruit ripeness. Given that the pattern $C^1éC^2əC^3$ often represents active participles (JL, *passim*), one is led to hypothesise that this term simply means 'ripe'.

(123)

ēnfí ɔl ḳéləʕ her axᵊrí śe lɔ

By saying everything our ancestors leave nothing for us to say

لم يترك السلف للخلف شيء (حكمة)

This means that the ancestors, having said a lot, have not left anything for their descendants to say. This is used in response to other proverbs (al-Shahri 2000, 101, 280).

The term *ɛnfí*, listed by JL under the root √ʔnf, and under the root √nfy by MLZ, normally means 'first, ancient' (JL, 4), but it can also mean 'forbear, ancestor' (MLZ, 931). The term *axᵊrí* usually means 'late, later, last; second; behind' (JL, 5) and is used here to contrast with *ɛnfí* and convey the meaning of 'descendant'. Compare the Mehri expression *ḥāwᵃlī l-ʿād kūlaʿ här āxᵃrī śī lā* 'Der Vorfahre hat dem Nachfahren nichts übrig gelassen' (Sima 2005, 83).

---

[30] See entry number **(41)** for further details about Gb-stem forms.

(124)

in ḳɔṭṭəʕ ḳɔṭṭəʕ

What has been paid is paid

ما تم دفعه قد زال

This is said when paying off a debt (al-Shahri 2000, 101, 280).

The less common relative pronoun *in* 'all that' (Rubin 2014, 72) is attested here.[31] The verb *ḳɔṭṭəʕ* < *ḳɔṭṭəʕ* is a perfective third person of a T1-stem, and is listed as 'to get cut' (JL, 154). However, the corresponding participial form *mekɔṭṭəʕ* is listed by MLZ (758), and not by JL, as 'compensation, or what is paid in exchange for the settlement of a debt' (العوض او ما يسدد من متاع بدل الدين). From a paremiological point of view, this proverb exhibits a strong element of tautology (Norrick 2015, 18).

(125)

e-nḳel máġˤreb mən ṭɛr šfret

The good person is known even when he is in the cradle

الذكي يُعرف حتى وهو لا يزال على فراش المهد

This saying is used to comment on the talents of a child (al-Shahri 2000, 101, 280).

The audio has *e-nḳel*, with a short vowel (presumably a definite article). However, the meaning given by JL (190), 'choice (livestock)', does not fit. Conversely, what one would expect here is *ẽnḳel* < **e-menḳel* 'active, energetic, heroic', from the same root (JL, 190). This, however, would raise questions as to the missing initial nasalised vowel. The passive participle *maġˤreb*

---

[31] It is also found in entry number **(9)** of the elicited proverbs.

means 'famous, well-known' (JL, 88). The term *šfrét* 'cradle' (MLZ, 478) is not recorded by JL.

(126)

in hē mən šútum yɔ́te b-e-gidrítᵊ

What falls from the sky will hit the ground

ما يسقط من السماء يستقر على الارض

This proverb means that actions have unavoidable consequences (al-Shahri 2000, 101, 281). The rare relativiser *in* (Rubin 2014, 72) is used here, as it is in entry number **(9)** of the elicited proverbs below. The verbal form *hē* is a perfective third person of a G-stem deriving from a doubly weak root √*hwy* meaning 'to fall' (JL, 100; al-Kathiri and Dufour 2020, 195). The verb *yɔ́te* is an imperfective 3.M.SG. of a Gb-stem from the root √*wty* meaning 'to come, come upon; to happen to be; to fall upon' (JL, 294; al-Kathiri and Dufour 2020, 194).

Additionally, MLZ (969) records this expression as إن هيئ من شُتم يوتئ بجدرت. Compare Mehri *l-hīn hwūh män (hītäm), ywōkaḇ-ärź* 'Wenn (etwas) vom Himmel fallt, landet es auf der Erde' (Sima 2005, 83).

(127)

ɔ́l šīʕ lɔ yənxērgʲɔ́l

Who doesn't hear, falls through the gap

من لم يسمع يسقط من خلال ثقب المنزل المهترئ

This is said upon noticing that someone is not listening to what is being said (al-Shahri 2000, 101, 281).

The quadriliteral verb *yənxērgʲɔ́l* is an imperfective 3.M.SG. of a ᵠN1-stem from the root √*xrgl* meaning 'to decline, get into difficulties' (JL, 304). Furthermore, JL (304) records a variant of this proverb: *ḏ-ɔl šĩʕ lɔʾ, yənxargɔ́l*. Sima (2005, 83–84) records a similar proverb, *aš-šäṣwūl ġrō lä, yäntᵃräšḥ*, which is translated with a rather different (albeit not totally divergent) meaning: 'Wer die (eigene) Rede nicht genau prüft, bringt (alles) durcheinander'.

(128)

ɔb yaʕrér ĩšáʕgʲəl

The closed door stops those who are in a hurry

الباب يوقف المستعجل

This is said upon giving up trying to get something from someone (al-Shahri 2000, 102, 281).

The verbal form *yaʕrér* is an imperfective 3.M.SG. of a G-stem from a geminate root √ʕrr meaning, among other things, 'stop something from going' (JL, 14). The participial form *ĩšaʕgʲəl* < *e-mešaʕgʲəl* is not listed by JL. However, MLZ (610) lists it as 'hurried' (المستعجل).

(129)

ɔ yaḥtégʲa ʕafɔ́r ar ɛd déhəḳ

The clouds only gather on the high mountains

لا يتجمع السحاب إلا على قمم الجبال

This is a comment about someone who turns out to be capable of sorting an issue which all others failed to sort. Therefore, the clouds are a metaphor for normal people, whilst the summit represents the wise person to whom the others turn (al-Shahri 2000, 102, 282).

The verbal form *yaḥtégʲa* is an imperfective 3.M.SG. of a T1-stem meaning, among other things, 'to come together' (JL, 106).

(130)

ɔ yəsɔkf l-ɔ̄rəm ar ɛ̃ltɛ̃́s̃ fəlɔ́h ɛ̃gᵊtɛ̃l

No-one lives beside the road except the unkind person or the generous person

لا يجلس على قارعة الطريق إلا البخيل او الكريم

This saying is used to express appreciation towards a good person, or disapproval towards a bad person. Al-Shahri (2000, 102, 282) asserts that in the olden days roads were very few in Dhofar, and those who lived near them were either good people who wanted to help travellers, or bad people who established their dwellings by the road for the convenience of it.

The term *ɛ̃ltɛ̃́s̃* < *ε-məltɛ̃́s̃* is not recorded by JL. MLZ (824) lists it as 'heedless, mean' (النظق . اللئيم). MLZ records this proverb within the above-mentioned entry as ايسُكْف لورم عر إيلتابش فلُه إيجتيل, and translates into Arabic as يجلس \ يسكن بالقرب من الطريق اللئيم \ الكري 'no one lives near the road except the wicked/the generous' (MLZ, 824). The term *fəlɔ́h* 'or' has an audible final [h], which is unexpected (Rubin 2014, 317). *ɛ̃gᵊtɛ̃l* < *e-məgᵊtɛ̃l* < √gml 'generous' is recorded by JL (76) as *məgtīl*.

(131)

ɔ yəsdíd b-ɔ yəbtidíd

They don't agree and they don't separate

لا يتفقون ولا يفترقون

This proverb normally refers to children who are supposed to be friends, but have frequent disagreements (al-Shahri 2000, 102, 282).

The verbal form *yəsdíd* is an imperfective 3.M.PL. of a G-stem from the geminate root √sdd and means, among other things, 'to agree on terms' (JL, 223). The verb *yəbtidíd* 'to separate' is a 3.M.PL. imperfective of a T1-stem derived from the root √bdd, which covers terms connected to the semantic field of 'separation' (JL, 22; MLZ, 117–18). The Mehri counterpart of this proverb is *l-yäsdīd wa-l-yäbtᵃdīd* 'Sie kommen nicht überein, (aber) sie trennen sich auch nicht' (Sima 2005, 84).

(132)

ɔ yəšḳə́ṭɔrn a-ʕiśśɔ́r

What a pity friends fall out

اللهم لا تتباغض الاصدقاء

This is used ironically when two evil individuals, who were friends, fall out with each other (al-Shahri 2000, 103, 283). The verbal form *yəšḳə́ṭɔrn* is an imperfective 3.M.PL. of a Š2-stem meaning 'to quarrel' (MLZ, 729: خاصم).[32] MLZ (729) additionally records this expression as أيشقوثرن أعشور. The literal meaning of this expression is 'Friends don't quarrel'.

(133)

ērɔ́t ɔ šḥalɔ́t gʲudᵊ lɔ ɔ tšḥalɔ́b ṣəbᵊlɔ́l lɔ

The animal which doesn't give milk after a birth will not give normal milk later on

التي لم تدر الولادة الدسم, فانها لن ترد حليباً صافياً فيما بعد

This proverb conveys that if one does not succeed in easy times, then one will certainly not succeed in harder times (al-Shahri 2000, 103, 283).

---

[32] This term is not recorded by JL.

The term *erɔ́t* < **ɛ berɔ́t* = relativiser + the auxiliary verb *ber* in the third-person feminine singular form (Rubin 2014, 164–68). The verbal forms *s̃halɔ́t* and *ts̃halɔ́b* are 3.F.SG. of the perfective and imperfective respectively, of a Š1-stem < √ḥlb meaning 'to be able to be milked' (JL, 109). The term *gʲud* means 'colostrum; beestings' < √gyd (JL, 81), and the term *ṣəbʕlɔ́l* is an adjective meaning 'pure', normally used for milk (JL, 243). Therefore, the literal meaning of this expression is '(she) who can't give colostrum, won't give milk'.

(134)

ērə ḥkum bə-gē̃s ɔl-ʕɔd a-ʕás̃ər ē de
The one who becomes old, no longer has any friends

الذي قد تقدم بالسن واصابه الوهن لم يعد صديق احد

This sentence may be uttered by an elderly person to remark that with old age comes loneliness (al-Shahri 2000, 103, 283).

The initial segment *er* must be interpreted as < **ɛ-ber* (see entry **(133)** above). The verbal form *ḥkum* is a perfective third person of a Ga-stem meaning 'to be old' (JL, 107). The term *gē̃s* is not recorded by the lexical sources used in this study. However, following al-Shahri's Arabic translation الذي قد تقدم بالسن, one would be tempted to postulate a noun meaning 'age' or 'weakness'. Alternatively, one might posit a G-stem verb *gē̃s/yəgɔ́̃s/yəgɔ́̃s* meaning 'to become weak':[33] in the latter case, the segment *bə* would stand for the coordinating conjunction. Sima (2005, 84) records a proverb that, in spite of some lexical divergences, is

---

[33] See al-Kathiri and Dufour (2020, 210–11) for a morphologically similar verb.

identical in meaning: *ḏ-bär wakbäth ḥakmōt, ḳulläm härbaʿt'yäh* 'Bei wem schon das Alter eingetreten ist, dem werden seine Gefährten weniger'.

(135)

ēr síni yum ɛ ɛmšín yəḥīl gʲub b-iššɔ́

Who saw the day of yesterday, he must carry a shield and a sword

من شاهد أحداث يوم امس يحب عليه ان ياخذ ترس وسيف

This is used as a comment about one's (or someone else's) overcautious behaviour (al-Shahri 2000, 103, 284).

The first segment is to be interpreted as *ɛ-ber*. The verbal form *síni* is a perfective third person of a Ga-stem meaning 'to see' (JL, 253). The term *iššɔ́* 'sword' is a feature of the eastern varieties of Jibbali/Śḥərɛ̄t. Compare the term *ištɔ́* used in the central and western varieties (al-Shahri 2007, 78).

(136)

ērsɛ́t ɛ̄-défər

Don't rub up against a bad person

تتلوث من تلوث السيئ

This is said when something bad happens as a result of the actions of a bad person (al-Shahri 2000, 103, 284).

The term *ērsɛ́t* < **e-mursɛ́t* 'dealing with a bad person' (MLZ, 861: التعامل مع الشخص السيئ) is not listed by JL, although the T1-stem verb *mutrəs* 'to be involved more and more in a problem thought at first to be small', listed under the corresponding root √mrs (JL, 174), indicates that the above noun has a semantic connection to this root. The literal meaning of this expression is 'dealings (of) the bad (person)'.

(137)

ēṭᵊlím yaḥṣizíl

The innocent person has the clear sound of a piece of metal being struck

المظلوم يرن كصوت المعدن النقي

This is said of someone who is innocent and, hence, speaks out vehemently (al-Shahri 2000, 104, 284).

The term *ēṭᵊlím* < *e-meṭᵊlím 'oppressed' (MLZ, 601: المظلوم) is not listed by JL, and here it means 'innocent' in relation to being accused of something. The imperfective 3.M.SG. of the ᵟH1-stem verb *yaḥṣíẑil* means 'to shake something, to drop it to make it ring' (MLZ, 244: هز الشيء \ أسقطه لإصدار رنين) < √ḥṣll, with the first /l/ > [ɫ] (JL, xiv; Rubin 2014, 26).

(138)

elkɛ́t ɛ ɛ-défər

The power of the bad

قوة السيئ أو اللئيم

This proverb is used as a comment about bad actions (al-Shahri 2000, 104, 284).

The term *ēlkɛ́t* < *e-melkɛt 'dominance, prevalence, control' (MLZ, 881: التغلب. الغلبة. السيط) is not recorded by JL.

(139)

ērét ɛ Ṣammún

The mirror of Damoon

مراة ضمّون

This is said as a comment about someone who wrongly feels physically perfect and is based on a folk story about a woman called Ṣammun, who had a mirror that made everyone look perfect (al-Shahri 2000, 104, 285).

The feminine personal name Ṣammún is formally comparable with ḍmn in Safaitic (al-Manaser and MacDonald 2017, passim), where it is, however, recorded as a masculine name.

(140)

bə ʕakʲbéts xɛr

I hope that the outcome will be better

اللهم اجعل عاقبتها او عاقبته خيراً

When something good happens, people utter this formula to express a wish that things remain as good as they are (al-Shahri 2000, 104, 285).

The preposition *bə* heads a prepositional phrase whose dependent is the term *ʕakʲbɛt*, which seems to be an Arabic loan < عاقبة 'end, outcome, upshot; issue, effect, result, consequence' (Wehr and Cowan 1976, 627).

The Arabic translation beginning with اللهم 'O God!' (Wehr and Cowan 1976, 24) indicates an invocation.

(141)

ber te śe fəlɔ́ terɔ́ktən

If they don't eat it they tread on it

أكلنّ شيئاً وإلا تدسنّ

This is said when someone ruins something, such that they are unable to take full advantage of it (al-Shahri 2000, 104, 285).

Rather unusually, this proverb uses the third-person feminine plural, which could be due to cattle being intended. The Ga-stem 3.F.PL. imperfective verb *terɔ́ktən* < √rkt means 'to step, to tread upon, put a foot on the ground' (JL, 211). Cf. Mehri *twūh w-lī träktän* '(Die Kühe, Kamelinnen, Ziegen) haben (das Gras) gefressen oder werden drauftreten' (Sima 2005, 84).

(142)

tɛ k-e-ṣinı̃t b-ɔ tġad šesᵊ lɔ

Eat with a midwife but don't accompany her

كل مع المربية ولكن لا ترافقها

This is used when a person takes advantage of another person being busy, to enhance his share of something to the detriment of the other (al-Shahri 2000, 105, 286).

The verbal form *tɛ* is an imperative of a G-stem from the doubly weak root √twy meaning 'to eat' (JL, 273). The term *ṣinı̃t* < √ḵnv 'nursemaid' is recorded by MLZ (774: المربية). The verbal form *tġad* is a subjunctive 2.M.SG. of a G-stem < √wġd 'to go' (JL, 288) followed by the preposition *k-* 'with' (Rubin 2014, 247–49), a combination that has been reported to mean 'to have sexual intercourse' (Rubin 2014, 386). However, in this case it is likely to mean 'to accompany'. The Mehri counterpart of this saying is *tēh k-ḵanyı̃t w-sēr šıs lä* 'Iß bei der Frau, die ein Kleinkind aufzieht, aber geh nicht mit ihr' (Sima 2005, 85).

(143)

tḥēl e-dinı́ in ḥōlɔ́t b-tɔ́ḵləʕ in ɔl iṣiźɔ́t

The earth carries what she can, and leaves what she cannot

تحمل الدنيا طاقتها وتترك ما لا تطيق

This proverb is often used to teach children that they should do what they can and leave the things they are not able to do to someone else (al-Shahri 2000, 105, 286).

The general sense of the proverb seems to be 'let the world carry its load and get rid of what it does not manage to carry'. The verbal form *tẖēl* is an imperfective 3.F.SG. of a Ga-stem meaning 'to load; to take; to carry' (JL, 111). The term *ḥɔ́lɔ́t* seems to be a diminutive of *ḥīlət* 'load, camel-load' (JL, 111). The second verbal form *tɔ́kləʕ* is a subjunctive 3.F.SG. of a Ga-stem meaning 'to let, allow'. The use of a subjunctive form here is unexpected, and points to a future meaning, with the future prefix *dḥa-, ḥa-,* or *a-* (Rubin 2014, 150–52) being either omitted or just inaudible. The third verbal form *iṣiẓ́ɔ́t* is a perfective 3.F.SG. of a Gb-stem < √wṣl meaning 'to arrive; to manage to shoulder a (physical or psychological) burden' (JL, 293). The use of the relativiser *in* is noteworthy.

(144)
təṣ́girér baʕlét ɛ-ḳuṇ
Only the one who has horns can scream

تصرخ ذات القرن وتعلي صوتها

This is said when someone is successful in a physical or verbal confrontation, to the detriment of someone else. According to al-Shahri (2000, 106, 286), the semantic connection between screaming and being successful derives from the fact that a goat lets out a scream-like vocalisation before butting another goat.

The verbal form *təṣ́girér* is an imperfective 3.F.SG. of a quadriliteral ᵠY-stem meaning 'to shriek, scream' (JL, 324). The corresponding proverb in Mehri is *baʕlīt ḳōn aśśᵃgīrūr* '(Nur) die (Ziege), die ein Horn hat, schreit laut' (Sima 2005, 85).

(145)

tə<u>k</u>béb fəló təṭɔ́x

You either get it burnt or cooked

تشوي أو تطبخ

This mean that there is a proper way to do something, and if it is not followed, the consequences can be unpleasant. This derives from the proper way to cook the beṭaḥ roots, *Gladiolus ukambanensis* (Miller and Morris 1988, 150), which is wrapping them in cow dung and roasting them (al-Shahri 2000, 106, 287).

The verb *təṭɔ́x* < √*ṭbx* is an imperfective 2.M.SG. of a Ga-stem meaning 'to wrap beṭaḥ in cow pats and bake' (JL, 274), whilst *tə<u>k</u>béb* is an imperfective 2.M.SG. of a G-stem from the geminate root √<u>k</u>bb meaning 'to roast' (JL, 140; MLZ, 725): شوي (على الجمر \ في الرماد الساخن). The difference in the meaning of these two verbs corresponds to the difference between the right way and the wrong way to carry out the roasting of beṭaḥ roots, and, *mutatis mutandis*, any other task.

(146)

tənʕaš a-ʕamit <u>d</u> ɔ kfe enúf

A person who is not able to do something should not pretend that he can

ثكلتة النخوة من عجز عن مساعدة نفسه

This is an expression that, according to al-Shahri (2000, 107, 287), is used when someone fails to complete a task that he was advised not to undertake beforehand.

The verb *tənʕa* is an imperfective 3.F.SG. of a Gb-stem < √*nʕw* and is reported to mean 'to elegize; to keen over the dead' (JL, 179). Al-Shahri translates this verb into Arabic as ثكل 'to be bereaved, to mourn' (Wehr and Cowan 1976, 105), which seems to be the most fitting translation in this case. The term ʕamit, translated by al-Shahri into Arabic as نخوة 'haughtiness, arrogance; pride, dignity, sense of honor, self-respect; high-mindedness, generosity' (Wehr and Cowan 1976, 950) is unattested in the lexica. The verbal form *kfe* is a perfective third person of a Ga-stem stem meaning 'to be enough' (JL, 128).

The literal meaning of this proverb may be tentatively rendered as 'The arrogance that cannot help itself bereaved him'.

(147)

ḥíki ĩrẑếm l-ēkḥált (l-ēkśéft)

The lid fits tightly on the mascara

تطابق الغطاء على المكحلة او على المكشيف

This is said of people who are alike, and usually applies to unpleasant people (al-Shahri 2000, 106, 287).

The verbal form *ḥíki* is a perfective third person of a passive G-stem meaning احكم إغلاقه 'to fit' (MLZ, 254).[34] The term *ĩrẑếm* < *e-mirẑếm from the root √rgm means 'cover, lid' (JL, 207). The term *ēkśéft* < *e-mekśéft is not recorded as such. However, compare the term *kśaf* 'A small wicker vessel with a lid in which a woman puts her belongings' (MLZ, 802: سلة صغيرة من الخوص لها غطا تضع فيها المرأ حاجياتها), not recorded in JL. The term in question is translated into Arabic as مكشيف (al-Shahri 2000, 287), a term which, despite being undoubtedly connected to the root √kšf, conveying 'discovery' (Wehr and Cowan 1976, 828–30), is not recorded in

---

[34] Ga- and Gb-stems have exactly the same morphological characteristics in the passive voice (al-Kathiri and Dufour 2020, 220).

the lexica. In Mehri, this proverb is recorded by Sima (2005, 85) as *ḥīḳi rījām l-ḥaḳḳath* 'Es paßt der Deckel zu seiner Dose'.

(148)

ḥa-leṣᵊm heš a-ʕiẑīt

I would make a continuous fast for him

سأصوم له صوم الخرساء

This is used sarcastically, with the opposite meaning. Therefore, the person in question is deemed not to be worthy of any consideration (al-Shahri 2000, 106, 288).

The verb *ḥa-leṣᵊm* is a 1.C.SG. future form of a G-stem deriving from a hollow root √ṣwm 'to fast' (JL, 243). The preposition *her* 'for' appears here in its monoconsonantal allophone *h-*, to which personal suffixes are attached (Rubin 2014, 243). The adjective *ʕiẑīt* seems to be the feminine counterpart of *ʕigɛm* 'dumb', recorded in JL (9) as *ʿigɛm*. Such a definition, rather divergent from the English translation of the expression, finds an explanation in the Arabic translation صوم الخرساء 'a silent fast' (al-Shahri 2000, 288).

(149)

xɔbs əllah xalḳét də āḥzíg'hum ṭad

People of evil appearance are tied with the same hobble

بئس او خابت من خلقة ذوي الرباط الواحد

This is said when giving up an argument with a group of related people who stand together (al-Shahri 2000, 106, 288).

The language of this proverb exhibits a strong influence from Arabic, as can be seen in the term *əllah* 'God', used in conjunction with the unrecorded interjection *xɔb*, which is rendered in Arabic (al-Shahri 2000, 288) with بئس 'how evil!' (Wehr and Cowan 1976, 39). Similarly, the term *xalkɛ́t* 'nature, creatures' (JL, 300) is best viewed as part of a mixed formulaic language (Johnstone 1972). It must be pointed out that the participial form *ãḥzíg̊* < **a-məḥzíg̊*, recorded in JL (122) as *maḥzeg* 'hobble', is found here with [i] as the stressed vowel instead of the expected [e].

(150)

xɔbš əllah ɛg̊eh ḏ ɔ yəṣtedɔ́f

The face which is never ashamed is a bad face

بئس وجه ذلك الذي لا ينثني من الخجل

This is a comment that people make either when a person is convinced by others to act wisely, or when a person refuses to act wisely (al-Shahri 2000, 107, 288).

The verb *yəṣtedɔ́f* < √*ṣdf* is an imperfective 3.M.SG. of a T1-stem, not listed by MLZ, meaning 'to dent, buckle' (JL, 235). However, al-Shahri's Arabic translation ينثني من الخجل 'to give up out of shame' suggests that this is the appropriate meaning in this case.

(151)

xīlṭét tenúfəʕ

The strange animal is useful

الخلطاء تفيد او مفيدة

This is used when an animal that is not part of one's herd suffers an accident, dies, or is stolen (al-Shahri 2000, 107, 289), which is made clearer in the Mehri counterpart of this expression *xalṭayt tkūn ʿašwēt ḏ-kōb* 'Das (fremde Tier, das) sich in die Herde hineinmischt, wird der Anteil des Wolfs' (Sima 2005, 85).

The term *xiltét*, feminine of *xalít̟* 'A person who dwells/settles down with a group of people who are not his people' (MLZ, 305: الشخص الغريب الذي يسكن \ يحل بقوم بقومه), is not listed in JL. The verbal form *tenufəʕ* is an imperfective 3.F.SG. of a Ga-stem meaning 'to be useful, of use' (JL, 181).

(152)

ḏ-ɔl ḥez k-e-gĩʕatᵊ lɔ yənufś

If you haven't slaughtered the stolen animal with the thief, you won't stay the night with them

من لم يشارك اللصوص في ذبح المسروقة يعود إلى منزله في المساء

This is said about someone who is accused of wrongdoing, and eventually turns out to be innocent (al-Shahri 2000, 107, 289).

The verbal form *ḥez* is a perfective third person of a G-stem deriving from the geminate root √ḥzz meaning 'to slaughter' (JL, 122). The term *gĩʕat* < √gmʕ is recorded in JL (76) as *gĩʕat* 'company, band of robbers'. The second verbal form *yənufś* is an imperfective 3.M.SG. of a Ga-stem meaning 'to go early in the evening' (JL, 182).

(153)

šáxbɛr ɛ bédərek bi yum̥

Ask the one who is one day older

أسأل من سبقك بيوم اي من هو اكبر منك بيوم

This proverb is quoted when a younger person, after pondering about a matter of concern, seeks the advice of an older person who, by virtue of experience, is able to sort out the problem (al-Shahri 2000, 107, 289). The verbal form *šaxbɛr* is an imperative of a Š1-stem meaning 'to ask', whilst *bédərek* is a perfective third person of a Gb-stem meaning 'to outrun'³⁵ (JL, 23), with a 2.M.SG. personal suffix *-k* attached (JL, 296). Compare the Mehri proverb *šaxbār ḏ-bār sābkūk b-sänn* 'Frag den, der dir schon an Alter voran ist' (Sima 2005, 86).

(154)

s̃əʕĩr ɛ̃ṣˤbɔ́r

The sides of the wadi are far apart

تباعدت اطراف الوادي

This is a comment about two things or individuals that have nothing in common (al-Shahri 2000, 108, 290).

The verb *s̃əʕĩr* seems to be a perfective third person of a Š2-stem, listed by JL (6) as *s̃ʕer* '(group) to think someone far away from you in position or opinion'. However, the vocalism of this verbal form differs from the norm. It would be tempting to posit a Š2-stem passive here. The term *ɛ̃ṣbɔ́r*,³⁶ likely to be the plural form of *ṣabər*, and recorded by MLZ (535) as حد المكان \ طرفه. شِق الوادي 'limit of a place, side, cleft', is not recorded by JL.

(155)

ṣˤəbɔts kin ḥel fəlɔ́ kin mišerˤd

Take wisdom from a lunatic or a senile old person

خذها من مسن حائل او من مجنون (الحكمة)

This can be used as a remark when a person who is old, or not of sound mind, speaks out. It can be used either straight or ironically,

---

³⁵ Compare سبق 'to precede' (MLZ, 118).

³⁶ The initial long vowel in the text is due to the coalescence of the definite article with the initial vowel of the term: *ɛ-ɛṣbɔ́r.

depending on the nature of what this person says (al-Shahri 2000, 108, 290).

The verbal form *ṣʼbɔṭs* is an imperative of a Gb-stem meaning 'to hold; to capture' (JL, 323) with a 3.F.SG. personal suffix *-s*. The term *mišerd* 'mad, evil' is listed under the root √*kwrd* by JL (138), and √*kbrd* by MLZ (784). In view of the Mehri cognate *mənkəwrəd* (ML, 219) the correct derivation seems to be from √*kwrd*. This proverb has two Mehri counterparts: *źaṭs män ḥaywal* and *źaṭ bählīt män mkawrät*, respectively 'Nimm sie (d.h. die Weisheit) vom Narren' and 'Nimm das (weise) Wort von den Verliebten' (Sima 2005, 86). In this expression, one can observe the use in context of the sparsely attested preposition *kin* 'from (someone)' (Rubin 2014, 249–50).

(156)

ʕagˤz l-ēšīn fékar də ʕɔnút

A little lazy, a year's poverty

عجز قليل فقر سنة

This is used as a warning not to procrastinate on a given matter (al-Shahri 2000, 108, 290).

The term *ʕagˤz* means 'laziness' (JL, 10). The term *šīn* < √*šyn* means 'for a time/while' (JL, 268), but the adverbial phrase *l-ēšīn* is hard to explain on account of the long vowel between the preposition *l-* and the term. According to MLZ (497), the temporal meaning of this word is widespread in the *Jabal Qamar* (western dialects), whereas it means 'truthfulness of speech' (صدق الكلام) elsewhere in the Jibbali/Śḥərɛ̄t-speaking area. The term *ʕɔnút* is the most common term for 'year' (JL, 20) in Jibbali/Śḥərɛ̄t.

(157)

ʕɔk ɔ śink mən e-ḳeraḥ ʕar īḏuntéś
So far, all you have seen of the donkey is his ears

لم تر من الحمار إلا اذنيه

This is said upon an unexpected event by a person who knows the likely reason for that event, to another person who does not know it and is, therefore, surprised (al-Shahri 2000, 108, 290).

It is noteworthy that the particle ʕɔd, which in this case conveys doubt, seems here to behave like the etymologically related auxiliary verb d-ʕɔd, although Rubin (2014, 186) states that ʕɔd "has just a single frozen form." The verbal form śink is a perfective 2.M.SG. of a Ga-stem meaning 'to see' (JL, 253). The term īḏuntéś is the plural definite form of iḏén 'ear' (JL, 1), with a 3.M.SG. personal suffix -ś attached. The corresponding Mehri proverb is 'ād l-śīnak män ḥayr är ḥayḏäntʲyäh 'Bis jetzt hast du vom Esel nur seine Ohren gesehen' (Sima 2005, 86).

(158)

ʕɔ́rɔ́t a-ʕēbdɔ́t ɔ́ṭaḥ bə xɔhi
The little sprat says, "the sand in my mouth"

قالت العومة (السمكة) الرمل في فمي

This proverb is used as a comment about a person who does not want to take a side in an argument (al-Shahri 2000, 109, 291).

The verbal form ʕɔ́rɔ́t is a perfective 3.F.SG. of an idiosyncratic Ga-stem (see al-Kathiri and Dufour 2020, 200–1) meaning 'to say' (JL, 13). The term ʕēbdɔ́t, translated by al-Shahri as 'little sprat' and العومة, seems to be a diminutive form related to ʕad 'sardine' (JL, 20). It is to be noted that Johnstone (1973, 101) lists the diminutive form of this term as ʕadebét. The term ɔ́ṭaḥ is the definite form of *bɔṭḥ* 'sand' (JL, 30). A part of this saying is found in Mehri as *bäṭḥ b-xōhi ahōräj lä* 'Mit Erde in meinem Mund spreche ich nicht' (Sima 2005, 86). This proverb may be regarded as a wellerism (see above, p. 22).

(159)

ʕɔ́rɔ́t e-ziginút əxer nur ʕar ʕɔr

The butterfly says that light is better than disgrace

قالت الفراشة النور افضل من العار

This is said as a warning not to disclose something that might spoil someone's reputation. The meaning of this proverb is rooted in a folk tale according to which a butterfly was asked by God whether it would rather throw itself into the fire or do something dishonourable. The butterfly chose the former option (al-Shahri 2000, 109, 291).

For the verbal form *ʕɔ́rɔ́t*, see the preceding entry **(158)**. The term *ziginút* 'butterfly' (JL, 316) is morphologically a diminutive (Johnstone 1973). The terms *nur* 'light' and *ʕɔr* 'disgrace' are Arabic loanwords. The latter is related to the root √ʕwr, which conveys defectiveness and deficiency (Wehr and Cowan 1976, 656).

(160)

ʕɔr ēnfí ɛ s̃əʕgél yəté nu

An impatient person eats uncooked food

من استعجل يأكل نيئاً

This proverb is mentioned upon a manifestation of inaccuracy due to being in haste (al-Shahri 2000, 109, 291). The first verbal form *s̃əʕgél* is a perfective third person of a Š1-stem meaning 'to hasten' (JL, 9), whilst the second one *yəte* is an imperfective 3.M.SG. of a G-stem from a doubly weak root meaning 'to eat' (JL, 273). Notwithstanding some lexical differences, the following Mehri proverb represents a semantically relevant counterpart: *aš-šaʿjūl yaʿṭōr* 'Wer sich beeilt, stolpert' (Sima 2005, 87). The initial segment *ʕɔ̄r ēnfī* 'the ancestor said' (not translated into English by al-Shahri) is a proverbial affix (Norrick 2015, 24), like *eḏīlín* 'so-and-so' found above.

(161)

ʕɔ̄rɔ́t ḥɔ̄t yɔtˀġ tɔ enḳél b-yɔ́ḳbər tɔ ɔ-défər

The snake said, "I hope that the good person will kill me and the bad person will bury me"

قالت الثعبان يقتلني الشارط ويقبرني الذليل

This is said when someone turns out not to be able to carry out a task properly due to lack of accuracy. The reference to the burial of a snake stems from a folk belief according to which the bones of a snake are as venomous as its bite, and an evil person will bury a snake improperly on purpose, so that its bones will sooner or later cause harm to a passer-by (al-Shahri 2000, 109, 292).

The two subjunctive 3.M.SG. verbal forms, *yɔtˀġ* and *yɔ́ḳbər*, are respectively an idiosyncratic G-stem (Rubin 2014, 37) and a Ga-stem, and are used here to express an optative sense (Rubin 2014, 147). The term *ḥɔ̄t* 'snake' is recorded in the lexical sources with an initial /h/ instead of /ḥ/ (JL, 100; MLZ, 966). However, before postulating a variant of this term, one should take into account the following: (1) al-Shahri transcribes <ه>, not <ح>, (2) the presence of a definite article could be in play here, causing [h] to geminate, and (3) /h/ may sound slightly more on the pharyngeal side when initial than when in other positions. As is the case with entry number **(125)** above, we encounter the term *enḵel* 'choice (livestock)'[37] (JL, 190) in the place of *ẽnḵel* < **e-menḵel* 'active, energetic, heroic', both < √*nḵl* (JL, 190).

(162)

ʕɔ̃r ēnfí e-kkəʕéb elṭím

The crockery can touch

العفش يتلامس

This saying is quoted when dealing with a minor issue to emphasise that some small problems in life are to be expected (al-Shahri 2000, 110, 292). The sense of this saying may be conveyed as follows: 'pieces of houseware are bound to knock each other', i.e., people living in the same house are bound to experience conflict. The term *kəʕéb* means 'pottery' (MLZ, 803: الوعاء, الإناء), and the verbal form *elṭím* is a perfective third person of a H1-stem meaning 'to slap oneself, bewail' (JL, 166). In light of the above, this expression is better translated as 'The ancestor said: the pottery is prone to shatter'.

(163)

ʕɔ̃r ēnfí e-ʕiṇ tšerḥɔ́ḵ b-faʕm telhɔ́ḵ

Our ancestors say that the eye can see things far away and the leg can make things close

قال السلف: العين ترى البعيد والرجل تقرب البعد

This is used as an encouragement not to give up on a difficult endeavour (al-Shahri 2000, 110, 292). The verbal forms *tšerḥɔ́ḵ*

---

[37] This form is presumably *e-nḵel*, with a definite article.

and *telḥɔ́ḳ* are, respectively, an imperfective 3.F.SG. of a Š1-stem meaning, among other things, 'to think (somewhere) is distant, far away' (JL, 210), and a subjunctive 3.F.SG. of a Gb-stem meaning 'to catch up with, overtake, run after' (JL, 163). The use of a subjunctive here is unexpected. As in entry number **(143)** above, the future prefix might be omitted or inaudible. Compare the Mehri saying *ʿayn tśäyn rähäḵ w-faʿm thäḵrōb* 'Das Auge sieht das Ferne, und der Fuß bringt (es) näher' (Sima 2005, 87).

(164)

ʕɔ̃r ēnfí mən gʲádəb tten ḥilɛ́t

In absence of anything else they can eat the dry leaves

من العدم تأكلن القديم من أوراق الشجر

This is used as a comment about a change which will likely not result in any worsening of the current circumstances (al-Shahri 2000, 110, 293).

The verbal form *tten* is a subjunctive (with optative force) 3.F.PL. of a G-stem meaning 'to eat' (JL, 273); the use of the 3.F.PL. probably refers to cattle. The term *ḥilɛ́t* (JL, 109) refers to the dry leaves of the *Anogeissus dhofarica* (Miller and Morris 1988, 102), called *sɔ́ġɔt* in Jibbali/Śḥərɛ́t (MLZ, 444), a term not listed in JL. See also entry number **(198)** below. Also, compare the Mehri saying *män xalsēt attawyän ḥallēt* 'Wegen des Mangels (an Grünfutter) fressen (die Tiere) das dürre Laub' (Sima 2005, 87).

(165)

ʕɔ̃r ēnfí skɔf e-kḥɔ her āʕlš

The breast-bone meat is waiting for its owner

قال السلف: انتظر مقدمة الصدر صاحبه

This is said when someone turns down something of good quality and accepts something else of lower quality. This is based on the fact that the flesh around the breastbone of cattle is considered a delicacy in Dhofar (al-Shahri 2000, 110, 293).

The verbal form *skɔf* is a perfective third person of a G-stem meaning 'to sit' (JL, 227). The term *kḥɔ* 'breastbone meat' is not recorded in Jibbali/Śḥərɛ̄t but can be found in Soqotri *kḥo* 'poitrine' (LS, 216).

(166)

ʕɔ̄r ēnfí ɔ yəṣér e-rumᵊḥ ar l-a-ʕəkkɔ́z

The spearhead is useless without the shaft

قال السلف: لا تقف الرمح إلا على سنها

This is a comment about a person who is not backed by a tribe or family, in spite of being good and/or strong (al-Shahri 2000, 110, 293).

The verbal form *yəṣér* is an imperfective 3.M.SG. of a G-stem deriving from the hollow root √ṣwr meaning 'to stand up' (JL, 243). The term *ʕəkkɔ́z* سن الرمح 'spear-head' (literally 'spear-tooth'; MLZ, 642) is not listed by JL. This expression is also found in MLZ (642) as أتصر أرمحت عر لعكُزس.[38] Cf. Mehri *yṣūr ramḥ är laḳōzäh* 'Die Lanze steht nur auf ihrem Schaft' (Sima 2005, 87).

(167)

ʕɔ̄r ēnfí ɔ təʕin ḏ ɔl ʕiní-k

Don't interfere in something which doesn't concern you

قال السلف: لا تعنِ من لم يُعنِكَ

---

[38] This variant in feminine in grammatical gender.

This is an encouragement to mind one's own business (al-Shahri 2000, 111, 294).

The verbal form *təʕin* is a subjunctive (as expected in a negative command) 2.M.SG. of a G-stem from the hollow root √ʕyn meaning 'to keep an eye on' (JL, 20).

(168)

ʕɔ̃r ēnfí ɔ téṣər ʕarə bə-ṭekəlk

Don't stop unless you are afraid of the consequences

قال السلف: لا تتوقف الا إذا خفت العواقب

This is said to someone who hesitates in an argument or in an action (al-Shahri 2000, 111, 294). The verbal form *téṣər* is a subjunctive 2.M.SG. of a G-stem deriving from √ṣwr 'to stand up' (al-Kathiri and Dufour 2020, 212; JL, 243; see also entry **(166)** above); al-Shahri's translation of this verb with the Arabic verbal form توقف 'to stop' (Wehr and Cowan 1976, 1092) suggests that the latter sense is meant here. The verbal form *ṭékəlk* is a perfective 2.M.SG. of a Gb-stem meaning 'to be suspicious, worried' (JL, 284).

(169)

ʕɔ̃r ēnfí bet təbáʕ

They are only imitators

قال السلف: قوم المقلّدين

This is a comment about a group of people who show no initiative (al-Shahri 2000, 111, 294).

The term *təbáʕ* 'followers' (Wehr and Cowan 1976, 90) is likely to be a relatively recent Arabic loanword: the absence of the intervocalic deletion of /b/ (Rubin 2014, 28–30) would point to a non-native origin. However, it is also possible that the first vowel [ə] in this term is an anaptyctic vowel by which the intervocalic deletion of /b/ is not triggered, in which case one cannot be certain as regards the etymological status of this term.

(170)

ʕɔ̃r ɛ̄nfí helk ɔl tbe

You missed the good grazing

قال السلف ويله من لم يأكل حيوانه

This is said by someone who has known a very good person in the past and implies that someone else has not known the person in question (al-Shahri 2000, 111, 294).

The verbal form *helk* is a perfective third person of a Gb-stem listed in JL (97) with two diverging meanings: 'to miss (1-) someone great who has died; to be very tired and thirsty'. The verbal form *tbe* must be a H1-stem < √*twy* 'to cause to eat, feed, allow to pasture' (JL, 273).

In light of the above, it is difficult to reconcile the literal meaning of the expression with the English and Arabic rendition provided by al-Shahri.

(171)

ʕɔ̃r hun īdenk ʕɔ̃r bɔh

They asked, "where is your ear?" "Here" he said, reaching round his head to point to the ear on the other side

قال اين اذنك ؟ قال : هنا

This is used when someone tries to complicate things, and is accompanied by the gesture of pointing to one ear using the opposite hand (al-Shahri 2000, 111, 295). The verbal form ʕɔ̃r is a perfective third person of an idiosyncratic G-stem meaning 'to say' (JL, 13).

(172)

ʕɔ̃r ɛd̪īlín yəgʲiblɛ́l ɛ̃ṣˤfɔ́r

So-and-so brings down the birds

فلان يسقط الطيور

This is a comment that can be made about either a good poet or a skilled liar (al-Shahri 2000, 112, 295).

The verbal form *yəgʲiblɛ́l* is an imperfective 3.M.SG. of a ᵠH1-stem meaning 'to drop one by one' < √gbl (MLZ, 175: أسقط (الواحدة تلو الأخرى), which exhibits reduplication of the last root consonant. The term *ɛ̃ṣˤfɔ́r = ɛ-ɛṣˤfɔ́r* is attested without the etymological initial /ʕ/, as in entry number **(26)** above.

(173)

ʕɔ̃r ɛd̪īlín bek əšũʕ wɛ̃h

I have heard 'Boo' before

قال فلان : سبق وسمعت كلمة واة

This is used to show courage in the face of a threat (al-Shahri 2000, 112, 295).

The use of the auxiliary verb *ber* followed by an imperfective indicative to convey a frequent action/event is described by Rubin (2014, 167).

The verbal form *əšũʕ* is an imperfective 1.C.SG. of a Gb-stem meaning 'to hear' (JL, 262). The interjection *wɛ̃h* is translated by al-Shahri (2000, 112) as 'boo!' in English and واة in Arabic (al-Shahri 2000, 295).

(174)

ġaśé kēdr īti l-e-nṣeníti

The big termite mound swallowed up the small one

علت بيوت النمل الكبيرة على بيوت النمل الصغيرة

This is said of lowly people who improve their condition and start to despise those who are as lowly as they once were (al-Shahri 2000, 112, 295).

The verbal form *ġaśe* is a perfective third person of a Ga-stem meaning 'to disappear behind (something)/to exceed the limits' (MLZ, 669: سار حتى توارى خلف المكان \ تخطاه \ تخطى الحط).[39] The term *kēdr*, a masculine plural corresponding to a singular form *śudar* 'conical termite mound' (MLZ, 489: بيت النمل المخروطي) is not recorded by JL.

(175)

ʕɔ̄r ɛd̠īlín ġumd d̠ə s̃īt

So-and-so is a Seeat set

فلان مثل أُفول أي مغيب نجوم الشييت

This is said of someone who is very lazy and not useful to anyone. The metaphor stems from a constellation named *s̃īt* in Jibbali/Śḥərɛ̄t, whose presence in the skies for about 40 days is traditionally believed to mark a period of laziness and illness. Moreover, this constellation is not very bright, so that its only use for the traditional lifestyle of Dhofar is indicating the passing of time (al-Shahri 2000, 112, 296).

The term *ġumd* means 'sunset' (JL, 86).

---

[39] This term is not listed by JL.

It is to be noted that the name of this constellation is a cognate of the term *s̃ín* 'for a time/while' (JL, 268; MLZ, 497).

(176)

farḥát tkin ʕas̃ɛ́s̃

Desire becomes fat

الرغبة تكون سمنة

This proverb serves as a reminder that people tend to see only the positive sides of something they want, and ignore the bad sides. It stems from a folk tale according to which a man who agreed to give his daughter in marriage to a suitor, on the condition that he brought a cow as the bride-price, later changed his mind when another suitor turned up, who was wealthier and more handsome. The father then rejected the cow of the first suitor, claiming that it was too thin and weak. The man then made his way back to his community, and as he was on the road, the wealthier suitor bought his cow to comply with the girl's father request, whereupon the cow was accepted. The first suitor then attended the wedding of the wealthy man and the girl, and upon being asked why that cow was turned down when offered by him, and it was accepted when offered by the other man, he replied *farḥát tkin ʕas̃ɛ́s̃* (al-Shahri 2000, 113, 296).

The term *farḥát* is assigned the meaning 'happiness' by JL (60). However, as pointed out in entry **(112)** of this collection, MLZ (695) has 'desire' (رغبة), in agreement with al-Shahri's (2000, 113, 296) translation. The verbal form is an imperfective 3.F.SG. of a Ga-stem meaning 'to be' (JL, 138).

(177)

farḳét tənúkəʕ bə ššaʕ

Panic brings flight

الخوف ياتي بالسرعة

This is said when someone accepts advice out of fear (al-Shahri 2000, 113, 297).

The term *šaʕ* 'flight, race' (MLZ, 478: الركض \ الجري) is not recorded by JL. A similar proverb in Mehri is recorded by Sima (2005, 88) as *färḳāt tnōkaʕ ab-bäḳẓ́* 'die Furcht bringt das Laufen'. The verbal form *tənúkəʕ* is an imperfective 3.F.SG. of a Ga-stem meaning 'to come' (JL, 187). Its meaning changes into 'to bring' when followed by the preposition *b-* (JL, 187).

(178)

fəlɔ́ məsɛ́ dūt fəlɔ ḏəhéb sáḥaḳ

Either light rain or a torrential downpour

يا مطر خفيف يا سيل جارف؟

This metaphor describes two extreme responses to an event, neither of which is satisfactory (al-Shahri 2000, 113, 297).

In this case, the term *məsɛ́* 'rain'[40] (Morris et al. 2019, 75) is feminine, as shown by its agreement with the verbal form *dūt*, which is likely a third-person singular feminine perfective of *dēm* 'to have lasted for a long time; (rain) to come everywhere' (JL, 42). However, Johnstone's texts provide contrasting evidence with regard to the grammatical gender of this term: it is treated

---

[40] In a second repetition, the speaker says *musɛ́*.

both as feminine (Rubin 2014, 442) and as masculine (Rubin 2014, 446).

(179)

kɔl śaʕb tegʼrér b-e-ḏəhḗs

A flood of water stays in its own wadi

كل وادي يجري من خلاله سيله

This is said when a person behaves as expected, or when priority in given to tribal ties over friendship (al-Shahri 2000, 114, 297).

The term *śaʕb* 'watercourse' (JL, 244) appears to be grammatically feminine, as shown by the agreeing verb. The verbal form *tegʼrér* is an imperfective 3.M.SG. G-stem from the geminate root √grr meaning 'to drag' (JL, 77). The segment *e-ḏəhḗs* is the definite form of *ḏheb* 'flood torrent' (JL, 45) with a 3.F.SG. personal suffix *-s* attached. Compare the Mehri proverb *käll śaʕb tjäyr bä-ḏhībäs* 'Jedes Tal führt seinen (eigenen) Wasserlauf' (Sima 2005, 88).

(180)

lə-kɔl erʼkíb letɔ́ts

Every beast of burden can only carry what he is able

لا تحمل الدابة الا قدرتها

This is said about a person who never tries to better him/herself, or as a criticism of something s/he has done (al-Shahri 2000, 114, 297).

The segment *letɔ́t-s* is difficult to account for, as a definite article would be expected to appear to the left of it, because of the presence of a suffixed possessive pronoun. Alternatively, the segment could be analysed as *l-etɔ́t-s* < l + definite article + *etɔ́t*

\+ third person singular suffixed possessive pronoun, but this would hardly shed any light on its meaning, and would make it even more difficult to justify it from a syntactic viewpoint. To complicate the matter further, the native speakers who could be contacted at the time of writing, and at a later time during the revision process, could not clarify its meaning.

However, its translation in Arabic (al-Shahri 2000, 114) is قدرة 'ability' (Wehr and Cowan 1976, 746). The Mehri counterpart of this proverb is *käll rkīb thōmäl är ḥmältäs* 'Jedes Lasttier trägt nur seine Last' (Sima 2005, 88).

(181)

kɔl ḳəṣerér b-e-ṭaʕmš

Every piece of grass has its own taste

لكل نباتة او عشبة طعم خاص بها

This comment is normally used to counter a nasty remark about a person who has good but hidden qualities coupled with less-than-appealing looks (al-Shahri 2000, 114, 298).

The term *ḳəṣərér* 'plant' is recorded neither in JL nor in MLZ, although both record the root √ḳṣr (JL, 152; MLZ, 750–751). This term is translated into Arabic as نباتة 'plant' (al-Shahri 2000, 298).

(182)

kɔl məṭᵊbaʕír yəšūnɛ l-ēṭbaʕírš

Every mud can be built from the same mud

كل طينة تُبنى من طينتها اي من فصيلتها

This is said of those who do not like to associate with people who are sharply different from them (al-Shahri 2000, 114, 298).

The participial form *məṭbaʕír* 'mud' is not recorded. However, it is connected to *ṭʕor* 'earth, clay' (Morris et al. 2019, 75), and the root √*ṭʕr* ~ √*ṭwʕr*, under which both JL (273, 281) and MLZ (584) list several terms connected with 'clay' and 'earth'. The verbal form *yəs̃ūnɛ* is an imperfective 3.M.SG. of a Š1-stem < √*bny* meaning 'to be able to be built' (JL, 27).

(183)

kɔl nīṭáf yənúṭuf d-ĩnzélš

Every drop drops on its place

كل قطرة تقطر في مكانها أي أسفلها تماماً

This is said when a person behaves as expected (al-Shahri 2000, 115, 298).

The term *nīṭáf* is a diminutive of *nuṭaf* 'drop' (MLZ, 921: قطرة), which is not listed in JL, although it does record the root √*nṭf* and the term *ənṭəfɔ́t* (plural *nṭɔf*) 'drop' (JL, 197). The preposition *d-* is an allomorph of *ɛd* 'to, until' (Rubin 2014, 228–30). The verbal form *yənúṭuf* is an imperfective 3.M.SG. of a Ga-stem meaning 'to drip' (JL, 197). The segment *ĩnzélš* is the definite form of *mənzél* 'place one lives at, homestead' (JL, 200) with a 3.M.SG. personal suffix *-š* attached. In the current usage of the speakers of eastern Jibbali/S̃ḥərɛ̃́t, this term simply means 'place'. This proverb can be compared with Mehri *käll nätf ynōṭaf är nxalyäh* 'Jeder Tropfen tropft nur auf das, was darunter ist' (Sima 2005, 88). Al-Shahri's use of 'to drop' instead of 'to drip' is an inaccuracy.

2. Proverbs and Linguistic Analysis

(184)

kɔl yum̥ b-ɛ̄kíls

Each day has its own angel

كل يوم بوكيلها

This comment is made when talking about the events of a specific day, on the basis of the folk belief whereby each day has a specific angel, and angels can be either good or bad (al-Shahri 2000, 115, 299).

The term *ɛ̄kíl* < **ɛ-ɛkíl*, derived from the root √wkl, is listed in JL (291) as 'agent', and as 'helper' in MLZ (980), and it is translated as 'angel' in English (al-Shahri 2000, 115), and وكيل in Arabic (al-Shahri 2000, 299).[41] Sima (2005, 89) lists a similar proverb in Mehri: *käll ḥyūm ba-ḥsōbäs* 'Jeder Tag hat seine (eigene) Abrechnung'.

(185)

k-ɔ́ź ənḥan̥ əb-bəʕél ūkún

We are with God and the owners of the place

نحن مع الله ومع اصحاب الملك

This is said by goat herders when they decide to move away from a place, and subsequently change their mind. According to al-Shahri (2000, 115, 299), the owner of the land has the power to protect those who are on it.

The term *ɔ́ź* 'God' appears here in its variant lacking a /ʕ/ < √bʕl (JL, 22). See also entry number **(56)** above.

---

[41] This term can be translated as 'representative, attorney, proxy' (Wehr and Cowan 1976, 1096).

(186)

kun śe ḏ ɔ yənúgʲəh

Is it as though dawn never comes

كالشيء او الليل الذي لا ينجلي

This is said to a person who asks the same thing all the time (al-Shahri 2000, 115, 299). The intonation of the speaker as well as the written version make it clear this is a question.

The verbal form *kun* is a perfective third person of a Ga-stem meaning 'to be' (JL, 138). The term *śe* 'thing' (JL, 259) also functions as an existential (i.e., 'there is'): the compound expression *kun śe* means 'there was/were' (Rubin 2014, 329). The verbal form *yənúgʲəh* is an imperfective 3.M.SG. of a Ga-stem meaning 'to dawn' (JL, 183). JL states that this verb can only be used in the feminine and lists the corresponding forms. However, it appears here in the masculine, as it refers to *śe*.

(187)

kɔ he her śēʕk aʕɔ̃r śe

When I've eaten my fill I don't say anything

هل انا اذا شبعت اقول شيئاً ؟

A person can use this expression after succeeding in convincing someone to do something in a certain way (al-Shahri 2000, 115, 300). The first verbal form is a perfective 1.C.SG. of a Gb-stem < √śbʕ meaning 'to be satisfied' (JL, 244). The second verbal form *aʕɔ̃r* is an imperfective 1.C.SG. of an idiosyncratic G-stem meaning 'to say' (JL, 13). Compare the Mehri counterpart *wkōh hīn śibʕak, aʕōmär śī* 'Warum, wenn ich satt bin, (soll ich noch) etwas sagen (d.h. mich beklagen)' (Sima 2005, 89).

(188)

lhes ɛ d-yəṭḥɔ́l ʕaḳ ɔ́ṭəḥ

Like the one who urinates in the sand

كمن يتبوّل في الرمل

This is said when someone's good actions go unnoticed (al-Shahri 2000, 116, 300).

The verbal form *yəṭḥɔ́l* is an imperfective 3.M.SG. of a T1-stem 'to pass water out of fear' (JL, 48)[42] and is preceded by the prefix *(v)d-*, which marks a circumstantial clause or indicates a progressive action (Rubin 2014, 158–61). See also entry number **(23)** above. Cf. Mehri *axāh hēh ḏ-yäṣbūb bräk rämäl* 'Wie der, der den Sand gießt' (Sima 2005, 89).

(189)

lhes bɔḏɔrɔ́t təgˤzéz

She reaps like she sowed

كما زرعت تحصد

This means that people have to live with the consequences of their actions, whether good or bad (al-Shahri 2000, 116, 300).

The first verbal form *bɔḏɔrɔ́t* is a perfective 3.F.SG. of a Ga-stem stem meaning 'to sow, cultivate' (JL, 23). The second verbal form *təgˤzéz* is an imperfective 3.F.SG. of a G-stem from the geminate root √gzz meaning 'to pluck (wild) fruit which comes once a year' (JL, 81).

Rather peculiarly, this proverb is expressed using the third-person feminine singular, which is mirrored in the corresponding

---

[42] The root is recorded as √ḏḥl by JL.

Mehri expression *l-hīs bäḏrōt ṯhōṣad* 'Wie sie gesät hat, so wird sie ernten' (Sima 2005, 89).

(190)

məḥerɛ́f kɔb l-aʕlš

I respect the dog for the sake of the owner

يُحترم الكلب لأجل صاحبه

This saying is used when those guilty of a crime are pardoned on account of the social standing of their tribe or family (al-Shahri 2000, 116, 300).

The participial form *məḥerɛ́f* is listed by JL (114) as 'shy, reserved', albeit in the form *moḥoruf*. The fact that it is used here to signify 'respected' offers a glimpse of the tribal culture of Jibbali/Śḥərɛ́t speakers, where seclusion and privacy may be viewed as unusual and, hence, a privilege for those who are respected by the community.

(191)

mergʲe ērġít yúnfəʕ

It is always expected that the nephew will be useful

من المُفترض من ابن الاخت ان يفيد خاله

This saying emphasises the importance of the relationship between a nephew and a (maternal) uncle and can be used sarcastically if the former fails to fulfil his obligations towards the latter (al-Shahri 2000, 116, 301).

The participial form *mergʲe* 'expected' is not listed in the lexical sources. However, it can be linked to the root √rgw, from which a number of verbs in the semantic field of waiting, delaying, and postponing are derived. The term *ērġít* 'nephew' (i.e., sister's son) is attested here without a possessive pronominal suffix (Rubin 2014, 87). The subjunctive 3.M.SG. of a Ga-stem *yúnfəʕ* < √*nfʕ* (JL, 181) is used here independently to convey deontic modality, i.e., 'should' (Rubin 2014, 147).

(192)

malḥít ṭer ʕakərūt

The jawbone is on the coccyx

فك على عصعص

This expression is used to describe an overcrowded place (al-Shahri 2000, 116, 301).

The term *məlḥet* عظمة الفك 'jawbone' (MLZ, 829) is recorded by JL (163) as *məẑḥet*, which could point to dialectal variation. The term *ʕakərūt* 'pelvis' is from √*ʕkrm* (JL, 10). The Mehri counterpart of this expression is *ḥābū bärhäm ġōṯi aṭ-ṭār ġōṯi* 'Die Leute sind schon Nacken an Nacken' (Sima 2005, 89), in spite of some evident lexical divergences.

(193)

moġorɔ̄t a-ʕín ā-ʕósər

The eye of the lover is known

تُعرف العين المحبة

This is said to describe someone who is in love and tries to deny it (al-Shahri 2000, 117, 301).

The participial form *moġorɔ̄t* 'known' < √*ġrb* must be the feminine counterpart of masculine *məġreb* (JL, 88). The long vowel in *ā-ʕósər* stands for the genitive exponent + a definite article. Compare the Mehri expression *yaġrōb ʻajbūn* 'Der Verliebte ist leicht zu erkennen' (Sima 2005, 90), with the same meaning.

(194)

mən ʕõk bɛss dəḥɔ́r a-aʕîtək

Either your grandfather or your grandmother

من جدك لاقى جدتك ؟

This is a remark on a solution which is actually worse than the problem (al-Shahri 2000, 117, 302).

The use of the preposition *mən* to mean 'instead of' is undoubtedly related to its disjunctive function (Rubin 2014, 303–4). The verbal form *dəḥɔ́r* is a perfective third person of a Ga-stem meaning 'to find someone, befall' (JL, 37).[43] This proverb is uttered as a question, as is evident by both the speaker's intonation and its Arabic translation, and would be best translated as 'instead of your grandfather only, did it find your grandmother (too)?', probably implying that an illness (or something equally undesirable) which initially afflicted only one person subsequently spread to another one, possibly as the result of an ineffective attempt to treat it.

(195)

mən bobɛ́h bɛss dəḥɔ́r ʕazəlɛ́t

Either leprosy or the plague?

من برص إلى جذام؟

Similarly to entry number **(194)** above, this is used as a warning not to opt for a solution that is worse or as bad as the problem (al-Shahri 2000, 117, 302), and it shares a similar sentential structure. The terms *bobɛ́h* < √bwb (MLZ, 145), not listed in JL,

---

[43] The vocalisation *dəḥɔ́r* is unexpected and may be due to a hesitation between the perfective *daḥár* and the imperfective *yədɔḥɔ́r*.

and ʕazəlɛ́t (JL, 21) are the names of two similar skin conditions related to leprosy. The former term, *bobɛ́h*, attests the uncommon phoneme /o/.

(196)

mən ṭəḳəlúnk ġəfɛr ʕánən ɔ-ġɔ́k

Instead of looking for the thaghloon, look after yourself

من بحثك لنا عن نبات الثقلون. اكفي عننا غيطك

This is said to people who volunteer for tasks clearly beyond their abilities, and stems from a folk tale according to which a group of people were gathered to discuss who should go to look for the *ṭəḳəlun* plant, but could not reach an agreement, whereupon a sick man, who was barely able to stand, and was not able to use the privy by himself, declared he would go. The others then replied using this sentence (al-Shahri 2000, 117, 302).

The term *ṭəḳəlun* indicates *Glossonema varians* (Miller and Morris 1988, 44). According to Miller and Morris, there exist three variants of this plant name, namely *ṭəḳəlum*, *ṭəḳəlob*, and *feḳelaw*. However, their distribution is presently unknown. The Ga-stem imperative *ġəfɛr* means 'to hide, to pardon' (JL, 84). The segment ɔ-ġɔ́k must be analysed as *ɛ-ġɔ́b-ək. The use of the term *ġɔ́b* 'excreta' < √ġbb here makes it rather clear that al-Shahri's English translation of this proverb uses a euphemism, and a more faithful, albeit rude, translation would be something like 'Instead of looking for *ṭəḳəlún*, spare us your shit!'.

(197)

mən ḥaggʲ lɔḳᵊbɔ́r tel šeríf

Instead of Haj I want to be buried close to the saint

بدلاً من الحج أُقبر عند السيد

This is used when accepting a small gift or a small part of what one really needs (al-Shahri 2000, 117, 303).

The Sharíf are held to be saints according to certain currents of Islam, so that when one cannot perform the Hajj within one's lifetime, one can be content with being buried in the proximity of a Sharíf. The use of a subjunctive lɔkˀbɔ́r expresses an optative meaning. The preposition *tel* means 'at, by, beside' (Rubin 2014, 263).

(198)

mən xalsɛ́t t-ten sɔ́ġɔt
If there is no other food they can eat the leaves of sughut
من العدم تأكلن شجرة السوغوت

This is said to those who resolve to do the opposite of what they have been advised to do (al-Shahri 2000, 118, 303).

For the meaning of the plant name *sɔ́ġɔt*, see entry number **(164)** above, which shares the same structure and Mehri counterpart.

(199)

mən maʕgíns lɛṣˀnax
Instead of fat meat we need acceptable meat
بدلاً من سمنتها المفرطة نريد سمنة صالحة للاكل

The proverb refers to a cow, and implies that, instead of hoping for a very filling meal and being disappointed by the lack thereof, the person who utters this sentence declares that recovering little fat from the animal is acceptable, and it is a feasible endeavour. Similarly to entry number **(196)** above, this is said to people who brag about being able to do something that is clearly beyond their abilities (al-Shahri 2000, 118, 303).

The term *maʕgín* < √ʕgn is listed in JL (10) as 'stew of fat and meat' and has here a 3.F.SG. personal suffix -*s*. The subjunctive 1.C.SG verbal form *lɛṣᵊnax* derives from a H1-stem of the root √ṣnx and means 'to find fat in a thin animal after slaughtering' (JL, 240). This form is used here to convey optativity. See also entries **(161)** and **(197)**. This expression can be more faithfully translated as 'Instead of fat meat, I'll be content with lean meat'.

(200)

her ɛ̄-rít ṣifɔ́t séhəl kɔbkɔ́b

If the moon is clear the stars are unimportant

اذا صفت القمر فلا تهم الكواكب

This is said when misfortune strikes a group of people, but one of them manages to emerge unscathed (al-Shahri 2000, 118, 304). The adjective *ṣifɔ́t* appears to be the feminine counterpart of *ṣofi* 'pure' (JL, 237), whilst *séhəl* means 'easy' (JL, 225), and seems to be intended as 'never mind' here: i.e., If the moon is bright, never mind the stars.

(201)

hiɛ yəṭɔ́rd aġəṣ́á

Love drives away hatred

الحب يطرد الكراهية

This is said of circumstances in which enmity between two groups is mitigated or overcome by the love or friendship between two individuals (al-Shahri 2000, 118, 304).

The term *hiɛ* means 'love', as its Arabic translation حب proves (al-Shahri 2000, 304). However, it is recorded neither in JL nor in MLZ, and one wonders whether it might be related to Arabic هوى 'love' (Wehr and Cowan 1976, 1040). The term *aġə́ṣá* < **e-baġə́ṣá* 'hatred' (MLZ, 136: بغض) is not recorded by JL. For an analysis of a verb that is morphologically similar to *yəṭɔ́rd* 'to send away, drive away' (JL, 279), see entries **(95)** of this collection and **(21)** of the MLZ collection.

(202)

her bek ḥa-lɔ́d ḏ fɔ́ṭɔx əlɔ́tɔġ

Instead of wounding a person I will kill him

بدلاً من أضرب الشخص لأجرحه افضل ان أقتله

This is said when someone is making things more complicated than they actually are (al-Shahri 2000, 118, 304).

The first verbal form is a complex and problematic one. For *ḥa-lɔ́d*, al-Shahri writes حلووت, which leads one to interpret it as a perfective 3.F.SG. of a Ga-stem < √*ḥlb* meaning 'to milk' (JL, 109). In actuality, حلووت stands for the pausal realisation of حلوود *ḥa-lɔ́d*, a 1.C.SG future form from a Ga-stem < √*lbd* meaning 'to shoot, strike hard, cut' (JL, 159). However, this interpretation too is problematic, in that the subjunctive form accompanying the future prefix *ḥa-* should be *l-ɔ́lbəd* and not the imperfective *lɔ́d*. Nevertheless, S. al-Amri believes that the form is correct and in current use, which leads one to wonder about the function of *ḥa-* + imperfective. The whole verbal form *her bek ḥa-lɔ́d* means 'if I'm about to strike', as shown by the use of the auxiliary *ber*, conjugated in the perfective 1.C.SG. Regarding *bek*, when followed by the future, this auxiliary conveys a proximative or avertative sense, i.e., to be about or to be nearly (Rubin 2014, 167). The term *fɔ́ṭx* means 'blow, wound in the head' (JL, 67). The verbal form *əlɔ́tɔġ* is an imperfective 1.C.SG. of a Ga-stem meaning 'to kill' (JL, 165). Overall, the literal meaning of this expression is best interpreted as 'If I were to wound (someone), I'd kill him instead'.

(203)

her šktɔ́rək tɔš effɔ́rkəš

If it looks to be too much, divide it up

اذا رأيته كثيراً فرّقه

This is said when people brag about their possessions, when they are in fact poor (al-Shahri 2000, 119, 304).

The verbal form *šktɔ́rək* is a perfective 2.M.SG of a Š1-stem < √ktr and means 'to think something is a lot' (JL, 137), whilst the segment *effɔ́rkəš* contains the H2-stem imperative *effɔ́rk* 'share!', listed in JL (61) as *efurk* 'to frighten; to make a parting'.

(204)

her šek a-ġagʲ e-difɔ́r yəlḥɔ́ḳk a-ʕazᵊm

Who has weak men, loses the bet

من مع القوم الضعفاء تُثبت عليه التهمة

This is used when someone is unsuccessful in an endeavour, despite having done everything to succeed. The specific example comes from a folk tale according to which a woman who was accused of being a witch, and who was actually innocent, could not prove her innocence because her accusers were powerful in the community, whilst she had no one by her side. This sentence is said to be what she uttered upon being condemned (al-Shahri 2000, 119, 305).

The verbal form *yəlḥɔ́kk* is a compound of a subjunctive (with optative force) 3.M.SG. of a Gb-stem meaning 'to catch up with, overtake, run after' (JL, 163), and the 2.M.SG. personal suffix *-k*. The term *ʕazᵊm*, besides meanings such as 'intention, aim' (JL, 21) and 'ordeal by fire' (a meaning not recorded by either JL or MLZ), has another meaning, as explained by al-Shahri (2000, 305): ويسمى بالشحرية (إغعزم) حيث إنه ياخذ ملتهبة بالنار ويحرق بها لسان المرأة 'In Shahri *ʕazᵊm* is the act of taking a red-hot iron and branding the tongue of a woman with it'. Overall, the literal meaning of this expression may be said to be 'if you have weak men, may the ordeal by fire catch you!'.

(205)
her ʕar kun xer̰ yəšɔ́ṣər
If there is rain the green will show
اذا كان هناك فعلاً غيث ستخضر الارض

This is said to those who promise to do something, but are strongly suspected to be either incapable of doing what they promise to do, or lying altogether (al-Shahri 2000, 119, 305).

The term *xer̰*, which is not reported by JL, means '(abundant) rain' (MLZ, 315: الغيث),. The verbal form *yəšɔ́ṣər* is an imperfective 3.M.SG. of a Ga-stem meaning 'to become green' (JL, 265).

(206)
her ġī kkelṭ ɔl ġī ĩšékəlṭ
Even if the speaker forgets, the listener doesn't
اذا نسي المتحدث لم ينس المتحدث إليه

This means that one should always remember who one is lying to, in order not to contradict oneself (al-Shahri 2000, 119, 305).

The term *kelṭ* is said to be the plural form of *kelṭɔ́t* 'story' (JL, 131; MLZ, 808: القصة, الأمثولةو الحكاية), but is used here with the meaning of 'speaker'. The first consonant [k] is geminated, perhaps because of the presence of a definite article. The participial form *ĩšekəlṭ* < *e-mešəkəlṭ* 'listener' is connected to the Š1-stem verb *šk̃əleṭ* 'to listen to a tale' (JL, 130). The perfective third person of the doubly weak G-stem verb *ġī* meaning 'to be wrong; to forget, loose, leave' < √ġwy is recorded by JL (91) as *ġe*. The unexpected /ī/ in the place of /e/ might be due to these doubly weak verbs often fluctuating between the two forms $C^1ī$ and $C^1ē$ (al-Kathiri and Dufour 2020, 216). S. al-Amri reports the variant *ɔl kɔṯ yəġī ɛ yəšékəlṭ*.

(207)

her hɔ̄t ʕɔzū̃t tɔkš̃ɛ́f yəhɛ̄ bəs ɔʕz rémᵊnɛm

When the snake wanted to behave badly, God threw it in the sea

اذا نوى الثعبان على الكفر والمنكر يرميه الله بحراً

This is said upon learning that a crime might have taken place, had the criminal not be hindered by circumstances (al-Shahri 2000, 120, 306).

The verbal form *ʕɔzū̃t* is a perfective 3.F.SG. of a Ga-stem < √ʕzm meaning 'to decide; to invite' (JL, 21). The Ga-stem subjunctive 3.F.SG. form *tɔkš̃ɛ́f* is from √kšf 'to do something very cruel; to uncover, examine; to be embarassed (at something odd)' (JL, 137). The verbal form *yəhɛ̄* is an imperfective 3.M.SG. of a G-stem from the doubly weak root √hwy meaning 'to fall' (JL, 100). Its use with the preposition *b-* to convey a causative meaning is hitherto unrecorded.

(208)

yəṣəḥɔ́k ḏ śíbir xɔh b-yəntəġɔ́ś ḏ śinifet

Only the one with the nice teeth can smile and the one with the long hair can show it off

يضحك ذو الفم الجميل وينفش الشعر ذو الشعر الكثيف

This is used either about someone who is very beautiful and loved by everyone, or someone who is not, but is unconcerned about the judgement of the community (al-Shahri 2000, 120, 306).

The verbal form *yəṣəḥɔ́k* is an imperfective 3.M.SG. of a Gb-stem meaning 'to laugh' (JL, 325). The term *śíbir* seems to be connected to the term *śəbrɔ́t* meaning 'perfection' (MLZ, 499: الإتقان), and is used in entry number **(116)** above as an adjective meaning 'beautiful'. However, the lack of intervocalic deletion of /b/ might point to a non-native origin. The term *śinifet* seems to be related to a root √śnf, which yields a Ga-stem verb that may be transcribed as *śɔnɔ́f*, meaning 'to stand in one's place frowning' (MLZ, 527: وقف في مكانه عابسا مكفهر الوجه). The verbal form *yəntəġɔ́ś* is an imperfective 3.M.SG. of a T1-stem < √nġś, meaning '(water, food) to be thrown away because it is dirty' (JL, 185). The abundance of doubtful forms raises the question as to whether we might be dealing with a formulaic, and hence mehrising and/or arabising, language (Johnstone 1972). The Arabic translation provided by al-Shahri, however, sheds some light on the literal meaning of this expression: 'He who has a beautiful mouth laughs, and he who has thick hair ruffles it'.[44]

---

[44] Compare Arabic نفش 'ruffles its feathers (bird)' (Wehr and Cowan 1976, 986).

(209)

yέbrəf ḏ ɔl bəʕέṣ

He who worries should support

من لم يطمئن الى قدرة صاحبه عليه مساندته

This is an encouragement to act on something instead of simply worrying about it (al-Shahri 2000, 120, 306).

The verb *yέbrəf* is an imperfective 3.M.SG. of a H1-stem meaning 'to support something not to make it fall' (MLZ, 125: سند شيئاً حتى لا يسقط), and is not listed in JL. The verbal form *bəʕέṣ* seems to be a perfective third person of a H1-stem < √bʕṣ, meaning 'to check something from a distance' (MLZ, 135: اطمئن الشيء من بعده). The initial vowel of the verbal form is lost due to the adjacency of a sonorant. This proverb is also recorded in MLZ (125) as يَبَرَّف أُل بَعَض. Al-Shahri's Arabic rendition of this expression translates as 'He who is not assured of his friend's ability, should support him', and may shed some light on its literal meaning.

(210)

yɔʕɔ́ṭ ʕar ε ḳeré

Only the person who has hidden something can find it

ينبش من اخفى

This is said when someone suddenly solves a vexing issue, which can either be the search for something physical, or the search for an explanation for something (al-Shahri 2000, 120, 307).

The verbal form *yɔʕɔ́ṭ* is an imperfective 3.M.SG. of a Gb-stem < √bʕṭ meaning 'to dig up' (MLZ, 134: نبش), and *ḳeré* is a perfective third person of a Ga-stem meaning 'to hide' (JL, 150).

2.0. *Muʿğam Lisān Ẓufār*

(1) MLZ, 156

ɛḏīlín əntəktɛ́k lhes e-ḵāḥáf o gʲūḏɛ́t

اذيلن انتكتك لهس قاحف اجوذات

⁴⁵فلان يغلي مثل قدر البر

So-and-so boils like a pot full of corn

This expression describes a very impatient, short-tempered person. The verbal form *əntəktɛ́k* is a perfective third person of a ᵠN1-stem meaning 'to boil' (MLZ, 156: غلى على النار). The noun *ḵāḥáf* is a diminutive form of *ḵaḥf* 'clay cooking-pot' (JL, 143). *gʲūḏɛ́t* means 'boiled corn/barley' (MLZ, 156: سليق البر \ الشعير). The relativiser is realised as [o] instead of the expected [ɛ]: this may be caused by the presence of a long rounded vowel in the leftmost position in *gʲūḏɛ́t*. In the introduction to JL (xxix–xxx), Johnstone describes a similar behaviour of the (almost homophonous) definite article when adjacent to a guttural consonant. He seems, however, not to include /g/ among the guttural consonants, and lists *e-* as the allophone of the definite article when adjacent to /g/ (JL, xxix). See also above, p. 36.

(2) MLZ, 217

ərdi bə ḥablɛ́tš ṭer ɛḏīlín

ردي بحبلتش ظئر اذيلن

رُمِي بحبله السري وراء فلان

His umbilical cord has been thrown after so-and-so

---

[45] MLZ does not provide an Arabic translation. This translation was devised by the authors.

People used to believe that if they threw a baby's umbilical cord at a person they admired, then the baby would take after that person. This expression is hence said in order to state that a person is very similar to another person. This tradition is described in al-Shahri (2000, 137, 327).

The verbal form *ərdi* is a passive perfective third person of a Ga-stem meaning 'to throw' (JL, 204). According to S. al-Amri, *ḥablɛ́t* does not mean 'umbilical cord' in his dialect, in which the term *šírɑ́ʕ* is used instead. However, JL (267) lists *šírɔ́ʕ* as 'navel' and MLZ (490) follows suit.

(3) MLZ, 301

ɛdīlín ɔ yəxéfər b-ɔ yaʕskɔ́r

اذيلن أُ يخفر بأُ يعسكُر

إن فلانا لا يؤمن الخائف ولا يحمى نفسه

So-and-so doesn't give protection and doesn't offer shelter

This is said of someone weak.

The form *yəxéfər* is a 3.M.SG. imperfective of a Ga-stem from the root √*xfr* meaning '(group) to give protection to a sick man by gathering and stating that he is given protection from ill health (as a counter-spell)' (JL, 298). The [e] vowel found between C¹ and C² in this verbal form instead of the expected [ə] is triggered by the presence of a guttural [x] (al-Kathiri and Dufour 2020, 194). The 3.M.SG. imperfective of a ᵠH1-stem derived from √*ʕskr* means 'to set up a temporary living quarter' (MLZ, 626: أقام التجمع السكني المؤقت) and is not recorded by JL.

(4) MLZ, 304

ɔ de yəxtelédən ṭer diní lɔ

أُ دئ يختلدن ظر ديني لو

لا أحد يتخلد في هذه الدنيا

No one in this world lives forever

This self-explanatory saying features an imperfective 3.M.SG. H2-stem verb < √xld 'to be eternal, live forever' (MLZ, 304: تجلد \ عاش إلى الأبد), which is not recorded by JL.

(5) MLZ, 314

ɛd̠ílín xḗ mən mun o-śúrəʕ

اذيلن خئ من مون أوشرع

فلان لم يأبه له أحد وتجاوزه الجميع

So-and-so is a gap between the sails

This is said of someone who is unimportant or uninfluential (especially within a family or a tribe).

S. al-Amri states that this expression is not typical of the dialect of his town. The term xḗ < √xwy means 'interstice, space' (JL, 311). The definite article before the term śúrəʕ 'sails' (JL, 254) is realised as [o]. As in item number **(1)** of this collection, this might be due to vowel harmony triggered by a rounded vowel in the leftmost position in the following segment. The pausal realisation of final /ʕ/ is [ḥ].

(6) MLZ, 328

ɛd̠ílín lhes e-ddesɔ́s

اذيلن لهس اَدَسُس

فلان مثل دسس

So-and-so is like the desɔ́s lizard

The *desɔ́s* is a small venomous lizard. S. al-Amri says this is a metaphor for a treacherous and disloyal person. According to JL (42), *desɔ́s* is a little venomous snake, an eavesdropper with bad intent, or a tiny mud snail. JL also lists, within the same entry, the similar proverb *ɛbrɛ́ ēdesɔ́s ḥa-yékən desɔ́s* 'the son of a snake will be a snake'.

(7) MLZ, 343

ɛdīlín ṭerš ēšdihikɛ́tə

اذيلن ظرش اَشْدّهُقتئ

فلان تتوالى عليه الزيارات

So-and-so, the visits are upon him

This is said of someone whose health is deteriorating. The term *ēšdihikɛ́tə* is the definite form of *mešdihikɛ́tə* 'abundance of visits to the ill' (MLZ, 343: كثرة الزيارات للمريض). However, MLZ lists the term as *mešdihɔkɛ́tə* (مِشدّهُقتئ).

(8) MLZ, 366

ɔ šeš ɔl ɛ́hɛl b-ɔ rgʲɛ́

اُ شش اُل إهَلْ بورجئ

ليس له أهل \ أصدقاء يرجو نفعهم

He has no family, nor does he have hope

MLZ states that this saying applies to those who have no friends. S. al-Amri, however, says that it applies rather to those who either don't have family or are cut off from it.

This expression exhibits two terms, *ɛ́hɛl* and *rgʲɛ́*, which may be suspected to be Arabic loans, meaning, respectively, 'family'

(MLZ, 983: أهل),[46] and 'the friends whose help is requested in the time of need' (MLZ, 366: الأصدقاء الذين يرجى نفعهم عند الحاجة).[47]

(9) MLZ, 427

ɛd̶īlín ərdé b səbṭát

اذيلن رَدَءِ بسبطت

استسلم للأمر ولم يعد يقدر على شيء

So-and-so has thrown the belt

The term *səbṭát* refers to the belt worn with traditional dress, and the meaning of the expression refers to someone who is giving up on something because of old age or illness. According to MLZ (427), however, *səbṭát* means 'a stick used to hit grains' (العصا الذي تضرب به سنابل الحبوب). The verbal form *ərdé* is a perfective third person of a Ga-stem meaning 'to throw' (JL, 204).

(10) MLZ, 434

ɛd̶īlín məḥík b səḥík

اذيلن محِق بسَحق

فلان يتسبب في إثارة إغاظة الناس وسخطهم

So-and-so, annoyance and oppression

According to S. al-Amri, this expression is used to describe an annoying and mean person. The semantics of the two terms *məḥík* and *səḥík* are not entirely clear. However, S. al-Amri suggests that they may be translated using the English terms 'annoyance' and 'oppression'. JL (170) records *məḥík* as '(person) tiresome, annoying', and the Ga-stem verb *šḥák* as 'to crush, grind fine' (JL, 226),

---

[46] This term is not listed in JL.

[47] This term is not listed in JL.

the latter's vocalism being altered in order to rhyme with the former.

(11) MLZ, 444

ɔ šek ɔ saʕi b-ɔ daʕi

اُشك اسيعي باُ ديعي

ليس معك من يسعي في حاجتك \ من ينافح عنك

You have neither someone to strive (for you) nor to speak out (for you)

According to S. al-Amri, this is said of someone who does not have anybody on their side, and cannot count on any help or support. The two terms *saʕi* and *daʕi* are clearly Arabic loanwords.

(12) MLZ, 480

šɔ́fɔlš défər

شُفلش دفر

إحساسه مرهف

His feelings are bad

The term *šɔ́fɔl*, besides its original anatomical meaning 'belly, entrails', also means 'feelings' (MLZ, 480). According to S. al-Amri, this describes someone who is ill-intentioned, judgmental, and cunning. He adds that the expression can be treated as either masculine or feminine, hence it can be formulated as *šɔ́fɔlš difirít*.

(13) MLZ, 516

dɛnu b-dɛnu menmunúhum štɔt

ذَنو بذَنو منمُنهم شطاط

بينهما بون شاسع

There is a big difference between this and this

S. al-Amri believes this self-explanatory expression to be very old. The term *ḏɛnu* is a singular masculine proximal demonstrative 'this' (JL, 47). For the last word in the expression, which is not recorded in JL, MLZ (516) records شطاط, which would be likely rendered as /śṭɛṭ/, but S. al-Amri pronounces *šṭɔṭ*.

(14) MLZ, 539

e-ṣɛrb beš ɛ̄ flɔk, e-défər yəsənúd enúf

اصَرب بش آفلك ادفر يسنُد أنف

الصرب فيه الخيرات حتى الإنسان الخامل الكسول لا يحتاج فيه لغيره

In the spring there are good things even for lazy people

Literally 'the spring has success, the bad (one) supports him-/herself'. According to MLZ (717), *flɔk* means 'success in trade' (النجاح في تجارة). The verbal form *yəsənúd* is an imperfective 3.M.SG. of a Gb-stem meaning 'to do something with help' (JL, 230) and adding the reflexive *enúf* gives it the meaning of 'to help oneself'.

(15) MLZ, 582

ɛḏīlín ɔ yəṭúrḳən beš śi lɔ

اذيلن أُ يطُرقن بش شّي لو

لا يؤثر فيه شيء

So-and-so is not hit by anything

S. al-Amri says this applies to someone resilient. Cf. the Arabic root √ṭrḳ 'knock, pound' (Wehr and Cowan 1976, 558–59), which in Jibbali/Śḥərɛ̄t produces a H2-stem verb that appears here in the 3.M.SG. imperfective.

(16) MLZ, 584

ṭaʕmέt ar diləmέt

طعمت عر دلمت

العطاء أفضل من البخل (بالطعام)

Generosity is better than being stingy

The non-occurrence of the term *xar* 'better' is unexpected. The term *ṭaʕmέt* 'giving food' (MLZ, 584) is used here to mean 'generosity'. The term *diləmέt* means 'stinginess' (MLZ, 337: البُخل) and is not recorded by JL.

(17) MLZ, 590

tob ar s̃ᵊṭaláġ

تُب عر شطلغ

⁴⁸جبنا سيرة القط جاء ينط

"Speak of the devil..."

Similarly to its English counterpart, this expression can be used when someone who is being talked about suddenly and unexpectedly shows up. The particle *tob ar* means 'indeed, truly' (Rubin 2014, 315). The verbal form *s̃ṭaláġ* is a perfective third person of a Š1-stem meaning 'to arrive upon being mentioned' (JL, 277; MLZ, 590: جاء عند ذكره).

---

[48] MLZ does not provide an Arabic translation for this expression. This is very close in meaning.

(18) MLZ, 591

ɛd̠ílín ṭaməšɛ́t b-ʕabrɛ́t

اذيلن طمبشت بعبرت

فلان أعمى البصر والبصيرة

So-and-so lacks sight and insight

The terms *ṭamšɛ́t* and *ʕabrɛ́t* mean, respectively, 'lack of insight' (MLZ, 591: قلة البصيرة) and 'blindness' (MLZ, 604: العمى). According to S. al-Amri, another similar expression, *ṭəmúš b ʕabɔ́r*, is a curse that means 'may you go blind and crazy'.

(19) MLZ, 608

ɛd̠ílín šeš ʕayt̠ɔ́t̠ d̠ serbɛ́t

اذيلن ششِ عِثث ذ سربت

فلان لديه عيال كُثر

So-and-so has the offspring of a ʕayt̠ɔ́t̠ and serbɛ́t

This expression predictably describes someone who has a big family.

The term *ʕayt̠ɔ́t̠* describes للماشية 'a very prolific insect whose eggs can be found on dried sardines... abundance of offspring' (MLZ, 608: حشرة تتطفل على سمك السردين المجفف والمخزن كعلف كثرة العيال). The term *serbɛ́t* means 'abundance of offspring' (MLZ, 438: كثرة العيال). S. al-Amri pronounces *ʕayt̠ɔ́t̠ zerbɛ́t*, with the segment /t̠d̠s/ coalescing into [z].

(20) MLZ, 624

l-ʕazíz ɛd̠ílín

لعزيز اذيلن

رحم الله فلان

May God help so-and-so

Said when grieving someone, to remark upon the good character of the person in question. The term ʕazíz is most probably an Arabic loan. This is also recorded by JL (20) as l-ʻazíz... 'God help... (a departed one)!'.

(21) MLZ, 633

yəfɔ́rd a-ʕiṭɔ́b

يفورد اعطب

يهرب عند رؤية شجرة العشرة

He flees the ʕaṭəb tree

The term ʕiṭɔ́b is the plural form of ʕaṭəb, a tree whose scientific name is *Calotropis procera* (Miller and Morris 1988, 42),[49] also listed in JL (18) as ʕaṭb. According to S. al-Amri, this tree looks like a human being in the darkness, so a person who flees it is a coward. The verbal form yəfɔ́rd is an imperfective 3.M.SG. of a Ga-stem meaning 'to stampede, panic' (JL, 59), not recorded by MLZ. S. al-Amri pronounces it with a long vowel, as al-Shahri does for the same verb in entry number **(95)** of the al-Shahri collection (al-Shahri 2000, 94, 270; Castagna 2022a, 41), and the long vowel in MLZ's Arabic-script transcription, with a و, seems to confirm this.

(22) MLZ, 634

ɛd̪īlín ɔ yaʕṭéṭ a-rɛšə lɔ

اذيلن أ يعطط رش لو

فلان لا يمرض

So-and-so doesn't rest his head

---

[49] Miller and Morris record the term as ʕuṭeb.

According to S. al-Amri, this means rather 'so-and-so is a workaholic' or 'so-and-so never stops working'. The verbal form *yaʕṭɛ́t*, an imperfective 3.M.SG. of a G-stem from the geminate root √ʕtt, is said by MLZ to mean 'to feel pain, to fall ill' (مرض \ وجع \ تألم), but S. al-Amri affirms that it means 'to rest'.

(23) MLZ, 656

ʕayún b-sūni b-hɛt lə ṭaʕbát ḏinú

اعيُن بسوني بهت لطبعت ذِنو

طوال الأعوام والسنين وأنت على هذا الطبع (السيء)

All these years, and you still have this (bad) habit

This expression is used as a reproach towards somebody who has had a bad habit for a long time. The terms *ʕayún* and *sūni* both mean 'years' (MLZ, 656: عَيُن يسوني : الأعوام), but *sūni* may be an Arabic loanword. Also, the term *ṭaʕbát* 'habit' (MLZ, 576: العادة) looks like an Arabic loanword. The term *ḏinú* is a singular feminine proximal demonstrative 'this' (JL, 44).

(24) MLZ, 663

a-ġarír ʕayér

اغَرِر عير

الغريب أعمى (لجهله بالناس والمكان)

He who is foreign is blind

MLZ states that this expression describes inexperienced young people. S. al-Amri, however, asserts that it applies to foreign people rather than young people, and the Arabic translation provided seems to agree with the latter meaning: note the Arabic meaning of the term *ġarír* provided by MLZ (663), 'strange, foreign' (غريب).

2. Proverbs and Linguistic Analysis

(25) MLZ, 667

ləksɛ́s id ġisɔ́t

لكسس غِسوت
تقوت

May I find it a wholesome hand

This is used to congratulate someone who has done a good job. The verbal form *ləksɛ́s* is a compound of *ləksɛ́*, a 1.C.SG subjunctive of a Ga-stem with an optative meaning 'to find' (JL, 135; al-Kathiri and Dufour 2020, 203) + a 3.F.SG personal suffix -*s*. The term *ġisɔ́t* seems to be an adjective indicating strength and health. MLZ (667) lists it in the feminine and provides little explanation as to its meaning. The Arabic translation, an imperative of a form V verb meaning 'to be or become stronger', does, however, shed some limited light on the overall meaning of this expression.

(26) MLZ, 698

eśśəbbɔ́t eddiní bə fərʕát

شِّيت اديني بفرّعُتْ

This is a formulaic expression: S. al-Amri affirms that the verbs are used only in this expression and are not found in any other context. Hence, its exact meaning is somewhat obscure, and MLZ does not give an Arabic translation. Nevertheless, it is used to comment on circumstances or situations that are worsening and becoming dangerously out of control. MLZ records شِّيت, but S. al-Amri reads *eśśəbbɔ́t* (H1-stem perfective 3.F.SG.), and remarks that the provided form is wrong. This form seems to derive from a III-weak root √śbw~y, although no relevant entries could be found at this time. However, MLZ (698) states that the Arabic expression قامت الدنيا و لم تقعد 'the world was turned upside down' is comparable to the Jibbali/Śḥərɛ́t expression.

(27) MLZ, 713

ɛdīlín beš fəkrɛ́t

اذيلن بش فْكْرَت

فلان أمره عجبا

So-and-so is behaving strangely

This is said of a person who is visibly troubled at a given time but is otherwise normal. According to MLZ (713), this expression is used in bewilderment and confusion, but it does not provide further explanation. The term *fəkrɛ́t* is related to the root √fkr, well known across Semitic, which conveys the meaning of 'thinking'.

(28) MLZ, 715

ɛdīlín ɔ yəfɔ́lgʲəš ġɛgʲ ʕak ḥagərɛ́tə lɔ

اذيلن أ يفُلجش غج عق حجرت لو

فلان لا يغلبه أحد في المرافعات القبلية

So-and-so's arguments cannot be refuted by anyone

This expression is used to describe someone who always seems to get his/her way in arguments. The verbal form *yəfɔ́lgʲəš* is a combination of an imperfective 3.M.SG. of a Ga-stem meaning 'to silence someone with superior argument' (JL, 57) and a 3.M.SG. personal suffix -š. The term *ḥagərɛ́t* means 'meeting to discuss (tribal) issues' (MLZ, 221: الاجتماع لمناقشة قضية ما).

(29) MLZ, 748

ɛd̪ilín ɔ ifferɔ́d ḳə́śśɛ́tə lɔ

اذيلن أ يفرُد قشّت لو

فلان لا يخيف \ ينفر شاة قاصية وحيدة

So-and-so doesn't (can't) stampede a lost goat

This is said of a cowardly person. S. al-Amri asserts that it rather describes a lazy person. The verb *ifferɔ́d* is an imperfective 3.M.SG. of a H1-stem meaning 'to stampede (transitive), frighten' (JL, 59). The term *ḳə́śśɛ́t* seems to mean 'a lost goat' (MLZ, 748), although it appears also to mean 'crazy'.

(30) MLZ, 774

ɛ̃ḳní dáhar

أَقْنِي دهر

الإنسان يحتاج إلى تربية وتوجيه طوال حياته

A child forever!

The term *ɛ̃ḳní* is the definite form of *məḳəní*, which according to JL (147) means 'baby'. However, MLZ (774) defines it as 'in the process of being raised' (في طور التربية), which might be a synonym to an extent. *dáhar* here means 'forever' (JL, 36; MLZ, 342: ابد, لبدهر). S. al-Amri states that this is used to describe someone whose attitude is childish. Therefore, the meaning provided by MLZ, 'the human being needs education and guidance throughout his life' (الإنسان يحتاج إلى تربية طوال حياته), is doubtful.

(31) MLZ, 785

titk elkobbí

تتك الكُبِه

تأكلك (الكبه)

May elkobbí eat you!

This is a (mild) reproach against a greedy, gluttonous person. The term *elkobbí* (MLZ, 785) is unknown to the author of MLZ. S. al-Amri enquired with his community and found that it may mean some sort of illness, but none of those whom he consulted was able to tell exactly which one. The verbal form *titk* is a subjunctive 3.F.SG. with optative force, implying that the subject *elkobbí* is feminine, in combination with a 2.M.SG. personal suffix -*k*.

(32) MLZ, 813

eḏílín ekmíl

اذيلن اكمِل

فلان سعى إلى حتفه \ جاءت ساعة موته

So-and-so's time has come

This self-explanatory expression features a H1-stem third-person verbal form meaning 'to finish (transitive), to be killed, to meet one's fate' (JL, 131). The rightmost vowel, normally [e], is raised to [i] in adjacent position to a nasal consonant.

(33) MLZ, 814

eḏílín beš kámən défər

اذيلن بش كَمْنْ دفر

فلان به مرض خبيث

So-and-so has a malicious illness

According to S. al-Amri, this expression can also be used to describe someone who has been bewitched. The term *kámən* means 'shape, nature, temperament; deadly disease which is not precisely known' (MLZ, 814: المرض. الطبع. السجية. الشبه. المثل. الشكل. الخبيث الفتاك الذي لا يعرف ما هو على وجه التحديد). The additional meaning of 'being bewitched' was suggested by one of S. al-Amri's informants.

(34) MLZ, 816

kɔnʕɔlɔ́t ḗ reš

كُنَّعُلْتُ آرش

الرأس المدبب إلى أعلى

A peak of a nose

This is said jokingly of someone who has a pointed head. The term *kɔnʕɔlɔ́t* is recorded by MLZ (816) as 'peak' (قمة).

(35) MLZ, 817

khal yit õl ɔ́tim

كَهَلْ يت أُوَّل آوتُم

استحل \ استمرأ أكل مال الأيتام

It is distasteful to eat the wealth of an orphan

This means that laying one's hands on the wealth of a weakling is not a commendable behaviour. The verbal form *khal* is a perfective third person of a Gb-stem meaning 'to be able to tolerate' (JL, 128). The verbal form *yit* is a subjunctive 3.M.SG. of a G-stem from the doubly weak root √*twy* meaning 'to eat' (al-Kathiri and Dufour 2020, 215). The segment *õl* is to be interpreted as

< *ɛ-mol 'the wealth' (JL, 176),⁵⁰ and the following segment ɔ́tim results from a sequence made up of the relativiser ɛ- and the term ótim 'orphan' (JL, 314).

(36) MLZ, 829

məlḥátᵊ ḍ ġɛgʲ

مَلْحَت ذ غج

رجل به بقية من شباب \ من قوة

A jawbone of a man

This idiomatic expression is used to describe a weak man. The term *məlḥát* 'jawbone' is recorded as *malḥít* in entry number **(192)** of the al-Shahri collection. Also, note the dialectal variant *məźḥet* (JL, 163).

(37) MLZ, 831

lɔ́ttəz əlḥá

لُتَزْ الحِئْ

تزاحمت اللحاء

(The) beards have crowded one another

According to MLZ (831), this expression is a 'metaphor for a stampede and intense crowding'. However, according to S. al-Amri, it rather symbolises an intense competition between two individuals or two groups, which can be either physical or intellectual. The beards symbolise manly strength and dignity.

---

⁵⁰ The literal meaning is 'livestock, capital', which in the culture of Jibbali/Śḥərɛ̄t speakers amounts to wealth.

As for the verbal form, lɔ́ttəz is a perfective third-person form of a T1-stem < √lzz meaning 'to shiver; to crowd one another; to have the jaws locked together' (JL, 167). The noun əlḥá is the plural form of ləhyέt 'beard' (JL, 163).

(38) MLZ, 891

nbaʕ yenbaʕ ɔź be-kεrəféfk

نْبْعْ ينْبْعْ اول بكرففك

أغرب عن وجهي ابعد الله وجهك

May God chase your face away

This expression is used as a wish not to see someone's face any more. According to S. al-Amri, it also carries the meaning of 'may you fall from God's grace'.

The use in sequence of the perfective and the subjunctive 3.M.SG. forms of a H1-stem meaning 'to chase away the evil' (MLZ, 891: طَرَدَ شر طِرظة) is noteworthy.

(39) MLZ, 897

εdịlín ɔ šeš négʲəm səʕídᵊ lɔ

اذيلن اُ شْبش نجم سعيد لو

فلان طالعه (اليوم) ليس طالع سُعد

So-and-so doesn't have a happy star

This is said when someone is struck by bad luck. The use of the term négʲəm for 'star' is peculiar. However, according to MLZ, this can mean 'star of destiny' (Wehr and Cowan 1976, 566) in addition to the likely imported Arabic meaning of 'star' as a celestial body. MLZ (897) specifies that this saying is used in a spontaneous manner, without a belief in stars or horoscopes being necessary: يقال ذلك بشكل عفوي دون الاعتقاد في النجوم \ الطالع.

(40) MLZ, 920

bɛr nɔ́ṭɔb ɛ-ḏbér

بر نْطُبْ إيذبر

فرش الجُعل جناحاه وطار

The scarab brushed its wings and flew

This expression is used as a metaphor for sunset. According to MLZ, it means 'the scarab brushed its wings and flew'; however, S. al-Amri states that the insect in question is a wasp rather than a scarab, despite the fact that MLZ translates the Jibbali/Śḥərɛ̄t term إيذبر ɛ-ḏbér into Arabic as الجُعل 'dung beetle; scarabaeus' (Wehr and Cowan 1976, 127). One might legitimately suspect that the similarity between the above-mentioned root and the root √dbr in Arabic (as well as other Semitic languages), whose meanings include 'wasp', might be responsible for a degree of semantic overlap. The verbal form nɔ́ṭɔb is a perfective third person of a Ga-stem meaning 'to shoot an arrow; to drive away' (JL, 196). According to MLZ (920), it can also mean 'to take something out' (أخرج الشيء). The presence of [ɔ] instead of the [u] expected adjacent to a nasal is noteworthy (Rubin 2014, 42–43). However, despite being very productive, the raising effect of nasals on adjacent vowels is not universal: for example, *kɔnɔṭɔt > kɔnṭɔt 'to die suddenly' (al-Kathiri and Dufour 2020, 184).[51]

---

[51] This form is a third-person 3.F.SG. of a Ga-stem (JL, 147).

(41) MLZ, 944

ɛ-kɛrˤféfš d-inyɛrən

اكرففش د ينيرن

وجهه يشيع نوراً

His face spreads the light

This is said of a good person.

The verbal form *d-inyɛrən* is an imperfective 3.M.SG. of a H2-stem meaning '(light) to glow' (JL, 198), with a circumstantial *d-* prefix (Rubin 2014, 158–61) attached (see also entries **(23)** and **(188)** of the al-Shahri collection above).

(42) MLZ, 950

kˤméz htɛf

كمز هِيْتْفَفْ

اقفز واصرخ[52]

Jump and shout!

S. al-Amri pronounces *htaf* for هِيْتْفَفْ. The meaning of this expression, made up of two imperatives of Ga-stems meaning respectively 'jump' (JL, 132) and 'to call out for help' (JL, 99), is 'if you don't agree, then jump and shout to see if somebody else will help you!' and it can be used in the heat of an argument by one of the parties to intimidate their opponent and cut short the dispute.

---

[52] Arabic translation by the authors. MLZ does not provide an Arabic translation of this expression.

(43) MLZ, 958

ɔl ġumúdk éhzəf ʕar ḥārɔ́tˤ lɔ

أُل غمُدكْ اهزفْ عر حارُتْ لو

أمسيت لا أهرب من النار \ الحية

(Tonight) I'm not able to escape a black (snake)

This is an expression used to describe a condition of extreme tiredness.

The verb *ġumúdk* is likely a perfective 1.C.SG. of a H1-stem recorded by JL (86) as *aġmíd* 'to be, appear in the evening', and the [u] between C^1 and C^2 is to be regarded as a phonologically neutral vowel which takes on the phonetic characteristics of the following stressed vowel, as is often seen in the eastern dialect of Jibbali/Śḥərɛ́t. The absence of intervocalic /m/ deletion seems to argue in favour of this. The segment *ʕar* is pronounced *ḥar* by S. al-Amri, probably due to regressive assimilation to the *ḥārɔ́t* segment to the right. The latter term, normally 'black (F.SG.)', is said by S. al-Amri to mean 'a black snake'.[53]

(44) MLZ, 963

ɔ tkɔs de xalí mən e-diní lɔ

أُ تكس دئ هْللْ من ديني لو

لا تجد أحدا خال من هموم الدنيا \ تعبها

You don't find anyone free from (the cares of) the world

This proverb is uttered to remind oneself or someone else that life is hard for everybody. The verbal form *tkɔs* is an imperfective 2.M.SG. of a Ga-stem meaning 'to find' (JL, 135; al-Kathiri and

---

[53] Indeed, the colour adjective *ḥɔ́r* is reported to mean 'black animal' among other things (JL, 120).

Dufour 2020, 203). S. al-Amri asserts that the term *xalí* 'empty, free' (MLZ, 308) should be used instead of هبال, as recorded by MLZ.

3.0. Jibbali Lexicon

(1) JL, 16

tob ʕar múʕṣam ḏə ġeg

He's a dull dog!

This is said of a dull and serious person.

According to JL (16), the term *múʕṣam*, a passive participle, means 'dull and serious (fellow)'. MLZ (631) does not ascribe to the term any meaning related to this semantic field, despite listing its other meanings related to tying/being tied tightly. S. al-Amri states that this expression should in fact be pronounced *maʕbṣím ḏə ġeg*ʲ: This could point to a */w/-infixed variant of the root, which subsequently became obsolete (Castagna and al-Amri forthcoming).

(2) JL, 24

ehĩt ɔ́ź

God's poor one!

This is a way to express sympathy for a poor person. MLZ does not record this term. In S. al-Amri's dialect, it is used in its diminutive form *mehĩnút ~ ẽhĩnút*, without adding ɔ́ź. It has the same meaning as Arabic *miskīn* 'poor, miserable; beggar; humble, submissive, servile' (Wehr and Cowan 1976, 909).[54]

---

[54] The term *miskīn* entered Jibbali/Śḥərɛ́t as a loanword, and its semantics shifted to "'I wish' or 'I hope' (usually implying an unlikely

(3) JL, 31 (also MLZ, 145)

ɛbóbnɛ

Please…

This particle, whose origin is obscure, is used to introduce an emphatic request: *ɛbóbnɛ hɛt* 'please (you)' (Rubin 2014, 316). S. al-Amri states that the shorter form *bob* may also be used.

(4) JL, 57

fɔlfɔlɔ́t ɖə ġeg[55]

a short and strong fellow

According to S. al-Amri, this expression describes someone who is strong and brave and can be relied on. JL (57) states that the term *fɔlfɔlɔ́t* means 'strong but not tall'. MLZ (717) defines it as 'a strong energetic man (regardless of height). This (term) applies to women as well' (الرجل الربعة القوي النشيط [ليس بالطويل ظـ القصير] وتطلق ايضا على المرأة).

(5) JL, 61

b-īfrɔ́ḳi!

By my hairline!

Said by women when swearing. According to JL (61), a woman's hairline is 'connected with honour and gentleness', hence the expression *məfrɔ́ḳ əḏ teṯ*, literally meaning 'a hairline of a woman', which describes a gentle woman.

---

scenario), in which case it is followed by the relative pronoun ɛ-/ð-" (Rubin 2014, 321).

[55] S. al-Amri renders JL *ġeg* 'man' as *ġegʲ* throughout the recordings.

(6) JL, 70

ɔ iferɔ́k̩ ar hegɛ́m ar ežédš défər

No one fears attacks except one whose root is bad

This is a proverb pointing to the fact that only the weak fear attack. The verb *iferɔ́k̩* is an imperfective 3.M.SG. of a Gb-stem meaning 'to be afraid, frightened' (JL, 61). S. al-Amri pronounces *egédš* instead of the expected *ežédš* 'his root',[56] and renders *hegɛ́m* as *heg^jɛ́m*.

(7) JL, 71

beš mən gədrét

He has from the ground

This idiomatic expression is said to mean 'he is possessed (by an evil spirit)' by JL. However, S. al-Amri disagrees with this, and states that the correct expression is actually *beš ənegdərét*, where the segment *ənegdərét* (probably to be analysed as *ə-negdərét*, with a definite article) is the name of an illness caused by sorcery. However, neither JL nor MLZ records this term.

(8) JL, 86

yəġmór ḥáṭək

May your fortune collapse!

A friendly curse.

---

[56] JL records numerous instances of dialectal variation involving a [g] ~ [ž] alternation.

Here the subjunctive 3.M.SG. of the Gb-stem verbal form *yəǵmór* has an optative meaning. The segment *ḥáṭək* is a compound of *ḥáṭ* 'luck' (MLZ, 246: حظ)[57] with a 2.M.SG. personal suffix *-k* attached.

(9) JL, 98
təd̰ḥɔ́fk həndét
May a demon slap you between the shoulder blades

A curse. As in expression number **(8)** above, the subjunctive form of the verb (in this case, a 3.F.SG. of a Gb-stem) has an optative meaning. According to S. al-Amri, the term *həndét* 'Indian (woman)' for 'demon' (JL, 98) stems from the popular belief that witches are from India.

(10) JL, 110
teḥtélək ɛ-lḥyétk
May your beard be shaved!

A curse whose actual meaning is 'may you be dishonoured!'. The verbal form *teḥtélək* is a subjunctive 3.F.SG. of a T1-stem < √ḥlk, and is again used optatively.

(11) JL, 111
he bɔś́ɔ́kk edés aḥyẽri
I've broken my string for her

This is an idiomatic expression alluding to the act of taking off one's clothes for the first time, which means 'she is my first wife': the term *aḥyẽri* 'my string' refers to the belt-string which kept a

---

[57] This term is not recorded by JL. It may be suspected to be an Arabic loanword.

man's clothes on in traditional Dhofari dress. The verbal form *bɔṣ́ɔ́kk* is a perfective 1.C.SG. of a Ga-stem meaning 'to tear' (JL, 33). The segment *edés* is made up of the preposition *ed* 'to' (Rubin 2014, 228–30) and the 3.F.SG. personal suffix -*s*.

(12) JL, 114

ɛ zógum l-ɔḥrɔ́f

He who closes his mouth when full of gold coins

This is an expression that describes a well-mannered person who speaks sparingly, politely, and always for a good reason. The preposition *l-*, whose peculiar semantics can be reconstructed to proto-MSAL (Kogan 2015, 468–69), is used here to express 'against, to the detriment of something' (Rubin 2014, 251). The term *ɔḥrɔ́f* (SG. *ḥarf*) means 'gold amulet; gold coin' (JL, 114). According to S. al-Amri, it can also be used with its Arabic meaning 'letter'. As for the verbal form *zógum*, it is a perfective third person of a Ga-stem, meaning 'to keep a closed mouth, keep absolutely quiet; to keep one's mouth shut' (JL, 316): S. al-Amri renders this form as *zóguim*.

(13) JL, 127

ʕar káfuhn ɛd d-isɔ́ṭ

What a big paw to hit with!

This is jokingly said to children who attempt to hit something with all their strength, but either miss their target or hit it clumsily. S. al-Amri's rendition is *ar kafférn ɛd d-isyɔ́ṭ*. The verbal form, an imperfective 3.M.SG. of a Ga-stem < √sbṭ meaning 'to beat, hit with a stick' (JL, 222), might be a variant in which the intervocalic /b/ results in a [əyv̄] sequence, instead of a plain long vowel [v̄] (Rubin 2014, 28; al-Kathiri and Dufour 2020, 185). The diminutive form *káfuhn* or *kafférn* (as rendered by S. al-Amri) has a non-diminutive counterpart *kɛf* 'paw, claw; palm of the hand' (JL, 127).

(14) JL, 130
keléb ḏə ġeg[58]
A little dog of a man

This describes a 'nasty, bad-mannered, whiskery, ugly, little fellow' (JL, 130). The diminutive form *keléb* corresponds to the non-diminutive *kɔb* 'dog'.[59]

(15) JL, 139
ḳətɛʕɔ́r mən défər
May you be struck motionless for being a nasty fellow!

A mild curse. It is reworded by S. al-Amri as *ḥa-ḳətɛʕɔ́r mən défər*. The verbal form *ḳətɛʕɔ́r* is a 3.M.SG. subjunctive of a T1-stem verb meaning '(man) to be paralysed by fear' (JL, 139). The use of the future particle *ḥa-* (Rubin 2014, 150) and the vocalism (Rubin 2014, 130) suggest the verbal form is a subjunctive. However, there is no trace of the *t-* verbal prefix which is expected to appear in a T1-stem. This might be due to assimilation of the phonetically strenuous sequence *[tḳ'].

---

[58] *ġɛgʲ* in S. al-Amri's pronunciation.

[59] < √klb with the loss of /l/ before a consonant (Rubin 2014, 35–37; al-Kathiri and Dufour 2020, 185).

(16) JL, 144
yəḳətél ḥask
May your brain shrink!

A friendly curse, this expression features a subjunctive 3.M.SG. of a T1-stem meaning 'to shrink; to feel dizzy after a knock on the head' (JL, 144) < √ḳll used as an optative. The term ḥas (with a -k 2.M.SG. personal suffix) means 'consciousness' (JL, 116).

(17) JL, 144
(ɛ) ḳelɛ́bk!
(O) little heart!

This expression, meaning 'poor fellow!', is made up of the optional vocative particle ɛ[60] (Rubin 2014, 307) and the diminutive form ḳelɛ́b < ḳɛlb + 2.M.SG. personal suffix: S. al-Amri, rather than ḳelɛ́b, pronounces ḳēlɛ́b, which appears to be the correct form for this diminutive pattern, as reported by previous studies (Johnstone 1973; Dufour 2016, 44–45).

(18) JL, 149
fɔʕɔ́r ḳeráḥ
A hornless bull

This is said of 'a weak, harmless fellow'. Interestingly, the adjective ḳeráḥ 'hornless; shaven-headed' is also the word for 'donkey' (JL, 149).

---

[60] Another vocative particle exists in some dialects of Jibbali/Śḥərɛ́t: ṭɛ (MLZ, 575) ~ tɛ (S. al-Amri).

(19) JL, 149

kɔbś bə-ġayr ḳerún

A ram without horns

Similarly to the expression above, this is used to describe 'a weak fellow, idiot'. S. al-Amri states that the correct form is *kɔbś mən ġayr ḳerún*, and *mən ġayr* does indeed appear to be the most common way to express 'without' in Jibbali/Śḥərɛ́t (Rubin 2014, 243). However, Rubin cites this very expression as the only occurrence of *bə-ġayr* throughout Johnstone's Jibbali/Śḥərɛ́t texts (Rubin 2014, 243).

(20) JL, 246

ʕɔ́śər śɔf

Old baldy

The literal meaning of this expression, 'ten hairs', is a clear reference to baldness. The plural term *śɔf* is based on a feminine singular *śfet* (JL, 246) and as such is counted by a grammatically masculine numeral (Rubin 2014, 277), in this case *ʕɔ́śər* 'ten' (JL, 17).[61]

(21) JL, 310

bə-xilk

By your uncle!

The meaning stated by JL is 'do as you please and don't worry about me'. S. al-Amri pronounces *bə-xillək* and adds that this expression is a polite way to tell someone they may do whatever

---

[61] This characteristic is widespread in the ancient Semitic languages, as well as in the other MSA languages (see above, p. 8).

they would like to do in a given situation, and not worry about the speaker. The use of the term for 'maternal uncle' in this expression is due to the cultural prominence of this figure. See also proverb number **(191)** of the al-Shahri collection, *mergʲe ērgít yunfəʕ* 'It is always expected that the nephew will be useful'.

(22) JL, 310
mən xɔk ed geśətk
From your mouth to your side!

This is said in retaliation for a curse. The term *geśət* means 'side' (of the body). S. al-Amri affirms that, in his dialect, the formula used is *mən xɔk ed ēdɛ́nk*, the latter term being the definite form of bedɛ́n 'body' (JL, 23) in combination with the 2.M.SG. possessive suffix -k.

(23) JL, 204
ber ɛrdi b-e-ḳélbəš ʕaḳ erémnəm
His heart has been thrown into the sea

This idiomatic expression means 'he has been bewitched' according to JL. However, S. al-Amri believes it to be a description of a careless, dull, and insensitive individual.

The verbal form *ərdi* is a passive perfective third person of a Ga-stem meaning 'to throw' (JL, 204), also used in entry number **(2)** of the MLZ collection. The term *ḳɛ́lb*, appearing here with a definite article and a 3.M.SG. personal suffix -š, means 'heart' (JL, 144) in a poetic sense, in contrast with the term *ub* (JL, 159) which refers to the physical heart. The preposition *ʕaḳ* 'in' is likely the result of grammaticalisation of a term deriving from the root √ʕmḳ, which yields terms related to 'middle' in Jibbali/

Śḥərέt (JL, 13) and 'depth' in Arabic (Wehr and Cowan 1976, 644). The term rέmnəm 'sea' (JL, 214) appears in this expression in the variant typical of the central and western dialects. S. al-Amri uses the variant rέmrəb. Furthermore, he states that this expression is not used in his dialect. Instead, he provides an alternative expression: berɔ́t het iditš ɛ remrəb 'his medicine has fallen into the sea', meaning that there is no hope of restoring someone's health. This expression features the preposition ɛ 'to, up to; until' (JL, 1). According to Rubin (2014, 229), this preposition is an allomorph of the synonymous preposition ɛd. However, he states that it occurs only once in Johnstone's field materials.

(24) JL, 170

e-défər yaʕḳɔ́r ʕaḳ āḥέn

The bad (person) falls short in hard times

This proverb underscores the bad person's lack of steadfastness, and their tendency to fail in critical times.

The verbal form *yaʕḳɔ́r,* not recorded in MLZ, is an imperfective 3.M.SG. of a Gb-stem meaning 'to fall short of duty' according to JL (11). The term *āḥέn* is the definite form of the plural noun *maḥέn* 'troubles' (JL, 170).

(25) JL, 214

ɛrmés bes!

Stick your hand in muck!

This is a scoffing remark.

According to JL (214), the verbal form *ɛrmés* is an imperative corresponding to a third-person perfective *rɔ̃s,* a Ga-stem deriving from the root √rms meaning 'to put the hand in dirt, excrement'. There exists a variant *duhúm bes*, which exhibits an imperative form of a Gb-stem whose perfective third person is *dɛhɛ́m* (JL, 36). JL (36) reports the meaning of this verb as 'to come to visit at an appropriate time'. However, S. al-Amri states that it means 'to lose'.[62]

(26) JL, 283

beš fúdət ṭirín

He is as mild (of as much use) as a hyena

According to JL (283), this expression describes a gentle person by comparison with a hyena: "Although it figures prominently in magic, being the servant and the mount of sorcerers it is, nevertheless, regarded as a mild, gentle animal."

In this expression, the term *fúdət* 'benefit, usefulness, advantage' (JL, 67) seems to be used as the first term of a construct chain *fúdət ṭirín* 'usefulness of a hyena'.

S. al-Amri affirms that this expression is unknown in his dialect, and provides an alternative version: *ɛḏilin hes ṭirín* 'so-and-so is like a hyena', which, however, means 'so-and-so is unreliable/useless'.

---

[62] Cf. the Š1-stem from the same root, *šədhím* 'to lose (in a game such as heads-or-tails); to lose in a draw (between two things not equally good)' (JL, 36; MLZ, 344).

4.0. Elicited Entries

(1)

ɛ̄hlɛ́t ɛrḥīt axɛ́r ar īdɛ́t

آهليت ارحيْت اخر ار ايْدت

A fair word is better than giving

This expression stresses the importance of fair speech. The terms *ɛ̄hlɛ́t* < *e-behlɛ́t and *īdɛ́t* < *e-midɛ́t mean, respectively, 'word' (JL, 24) and 'giving' (JL, 168).

(2)

fɛ́ḳər ɔl ʕīb lɔ

فكر اول عيب لو

Poverty is no defect

This expression is used to exhort the listener not to mistake poverty for guilt. The terms *fɛ́ḳər* and *ʕīb* appear to be Arabic loanwords. In particular, *ʕīb* and the related verbal forms are recorded as having meanings related to oath-breaking (JL, 19–20), with only MLZ (654) recording the gloss 'defect'.

(3)

axɛ́r aḥbɛ́t ḳiṭɛ́t ar aḥbɛ́t śtəbɛ́t

اخر احبت قيظات عر احبت شْتِبات

A summer dwelling is better than a winter dwelling

This expression is used to state that something is obviously better than something else. This stems from the easier life that animal herders lead in the summer, versus the more physically demanding activities that are carried out in the winter. The two feminine denominative adjectives *ḳiṭɛ́t* and *śtəbɛ́t* can be regularly derived from ḳoṭ 'summer' (JL, 157) and śétɛ 'winter' (JL, 257) respectively.

(4)

i-míh her ḍáʕar ɔl ʕɔd yəsḥəféś lɔ

ايميه هر ذعر اول عود يبشحفتش لو

The spilt water cannot be collected

The meaning of this proverb is close to English *cry over spilt milk*. The first verbal form *ḍáʕar* is a perfective third person of a Gb-stem meaning 'to spill, pour' (JL, 44). The second verbal form *yəsḥəféś* is an imperfective 3.M.SG. of a Š1-stem derived from √ḥfś 'to be able to be collected' (JL, 105). MLZ does not record this term.

(5)

ɔ ikín məndɔ́x ʕar bə śɔ́ṭ

او يكن مندوخ عر بشّوط

There is no smoke without fire

Like the similar English expression, this means that the presence of one thing implies the presence of another. The term *məndɔ́x* 'smoke' (JL, 180; MLZ, 903) appears here in its non-definite form. It is not uncommon for this term to take a definite form even when syntactically indefinite: for example, *išerɔ́k ĩndɔ́x* 'it makes smoke' (Castagna 2018, 303).

(6)

ɔ ikín məšənɔ́x ar mən śəḳé

او يكن مشنوخ ار من شّقا

There is no rest but through toil

This proverb reminds the listener that only those who work hard have the right to rest.

Rather curiously, neither JL nor MLZ records the term *məšənɔ́x* as 'rest', although both record the root √šnx with meanings related to this semantic field (JL, 263; MLZ, 484–85). The term *śəḳɛ́* 'toil' is recorded by MLZ (522)—but not by JL—as 'hardship', among other meanings: شقاء, مشقة, العمل الشاق. ارهاق. الاعياء من شدة العمل.

(7)

araḥᵊmún ɔl zum ḳeráḥ ḳerún lɔ

ارحمن اول زوم قرح قرون لو

God didn't give horns to the donkey

This proverb serves as a reminder that those who are weak should not attempt to get involved in activities that require strength. The verbal form *zum* is a perfective third person of an idiosyncratic Ga-stem meaning 'to give' (JL, 295; al-Kathiri and Dufour 2020, 199–200). The term *araḥᵊmún* is, along with *ɔ́ź*, one of the most used names for God (JL, 210; MLZ, 368).

(8)

ɛḏīlin ebṣ́ɛ́ ḏərbɛ́t

اذيلن ابضا ذربيت

So-and-so has grown a hump

This is said as a comment on a person of humble origin who attains success and power in life but becomes haughty and ruthless in the process. The hump in a pastoral society symbolises welfare and health. The verbal form *ebṣ́ɛ́* is a perfective third person of a H1-stem derived from √wṣ́y meaning 'to grow (transitive)' (JL,

2. Proverbs and Linguistic Analysis

296). The term ḏərbét 'hump' is not recorded in JL. MLZ (349), however, records it as سنام البعير 'camel hump'.

(9)

ɔ yəfɔsk ar in ġɔ́tbər ṭerš ɛdité

او يفسك ار ان غُتبر ظيرش اديتا

It won't be accomplished unless hands meet upon it

This proverb corresponds rather literally to English *Many hands make light work*. For the relative pronoun *in*, also used in entry **(124)** of the al-Shahri collection, see Rubin (2014, 72). The verbal form *yəfɔsk* is an imperfective 3.M.SG. of a Ga-stem meaning 'to finish (with a meeting, a problem, with something)' (JL, 63). *ġɔ́tbər* is a perfective third person of a T1-stem from √ġbr 'to meet one another' (JL, 82). The term *ɛdité* is the plural of *ed* 'hand' (JL, 313).

(10)

ɔ śi ar tirɔ́k

او شّي ار تيروك

There is nothing like your soil

The meaning of this expression is similar to the English saying *There's no place like home*. The segment *tirɔ́k* stands for *tirɔ́b* 'soil' in conjunction with the 2.M.SG. personal suffix *-k* 'your soil', which triggers /b/ intervocalic deletion.

(11)

ɛ-rḥím ɔ yəṭyūr lɔ

آ رحيم او بشيور لو

(Even) the good doesn't come to ripeness

This expression means that even the best things in life have defects and must come to an end. The verbal form *yəṭyūr* is an imperfective 3.M.SG. of a Gb-stem from the root √*ṭmr* meaning 'to ripen, come to fruition' (JL, 285).

(12)
kɔl śe heš fərkɛ́t
كوشّيء هش فركت
There is a trick for everything

This means that there is a way to do everything. Its meaning is similar to that of the Latin proverb *est modus in rebus*. The term *fərkɛ́t* 'trick' is not recorded in either JL or MLZ. Instead, the root √*frk* is said to relate to leaving one's spouse or loading/polishing a gun (JL, 60–61; MLZ, 700).

(13)
šfɛḳˀ bə teṯ ḏ ɔ tfeṭún ḳɔ̄r ɛ īsˀ lɔ
شفق بتث ذو تفطن قور آيس لو
Marry a woman who doesn't remember her father's grave

This proverb underscores the importance of marrying a woman who is not under the influence of her father's authority.

The verbal forms *šfɛḳ* and *tfeṭún* are, respectively, an imperative of the Ga-stem *šfɔḳ* 'to get married' (JL, 260), and an imperfective 3.F.SG. of a Gb-stem *féṭən* 'to remember' (JL, 66). The use of the relativiser *ḏ*- instead of *ɛ*- is slightly unusual: some speakers regard *ḏ*- as a Mehrism, and *ɛ*- as the proper Jibbali/Śḥərɛ́t relativiser (Rubin 2014, 68). However, *ḏ*- is not uncommon, and most speakers seem to use the two relativisers interchangeably. The segment *īs* is to be interpreted as *iy* 'father' (JL, 1) + a 3.F.SG.

personal suffix -s. An almost identical proverb exists in Mehri: *hām təḥōm təhārəs, hārəs bə-tēṯ ḏ-əl təftōn aḳōbər ḏə-ḥāmēs əlā* (ML, 28).

(14)
her a-tdəʕá dəʕá ḥanúf bə xar

هر اتدعا دعا حنوف بخر

If you wish, wish yourself well

This expression is an exhortation to self-respect and self-love.

The future form consists of the *a-* prefix + a 2.M.SG. subjunctive *tədʕá*,[63] and the imperative *dəʕá* is reminiscent of the verbal morphology of Gb-stems. However, this verb, which is used here to mean 'to wish', is likely to be an Arabic loan. Compare the corresponding entry in JL (34), which gives the meaning 'to curse' (JL, 34), whereas MLZ (330) gives دعا.[64] A similar expression is recorded in Mehri by the *Mehri Lexicon*: *āmōr ḥāwəláy: əmtōni ḥənáfk bə-xayr w-əl təmtōni ḥənáfk śarr əlā* (ML, 382).

(15)
ε-ṭifér ɔ yəs̃xanɔ́t mən te lɔ

اظفار او يشخنوط من تي لو

Fingernails don't stem from the flesh

The meaning of this expression is that kinsfolk should stick together in hard times, regardless of the disagreements they may have in daily life.

---

[63] This segment is rendered as [ddaʕ] by S. al-Amri.

[64] This highly polysemic Arabic verb means, among other things, 'to call, to pray to God, to wish well' (Wehr and Cowan 1976, 282).

The term *ṭifér* 'finger or toe-nail' (JL, 48) is singular, although the meaning of this expression implies a plural. The verbal form *yəŝxanɔ́t* is an imperfective 3.M.SG. of a Š1-stem deriving from the root √xnṭ, meaning 'to come out, away from; to get out' (JL, 303). The vowel [ɔ] instead of [u] after a nasal is noteworthy. The term *te* 'meat' (JL, 273) derives from the root √twy, which also yields terms in the semantic field of eating in the MSA languages at large.

(16)

ɛ d-ŝəʕṣér yərɔ́ṭɔf

آ دشعصير يرطف

He who gives something (out of generosity) has it returned

This saying encourages the listener to be generous, by reminding them that generosity will be rewarded sooner or later.

This meaning is conveyed in a rather idiomatic way: the verbal form *d-ŝəʕṣér*, which follows the ɛ relativiser, is a third-person perfective of a Š1-stem < √ʕṣr meaning 'to be squeezed; to be pumped (subtly) for information' (JL, 17), with a d- circumstantial prefix attached. The function of this prefix with the perfective is not as straightforward as it is with the imperfective. In this case, however, it seems to express a stative function (Rubin 2014, 163). The second verbal form *yərɔ́ṭɔf* is an imperfective 3.M.SG. of a Ga-stem meaning 'to repeat' (MLZ, 382: عاود الشيء \ كرره), not recorded by JL. Therefore, the literal meaning of the expression is 'He who deprived himself (of his wealth/possession of out generosity), will have them repeated (returned)'. S. al-Amri confirms that the literal meaning of this expression is substantially divergent from its actual meaning.

(17)

aġád h-e-gizərɛ́t, ōṭəl āḥtəl b-e-gizərɛ́t

اغاد هاجزرات اوثل آحتل باجزرات

He went to get horns and returned without ears

This expression is very similar in meaning to entry number **(7)** of the al-Shahri collection, in that it exhorts the listener not to engage in a dangerous activity that will likely result in trouble and can be used also when the trouble has already happened.

The verbal form *aġád* is a perfective third person of an idiosyncratic Ga-stem < √wġd meaning 'to go' (al-Kathiri and Dufour 2020, 197). The term *e-gizərɛ́t* 'the machet' (JL, 82) has a *h-* prefix: this prefix is best viewed as the monoconsonantal base of the preposition *her* 'for, to' (Rubin 2014, 243), although this is normally only used before personal suffixes. The verbal form *ōṭəl* appears to be an unrecorded variant of *éṭəl*, a perfective third person of a I-weak Gb-stem meaning 'to follow, chase' (JL, 5). The term *āḥtəl* must be the definite form of an unrecorded variant of *máḥtəl* 'chopper' (JL, 119) *a-báḥtəl*.

In view of the above, the literal translation of this expression is 'he went for the machet, he chased the chopper and the machet'.

(18)

ɔ ḳenɪ́š iźák iź šeš lɔ yəḳúnš ɛ̄kət

او قنيش إلاك إل بش لو يقونش آقت

Experience is the best teacher

This self-explanatory proverb is a near-equivalent of English *Experience is the best teacher*.

The verbal forms *kenī́š* and *yəkúnš* are, respectively, a perfective third person and an imperfective 3.M.SG. of a III-weak Ga-stem meaning 'to rear, look after, bring up' (JL, 147), with a 3.M.SG. personal suffix -*š* attached. The idiomatic phrase *iẓ́ák iẓ́ šeš* 'his relations' literally means 'those of his', and is recorded as *iẓ́ɔ́k iẓ́ šəš* by JL (44). The term *ɛ̄kət* must be analysed as *ɛ-ɛkət, a noun meaning 'time' (JL, 291). The literal meaning of this expression is 'he who is not taught by his family is taught by time'.

(19)

yəḳúdum záḥar əl-fɛ́nɛ ɛ-ṭalʕayt

يقدم زاحر لفانا اظلعات

Cross your bridges when you come to them

This proverb describes someone who worries about troublesome events before these events take place.

According to JL (141), the verbal form *yəḳúdum* is an imperfective 3.M.SG. of a Ga-stem meaning 'to come to someone'. However, considering its meaning in this context, this verb is probably best viewed as an Arabic loan deriving from the measure I verb *ḳadama*, whose meanings include 'to get something' (Wehr and Cowan 1976, 747). The term *záḥar*, which is not recorded by JL, means 'sediment that remains at the bottom of a pot after emptying what is in it' (MLZ, 408: الرواسب والقذي الذي يبقى في الإناء بعد إفراغ ما فيه). S. al-Amri, however, affirms that it also means a sort of medicine or ointment that is used to treat animals for infections in their paws that cause them to limp. Accordingly, the term *ṭalʕayt*,[65] not recorded by JL, means 'limp' (MLZ, 600: العرج, كساح), and is preceded by the preposition *əl-fénɛ* 'before, in front of, ago' (Rubin 2014, 242). All in all, the literal meaning of this proverb is 'he gets the ointment before (the animal) limps'.

(20)

e-défər ɔ yəʕterér ar e-dɔ́fərš° lɔ

ادفر او يعترير ار ادوفرش لو

Nothing stops the bad person except his badness

In a similar fashion to entry number **(19)** of the al-Shahri collection, this proverb is a comment on the self-destructive tendencies of evil people.

The verbal form *yəʕterér* is an imperfective 3.M.SG. of a Š1-stem deriving from the root √ʕrr, meaning 'to be blocked, dammed' (JL, 14). The particle *ar* 'except' (Rubin 2014, 312) is followed by the term *dɔ́fər* 'badness' (JL, 35) with a 3.M.SG. personal suffix -*š* attached.

---

[65] According to Rubin (2014, 41), /a/ may be realised as [aj] after /ʕ/ and /ġ/. See also entry number **(52)** of the al-Shahri collection.

3. CONCLUSIONS

Overall, the linguistic analysis of these collections of proverbs yields some results upon which it is worth reflecting.

1.0. Phonetics and Phonology

1.1. The Realisation of /g/

With regard to Ali al-Shahri's dialect, which is that of Ṭawi Aʕtír, a town in the hills to the north-east of Wadi Darbat (Dhofar), it falls within the eastern branch of Jibbali/Śḥərɛ̃t. The realisation of /g/ in his recording can be summarised as follows:

- /g/ is realised as [g] six times before fronted vowels,[1] and twice before ultra-short non-phonological vowels;[2]
- /g/ is realised as [gʲ] six times before fronted vowels,[3] 13 times before non-fronted vowels,[4] three times before ultra-short non-phonological vowels,[5] once in pre-consonantic position,[6] and five times in final position.[7]

---

[1] Entries **(1)**, **(11)**, **(13)**, **(93)**, **(152)**, and **(199)** of al-Shahri's collection.

[2] Entries **(179)** and **(189)** of al-Shahri's collection.

[3] Entries **(54)**, **(100)**, **(108)**, **(134)**, **(150)**, and **(172)** of al-Shahri's collection.

[4] Entries **(17)**, **(45)**, **(68)**, **(83)**, **(89)**, **(106)**, **(110)**, **(127)**, **(128)**, **(129)**, **(135)**, **(164)**, and **(186)** of al-Shahri's collection.

[5] Entries **(11)**, **(70)**, and **(179)** of al-Shahri's collection.

[6] Entry **(149)** of al-Shahri's collection.

[7] Entries **(1)**, **(16)**, **(114)**, **(197)**, and **(204)** of al-Shahri's collection.

As for S. al-Amri's recordings, his recordings reveal, on a smaller scale,[8] a parallel state of affairs:

- /g/ is realised as [g] three times before non-fronted vowels;[9]
- /g/ is realised as [gʲ] four times before non-fronted vowels,[10] five times in final position,[11] and once before a fronted vowel.[12]

In light of this, it would be tempting to posit that /g/ is actually realised as [gʲ] in both varieties, and the *yod*-coloured off-glide is perceptually much more prominent before non-fronted vowels. However, only a detailed phonetic analysis might confirm this. Perceptually speaking, [gʲ] seems to be the most frequent realisation in both dialects.

1.2. The Pausal Realisation of /l/

Al-Shahri consistently renders /l/ as a devoiced alveolar tap [ɾ̥] in final position.[13] In S. al-Amri's recordings, the /l/ phoneme occurs only once in final position and, as in al-Shahri's recordings,

---

[8] Al-Shahri's collection is made up of 210 entries, whereas the other collections (MLZ, JL, and elicited entries) account for 74 entries in total.

[9] Entries **(28)** of MLZ, and **(7)** and **(22)** of JL.

[10] Entries **(8)**, **(28)**, and **(39)** of MLZ, and **(6)** of JL.

[11] Entries **(28)** and **(36)** of MLZ, and **(1)**, **(4)**, and **(14)** of JL. This realisation occurs only in the term *ġegʲ*.

[12] Entry **(12)** of JL.

[13] Entries **(27)**, **(122)**, **(125)**, and **(155)** of al-Shahri's collection, that is, in all occurrences of final /l/.

it is realised as [r̥].¹⁴ Despite the limited number of tokens in this study, S. al-Amri's natural speech shows that this pausal realisation regularly occurs in his dialect too. Furthermore, some degree of hesitation between forms with final [l] and [r] in the literature, e.g., bīdol ~ bīdor 'Sarcostemma viminale' (Miller and Morris 1988, 50) and daġál ~ daġár 'to prick' (JL, 35; MLZ, 331), suggests that this feature might not be limited to the eastern dialects of Jibbali/Śḥərέt.

1.3. /ɛ/ > [ɔ]

In al-Shahri's dialect, certain terms and verbal forms which normally exhibit a final [ɛ] have [ɔ] instead: t̰ɔ́dɔ, recorded by JL (283) as t̰ɔ́dɛʼ 'bosom, breast; nipple and breast'; gɔ́fɔ, recorded as gɔ́fɛʼ 'shadow' (JL, 72); yəšeṣɔ́fɔ,¹⁵ recorded as yəšeṣɔ́fɛ 'to gather news, find out' (JL, 237); and aʕtɔ́dɔ, recorded as aʕtede¹⁶ 'to attack' (JL, 7).¹⁷

One might legitimately suppose that the vowel quality of the stressed vowel influences that of the following unstressed final vowel, where this vowel is part of the root, but this mechanism does not appear to be straightforward. For one thing, there are not enough data available to posit a phonological rule. Besides, the case of aʕtede < √ʕdw casts additional doubts upon this problematic state of affairs: according to Dufour (2016, 101), the

---

[14] Entry **(32)** of MLZ.

[15] A 3.M.SG. imperfective of a Š1-stem < √ṣfv.

[16] A third-person perfective of a T2-stem < √ʕdw

[17] These forms are found respectively in entries **(40)**, **(45)**, **(94)**, and **(103)** of al-Shahri's collection.

stressed vowel of the third-person perfective of a T2-stem derived from a III-weak root is [ɔ]. Therefore, the 'regular' verbal form should be *aʕtɔdɛ, rather than aʕtedɛ, as reported by JL. One should, however, always bear in mind that the data reported by JL should not be absolutely relied upon, especially with regard to vocalism, notwithstanding the undoubted value of this pioneering work.[18]

This process is unknown to S. al-Amri's dialect.

2.0. Morphology

2.1. The Plural Relativiser *iź* as a Genitive Exponent

The plural relativiser *iź* (Rubin 2014, 68) is used once as a genitive exponent (that is, a particle which functions in a similar way to the English preposition *of* and is often found in MSA languages and other Semitic languages).[19]

2.2. /ī/ in Passive Verbal Forms

The verbal forms *ṭkīʕ*[20] (H1-stem) 'to look' (JL, 276), *eʕilik̇* (H2-stem) 'to hang (transitive)' (JL, 12), and *axnīṭ* (H1-stem) 'to take

---

[18] The pitfalls of relying upon JL are summarised by al-Kathiri and Dufour (2020, 172): "The verbal paradigms of the *Jibbāli Lexicon* are few in number, marred with typos or ambiguous abbreviations, and, one may suspect, not always totally accurate; moreover, the transcriptional system adopted often blurs crucial phonological facts, and in particular the position of stress."

[19] Entry **(21)** of the al-Shahri collection.

[20] For *eṭkīʕ*, with the loss of the initial vowel due to a phonological process described by al-Kathiri and Dufour (2020, 183).

out' (JL, 303) exhibit an unexpected long vowel /ī/.[21] This could be a feature of the speaker's dialect. However, it must be pointed out that *axniṭ* appears with the expected short vowel in entry **(52)**.

2.3. Negation

In Jibbali/Śḥərɛ́t, the unmarked negator for both verbal and nominal phrases is the circumfix ɔ(l)... lɔ (Rubin 2014, 330). However, the element ɔ(l) appears without the element lɔ in several circumstances throughout the collections examined, many of which differ from the attested uses of the stand-alone morpheme ɔ(l) (Rubin 2014, 332–34). Remarkably, ɔ(l) is found as a negator of simple verbal phrases.

3.0. Lexis

3.1. 'Mehrising' Language

Four entries in al-Shahri's collection attest to the poetic admixture of Jibbali/Śḥərɛ́t and Mehri described by Johnstone (1972).[22] The examples in this corpus range from single lexical items to verbal forms and morphology.

3.2. Previously Unattested Terms

The analysis of these proverb collections has yielded a substantial number of terms which do not appear in the written sources. Here follows a summary of said terms in English alphabetical order.

---

[21] Entries **(27)**, **(28)**, and **(45)** of the al-Shahri collection respectively.

[22] Entries **(13)**, **(92)**, **(108)**, and perhaps **(208)** of the al-Shahri collection.

Entry **(146)** al-Shahri: ʕamit 'haughtiness, arrogance; pride, dignity, sense of honour, self-respect; high-mindedness, generosity' < √ʕmy.[23] A semantic shift of the Arabic root √ʕmy 'blindness, ignorance, folly' (Wehr and Cowan 1976, 647) is not to be ruled out.

Entry **(204)** al-Shahri: ʕazᵊm 'ordeal by fire' < √ʕzm. This root primarily yields terms that fall into the semantic field of decision and invitation (JL, 21; ML, 39). However, it is interesting to note Arabic عزيمة 'spell, incantation' (Wehr and Cowan 1976, 611), from which Gəʕəz ዐሠመ 'conjure, cast spells' derives (Leslau 1987, 81).

Entry **(31)** MLZ: elkobbí 'illness'. According to S. al-Amri, this term is very old, and its semantics are not transparent. All his informants agree upon this term indicating an illness, but no one knows exactly of which sort.

Entry **(26)** MLZ: Both the verbal form شيت reported in this proverb (MLZ, 698) and S. al-Amri's rendition eśśəbbɔ́t (H1-stem perfective 3.F.SG.) seem to derive from a III-weak root √śbw~y. However, this verb, whose semantics are uncertain, is, in S. al-Amri's opinion, used only within this expression, and it is not recorded by the lexical sources.

Entry **(21)** al-Shahri: the plural form ẽžed < *e-mežed 'labour pains' must correspond to a singular *megdét < √gdy on the basis of similar CvCvC forms, for example, mɛrṭet/ mirέṭ 'instruction, message, parcel' (JL, 173). Cf. Arabic

---

[23] This word translates the Arabic term نخوة (Wehr and Cowan 1976, 950).

جدي 'kid, young billy goat' (Wehr and Cowan 1976, 115). Leslau (1987, 183) cites Hebrew *gədī*, Aramaic–Syriac *gadyā*, and Phoenician and Ugaritic *gdy* 'kid'.

Entry **(121)** al-Shahri: *ḏēh* 'misfortune, distortion', derived from √*ḏbh* on the basis of the H1-stem verbal form أذّبَه meaning 'to distort, to seek/try to distort something' (MLZ, 349: شوه, سعى \ حاول تشويه الشيء). No reliable cognates of this root seem to exist in other MSA languages or Semitic at large.

Entry **(59)** al-Shahri: *ḏelɛ́* 'early morning' < √*ḏly*, a variant of *ḏelɛ́b* (JL, 46) carrying the same meaning. The term is listed as *ḏélɛʾ* in ML, as the Jibbali/Śḥərɛ̄t translation of Mehri *ḏáwbən* 'morning' (ML, 560).

Entry **(134)** al-Shahri: G-stem verb *gēš/yəgɔ́š/yəgɔ́š* meaning 'to become weak, be debilitated'.[24] The Gəʕəz root √*gys* offers an interesting, although not necessarily illuminating, parallel in that it indicates 'morning, tomorrow' (Leslau 1987, 208), hence the future and becoming old.

Entry **(25)** MLZ: *gisɔ́t* 'wholesome (F.SG.)'. Unrecorded as an adjective, and with no known masculine counterpart, this term has no readily detectable counterparts in the rest of MSAL or Semitic at large.

Entry **(70)** MLZ: *ḥagⁱəlɔ́* 'in the open', a masculine plural *nisbah* adjective with adverbial force, corresponding to an unattested singular **ḥagⁱəlí*. In MSAL (JL, 106; ML, 171), √*ḥgl* refers to the pasturing of animals. However, in Semitic at

---

[24] See al-Kathiri and Dufour (2020, 210–11) for a morphologically similar verb.

large, it indicates enclosures and rings (Leslau 1987, 228), which points to a peculiar development in MSAL.

Entry **(17)** elicited: The preposition *her* appears as its monoconsonantal base *h-*, although no personal suffixes are attached to it.

Entry **(77)** al-Shahri: *kelɛ́* 'wolf'. This term follows the same *CeCɛ* pattern as *ḏelɛ́* 'early morning' (entry **(59)**), and shares with the latter the same apparent loss of /b/ as third root consonant, as well as semantics that match those of the /b/-final root.

Entry **(165)** al-Shahri: *kḥɔ* 'breastbone meat', presumably < √*kḥw*. Cf. Soqotri *kḥo* 'poitrine' (LS, 216).

Entry **(181)** al-Shahri: *kəṣərɛ́r* 'plant' < √*kṣr*.

Entry **(180)** al-Shahri: The dubious term *letɔ́t* 'load' < √*ltt* ~ √*lty* ~ √*ltw*, which seems to be devoid of Semitic cognates.

Entry **(191)** al-Shahri: *mergʲe* 'expected' < √*rgw*. This root yields other terms consistent with 'expected' in Jibbali/Śḥərɛ̃t and Mehri (JL, 207; ML, 319).

Entry **(6)** elicited: *məšənɔ́x* 'rest'. A participial form derived from the root √*šnx*, which yields various terms related to 'rest' in Jibbali/Śḥərɛ̃t (JL, 263). Compare also Soqotri *šínoh* 'heure de la nuit' (LS, 419).

Entry **(182)** al-Shahri: *məṭbaʕír* 'mud' < √*ṭʕr* ~ √*ṭwʕr*. These roots yield several terms connected with 'clay' and 'earth' (JL, 273, 281; MLZ, 584). One may raise the question as to whether we are dealing with two distinct roots, or simply with a *-b-* infix derived from PS **w* and most commonly found in certain plural patterns (al-Aghbari 2012, 26–27), but far from rare in other contexts, including in some obsolescent verbal classes.[25] See also the commentary to entry number **(1)** of the JL collection below.

Entry **(90)** al-Shahri: *mibdí* 'exaggerated' < √*bdy* = 'to lie' (JL, 23; ML, 43; LS, 82).

Entry **(89)** al-Shahri: The H2-stem participial form *mugʲū́ś* 'gone at late night' derives from √*gmś*, despite the corresponding verb being listed under the root √*gwś*.

Entry **(7)** JL: *ə-negdərét* 'illness caused by sorcery'. Similarly to *elkobbí*, this pathonym is held to be very old by S. al-Amri's informants. No one, however, was able to provide clues as to the illness to which it refers, except that it may be caused by sorcery.

Entry **(27)** al-Shahri: *śəʕil* 'strength' < √*kʕl*. A semantic connection with the basic meaning of 'swollen testicles' in MSAL (JL, 124; ML, 200) is possible, but not secure.

3.3. Newly Attested Variants of Previously Attested Terms

In addition to the previously unattested terms listed above, the analysis also yielded some variants of previously recorded terms:

Entry **(149)** al-Shahri: the participial form *aḥzígʲ* < **a-məḥzígʲ*, recorded in JL (122) as *maḥzeg* 'hobble', has an [i] as the stressed vowel instead of the expected [e].

---

[25] For example, the verbs *ənxablés* 'to grieve deeply' < √*xls*, and *ənẓəbxér* 'to have brown marks on the teeth' < √*gxr*.

Entry **(17)** al-Shahri: the diminutive form ʕālˀgʲán '2–4 year old camel' < √ʕlg, recorded as ʕálgɛ́n '2–4 year old camel' in JL (12), is attested here with a long vowel instead of a short one. The form with a long vowel matches one of the diminutive patterns described by Johnstone (1973).

Entry **(3)** JL: *bob*, a variant of *ɛbóbnɛ* 'please' in S. al-Amri's dialect (JL, 31; MLZ, 145).

Entry **(25)** JL: The verb *dɛhɛ́m*, not recorded by MLZ, and recorded by JL as 'to come to visit at an inappropriate time', also means 'to lose in a draw, in a heads-and-tails game'.

Entry **(6)** JL: *egéd*š instead of *ežédš* 'his root' (JL, 70).

Entry **(147)** al-Shahri: the term *ɛ̄kśɛ́ft* < *e-mekśɛ́ft* is likely a hitherto unrecorded variant of the term *kśaf* 'a small wicker vessel with a lid in which a woman puts her belongings' (MLZ, 802: سلة صغيرة من الخوص لها غطا تضع فيها المرأة حاجياتها).

Entry **(12)** elicited: *fərkɛ́t* 'trick'. In Jibbali/Śḥərɛ̄́t and Mehri, the root √frk has meanings connected to leaving one's spouse and loading/polishing a gun (JL, 60–61; ML, 99; MLZ, 700). The Akkadian verbal form *parāku* 'to hinder, to thwart, to oppose, to frustrate, to foil, to stand in the way' (Black 2000, 265) might offer a clue as to the origin of the MSAL semantics, which are, however, best viewed as an independent development.

Entries **(83)** and **(89)** al-Shahri: The verb *gʲūś* 'to go late at night', corresponding to the hitherto unrecorded participial form *mugʲūś* (see above, p. 223), is listed by MLZ under the root √gwś. However, al-Shahri pronounces it with

3. Conclusions

a clearly audible nasalised vowel, which would point to the root being actually √gmś.

Entry **(48)** al-Shahri: *ḥabbərrḗdi* 'Kleinia saginata' appears here with an initial /ḥ/ and a geminate /r/, in contrast with the recorded form *hubberādi* (Miller and Morris 1988, 110). This seems to be confirmed by MLZ (214), which records حبرادي بيطُف.

Entry **(36)** al-Shahri: *ḥuṃ* 'charcoal' (JL, 111; MLZ, 269: الفحم) here means 'splinter of wood'.

Entry **(148)** al-Shahri: the adjective *ʕiẑiẗ* seems to be the feminine counterpart of *ʕigɛm* 'dumb' < √ʕgm (JL, 9; MLZ, 610: أصيب بالخرس).

Entry **(13)** JL: *kaffɛ́n* instead of *káfuhn*. Both are diminutive forms of *kɛf* 'paw, claw; palm of the hand' (JL, 127).

Entry **(206)** al-Shahri: The term *kelṭ*, reported to be the plural form of *kelṭɔ́t* 'story' (JL, 131; MLZ, 808: القصة, الأمثولةو الحكاية), is used with the meaning of 'speaker'.

Entry **(99)** al-Shahri: The term *kiśɛ́t* 'wolf' (JL, 153; MLZ, 748: ذئب) is here given the meaning 'animal'.

Entry **(156)** al-Shahri: the adverbial phrase *l-ɛ́sīn* 'for a while'. According to MLZ (497), the temporal meaning of this adverbial phrase is typical of the western dialects of Jibbali/Śḥərɛ́t spoken in *Jabal Qamar*.

Entries **(48)** and **(49)** al-Shahri: the preposition *lhes* 'like' causes a following vowel to become lengthened, which leads one to speculate as to whether the underlying form could be **lhes ɛ*, perhaps through analogical levelling after the pattern of a compound preposition such as *ḥaṣ ɛ* or *ḥakṭ ɛ* (Rubin 2014, 361–63, 371–72).

Entry **(1)** JL: *maʕbṣím* is a variant of *múʕṣam* 'dull and serious (fellow)' (JL, 16), which points to *w-infixed verbal form (Castagna and al-Amri forthcoming). See also the commentary to entry **(182)** of the al-Shahri collection above.

Entry **(2)** JL: The terms *mehĩnút ~ ẽhĩnút* are diminutives of *ehī̃t* 'poor man' (JL, 24).

Entry **(20)** al-Shahri: the term *mɛ̃l* 'fullness' (JL, 171) functions here as the head noun of a construct chain.

Entry **(192)** al-Shahri: the term *məlḥet* عظمة الفك 'jawbone' (MLZ, 829) is recorded by JL (163) as *məẑḥet*, which could point to dialectal variation.[26]

Entry **(157)** al-Shahri: the particle *ʕɔd* seems here to behave like the etymologically related auxiliary verb *d-ʕɔd*, although Rubin (2014, 186) states that *ʕɔd* "has just a single frozen form."

Entries **(116)** and **(208)** al-Shahri: The adjective *ṣəbrɔ̃t* 'perfect' is not recorded in JL. However, MLZ (499) records it with the meaning الاتقان 'perfection'. The term *śíbir* seems to be a cognate of the above term < √sbr ~ √swr.

Entry **(13)** MLZ: *šṭɔṭ* 'distance, vast gap' is recorded as شطاط (MLZ, 516: البون الشاسع. البُعد), which would likely be rendered as /śṭɛṭ/.

---

[26] And indeed, Johnstone (JL, 163) states that *məlḥet* is the eastern variant of central Jibbali/Śḥərɛ̃t *məẑḥet*. However, according to S. al-Amri, the alleged eastern variant does not exist.

Entry **(146)** al-Shahri: The verbal form *tənʕa* < √nʕw is reported to mean 'to elegize' (JL, 179). However, al-Shahri translates this verb into Arabic as ثكل 'to be bereaved, to mourn' (Wehr and Cowan 1976, 105).

Entry **(16)** MLZ, *taʕmɛ́t* 'giving food' (MLZ, 584: إطاء الطعام) is used here to convey 'generosity'.

Entry **(22)** MLZ, *yaʕtɛ́ṭ* 'to rest' vis-á-vis 'to feel pain, to fall ill' (MLZ, 634: مرض \ وجع \ تألم).

4.0. Arabic Translation of *Jibbali Lexicon* and Elicited Entries

This section provides an Arabic rendition of the entries from the *Jibbali Lexicon* and the elicited entries.

4.1. JL

(1) *tob ʕar múʕṣam də ġeg*—إنه رجل ممل

(2) *ehīt ɔ́ź*—يا له من مسكين

(3) *ɛbóbne*—... ان استحلفك بالله

(4) *fɔlfɔlɔ́t də ġeg*—هذا الرجل يُعتمد عليه في المواقف الحرجة

(5) *b-ĩfrɔ́ki*—بوجهي

(6) *ɔ iferɔ́k ar hegɛ́m ar eẑɛ́dš défər*—لا يحاب العدو إلا الضعيف

(7) *beš mən gədrɛ́t ~ beš ənegdərɛ́t*—إنه مسكون

(8) *yəġmór ḥáṭək*—ساء حظك

(9) *tədḥɔ́fk həndɛ́t*—لطمتك الساحرة

(10) *teḥtɛ́lək ɛlḥyɛ́tk*—اهانك الله \ فلتهن

(11) *he bɔṣɔ́kk edɛ́s aḥyɛ̃ri*—هذه اول زيجة لي

(12) *ɛ zógum l-ɔhrɔ́f*—شخص حكيم

(13) *ʕar káfuhn ɛd d-isɔ̄ṭ*—يا للشفقة إنه صغير ليضرب

(14) keléb də ġeg—إنه رجل نذل

(15) kəteʕór mən défər—يا لك من مهمل

(16) yəkətél ḥask—يا لك من مزعج

(17) (ε) kelɛ́bk!—يا مسكين

(18) fɔʕór kəráḥ—ثور من غير قرون

(19) kɔbś bə-ġayr kərún—كبش من غير قرون

(20) ʕóśər śɔf—اصلع

(21) bə-xilk—كما تريد

(22) mən xɔk ed geśətk—من فمك لبدنك

(23) ber ɛrdi b-ekɛ́lbəś ʕak erémnəm—إنه شخص بليد

(24) e-défər yaʕkɔ́r ʕak āḥén—الجبان يتراجع في الشدائد

(25) ɛrmɛ́s bes!—اتركها لنفسك (بطريقة سلبية)

(26) beš fúdət ṭirín—فلان عديم الفائدة

4.2. Elicited Entries

(1) ḗhlét ɛrḥĩt axér ar ĩdét—الكلمة الطيبة خير من العطاء

(2) fekər ɔl ʕĩb lɔ—الفكر ليس عيباً

(3) axér aḥbét kiṭét ar aḥbét śtəbét—المنزل الصيفي خير من المنزل الشتوي

(4) i-míh her ḏaʕr ɔl ʕɔd išḥəfɛ́ś lɔ—لا تبكي على الحليب المسكوب

(5) ɔ ikín məndɔ́x ʕar bə śɔ́ṭ—لا يوجد دخان بدون نار

(6) ɔ ikín məśənɔ́x ar mən śəkɛ́—لا توجد راحة إلا بعد شقاء

(7) arəhəmún ɔl zum kəráḥ kərún lɔ—الله لم يعطي الحمار قرون

(8) ɛdīlin ebśɛ́ dərbét—فلان صار له سنام

(9) ɔ ifɔsk ar in ġótbər ṭerš aditɛ́—ما اجتمعت عليه الايدي \ الإتحاد قوة ينجز

(10) ɔ śi ar tirɔ́k—لا شيء كالوطن

(11) ɛrḥím ɔ ityūr lɔ—الزين لا يكتمل

3. Conclusions

(12) kɔl śe heš fərkɛ́t—لكل مشكلة حل

(13) šfɛkʰ bə tet̯ d̯-ɔ tfet̯ún kɔ̄r ɛ īsʰ lɔ—لا تتزوج من إمرأة تتذكر موت ابيها

(14) her a-tdəʕá dəʕá ḥanúf bə xar—إذا دعوت ادع لنفسك بالخير

(15) ɛ-t̯ifɛ́r ɔ yəŝxanɔ́t mən te lɔ—خشمك منك لو كان عوج

(16) ɛ d-ŝəʕṣér yərɔ́t̯ɔf—من جاد عاد

(17) aġád h-e-gizərɛ́t, ōt̯əl āḥtəl b-e-gizərɛ́t—سارت تبغي قرون رجعت بلا ذنين[27]

(18) ɔ kenîš iźák iź šeš lɔ yək̯únš ɛ̄k̯ət—لي ما يادّبه اهله يادّبه الزمان

(19) yək̯údum záhar əl-fɛ́nɛ ɛ-t̯alʕayt—استبق الحدث

(20) e-défər ɔ yəʕterér ar e-dɔ́fərsʰ lɔ—الطبع يغلب التطبع

---

[27] The feminine gender in the Arabic translation of this proverb implies a she-goat as its subject.

BIBLIOGRAPHY

Abbreviations

JL = Johnstone, Thomas M. 1981. *Jibbali Lexicon*. London: Oxford University Press.

LS = Leslau, Wolf. 1938. *Lexique Soqotri (Sudarabique Moderne)*. Paris: C. Klincksieck.

ML = Johnstone, Thomas M. 1987. *Mehri Lexicon and English–Mehri Word-List*. London: School of Oriental and African Studies.

MLZ = al-Maʕšanī, Aḥmad bin Maḥad. 2014. *Muʕgam Lisan Ẓufar*. Beirut.

Other Works

al-Aghbari, Khalsa. 2012. 'Noun Plurality in Jebbāli'. PhD dissertation, University of Florida.

al-Jahwari, N. 2018. 'نقش حجري من منطقة جعلان بني بوحسن، المنطقة الشرقية من سلطنة عمان'. *Journal of Arts and Social Sciences* 9 (2): 97–109.

al-Kathiri, Amir Azad Adli, and Julien Dufour. 2020. 'The Morphology of the Basic Verbal Stems in Eastern Jibbali/Śḥrɛ̄t'. *Journal of Semitic Studies* 65 (1): 171–222.

al-Manaser, Ali, and Michael C. A. Macdonald. 2017. 'The OCIANA Corpus of Safaitic Inscriptions: Preliminary Edition'. In *The Online Corpus of the Inscriptions of Ancient North Arabia (OCIANA)*, edited by Michael C. A. Macdonald, Ali al-Manaser, and María del Carmen Hidalgo-Chacón Diez.

Oxford: Khalili Research Centre. http://krc.orient.ox.ac.uk/resources/ociana/corpora/ociana_safaitic.pdf, accessed 3 July 2024.

al-Maʕšanī, Muḥammad ibn Sālim. 2003. لسان ظفار الحميري المعاصر. جامعة السلطان قابوس. مسقط. Muscat: Ǧāmiʕat al-Sulṭān Qābūs.

al-Shahri, ʕAli Aḥmad. 1994. ظفار كتاباتها ونقوشها القديمة: كيف ابتدينا وكيف ارتقينا بالحضارة الانسانية من شبه الجزيرة العربية. Dubai: Sharikat Dār al-Ghurayr li-l-Ṭibāʕa wa-l-Nashr.

———. 2000. لغة عاد (*The Language of Aad*). Salalah.

al-Shahri, Sālim Suhayl ʕAli. 2007. 'The Shahri Language and Its Relationship with Classical Arabic: A Comparative Study'. MA dissertation, Yarmuk University, Jordan.

Bellem, Alex, and Janet C. E. Watson. 2014. 'Backing and Glottalization in Three SWAP Language Varieties'. In *Arab and Arabic Linguistics: Traditional and New Theoretical Approaches*, edited by M. E. B. Giolfo, 169–207. Oxford: Oxford University Press.

———. 2017. 'South Arabian Sibilants and the Śḥərɛ́t š̃ ~ š Contrast'. In *To the Madbar and Back Again: Studies in the Languages, Archaeology, and Cultures of Arabia Dedicated to Michael C. A. Macdonald*, edited by Laila Nehme and Ahmad al-Jallad, 622–43. Leiden: Brill.

Bendjaballah, S., and P. Ségéral. 2014. 'The Phonology of "Idle Glottis" Consonants in the Mehri of Oman (Modern South Arabian)'. *Journal of Semitic Studies* 59: 161–204.

Bittner, Maximilian. 1913. 'Characteristik der Šḫauri-Sprache in den Bergen von Dofâr am Persischen Meerbusen'. *Anzeiger der Kaiserlichen Akademie der Wissenschaften in Wien* 50 (9): 81–94.

Black, J. 2000. *A Concise Dictionary of Akkadian*. SANTAG 5. Wiesbaden: Harrassowitz.

Carter, H. J. 1845. 'Notes on the Ghara Tribe, Made During the Survey of the Southeast Coast of Arabia, 1844–45'. *Journal of the Bombay Branch of the Royal Asiatic Society* 2 (9): 195–201.

Castagna, Giuliano. 2018. 'A Sketch of the Kuria Muria Language Variety and Other Aspects of Modern South Arabian'. PhD thesis, University of Leeds.

———. 2022a. 'A Collection of Jibbali/Śḥərɛ́t Proverbs from Ali al-Shahri's Publication *The Language of Aad*'. *Old World: Journal of Ancient Africa and Eurasia* 2: 89 pages. https://doi.org/10.1163/26670755-01010009

———. 2022b. 'Etymological Investigations on Jibbali/Śḥərɛ́t Anthroponyms'. In *The IOS Annual*, vol. 22, *"Telling of Olden Kings"*, edited by Yoram Cohen, Amir Gilan, Nathan Wasserman, Letizia Cerqueglini, and Beata Sheyhatovitch, 96–118. Leiden: Brill.

Castagna, Giuliano, and Suhail al-Amri. Forthcoming. 'The Morphology of Some Obsolescent Non-triliteral Verbal Classes in Eastern Jibbali/Śḥərɛ́t'.

Dufour, Julien. 2016. 'Recherches sur le verbe subarabique moderne'. Habilitation thesis, École Pratique des Hautes Études.

Eades, Domenyk, and Miranda J. Morris. 2016. 'The Documentation and Ethnolinguistic Analysis of Modern South Arabian: Harsusi'. Endangered Languages Archive (ELAR).

http://hdl.handle.net/2196/00-0000-0000-000F-0522-6, accessed 3 July 2024.

Fresnel, Fulgence. 1838. 'Note sur la langue hhymiarite'. *Journal Asiatique*, 3rd ser., 6: 79–84.

Gasparini, Fabio. 2018. 'The Baṭḥari Language of Oman: Towards a Descriptive Grammar'. PhD thesis, University of Naples.

Hofstede, Antja Ida. 1998. 'Syntax of Jibbāli'. PhD thesis, University of Manchester.

Hrisztova-Gotthardt, Hrisztalina, and Melita Aleksa Varga. 2015. 'Introduction'. In *Introduction to Paremiology*, edited by Hrisztalina Hrisztova-Gotthardt and Melita Aleksa Varga, 1–6. Warsaw: De Gruyter Open Poland. https://doi.org/10.2478/9783110410167.i

Johnstone, Thomas M. 1972. 'The Language of Poetry in Dhofar'. *Bulletin of SOAS* 35: 1–17.

———. 1973. 'Diminutive Patterns in the Modern South Arabian Languages'. *Journal of Semitic Studies* 18: 98–107.

Kispál, Tamás. 2015. 'Paremiography: Proverb Collections'. In *Introduction to Paremiology*, edited by Hrisztalina Hrisztova-Gotthardt and Melita Aleksa Varga, 229–42. Warsaw: De Gruyter Open Poland. https://doi.org/10.2478/9783110410167.10

Kogan, Leonid. 2015. *Genealogical Classification of Semitic: The Lexical Isoglosses*. Berlin: De Gruyter.

Leslau, Wolf. 2006. *Comparative Dictionary of Ge'ez (Classical Ethiopic): Ge'ez–English, English–Ge'ez—With an Index of the Semitic Roots*. Wiesbaden: Harrassowitz.

Lonnet, Antoine. 2006. 'Les langues sudarabiques modernes'. *Faits de Langues* 27: 27–44.

———. 2008. 'La marque -i de féminin en (chamito-)sémitique et son développement en sudarabique moderne oriental'. *Aula Orientalis* 26: 117–34.

———. 2009. 'South Arabian, Modern'. In *Encyclopedia of Arabic Language and Linguistics*, vol. 4, Q–Z, edited by Kees Versteegh et al., 296–300. Leiden: Brill.

———. 2017. 'Modern South Arabian *ikōtəb* is Not Necessarily *iparras* or *yənaggər*'. In 'Description and Analysis of the Modern South Arabian Languages', edited by Sabrina Bendjaballah and Philippe Ségéral, special issue, *Journal of Afroasiatic Languages and Linguistics* 9: 265–90. Leiden: Brill.

Mac Coinnigh, Marcas. 2015. 'Structural Aspects of Proverbs'. In *Introduction to Paremiology*, edited by Hrisztalina Hrisztova-Gotthardt and Melita Aleksa Varga, 112–32. Warsaw: De Gruyter Open Poland. https://doi.org/10.2478/9783110410167.5

Miller, Anthony G., and Miranda Morris. 1988. *Plants of Dhofar, the Southern Region of Oman: Traditional, Economic and Medicinal Uses*. Muscat: Office of the Advisor for Conservation of the Environment, Sultanate of Oman.

Morris, Miranda. 1997. 'The Harvesting of Frankincense in Dhofar, Oman'. In *Profumi d'Arabia: Atti del convegno*, edited by A. Avanzini, 231–47. Rome: L'Erma di Bretschneider.

———. 2002. 'Plant Names in Dhofar and the Soqotra Archipelago'. *Proceedings of the Seminar for Arabian Studies* 32: 47–61.

———. 2007. 'The Pre-literate, Non-Arabic Languages of Oman and Yemen: Their Current Situation and Uncertain Future'. *The British-Yemeni Society Journal* 15: 39–53.

———. 2016a. 'The Documentation of Modern South Arabian Languages: Bathari'. Endangered Languages Archive (ELAR). http://hdl.handle.net/2196/8e11823b-313b-49e0-8e89-7acf82102a56, accessed 3 July 2024.

———. 2016b. 'The Documentation and Ethnolinguistic Analysis of Modern South Arabian: Hobyot'. Endangered Languages Archive (ELAR). http://hdl.handle.net/2196/6711db6a-16e8-4f48-be19-3bf9b59a7a0c, accessed 3 July 2024.

———. 2017. 'Some Thoughts on Studying the Endangered Modern South Arabian Languages'. In 'Description and Analysis of the Modern South Arabian Languages', edited by Sabrina Bendjaballah and Philippe Ségéral, special issue, *Journal of Afroasiatic Languages and Linguistics* 9: 9–32. Leiden: Brill.

Morris, Miranda, and ʕAwaḍ Ahmad al-Shahri. 2017. 'Drink Long and Drink in Peace: Singing to Livestock at Water in Dhofar, Sultanate of Oman'. In *To the Madbar and Back Again: Studies in the Languages, Archaeology, and Cultures of Arabic Dedicated to Michael C. A. Macdonald*, edited by Laila Nehme and Ahmad al-Jallad, 610–21. Leiden: Brill.

Morris, Miranda, Janet C. E. Watson, and Domenyk Eades. 2019. *A Comparative Cultural Glossary across the Modern South Arabian Language Family*. Oxford: Oxford University Press.

Naumkin, Vitaly, Leonid Kogan, Dmitry Cherkashin, Maria Bulakh, Ekaterina Vizirova, ʕisa Gumʕan al-Daʕrhi, and Aḥmad ʕisa al-Daʕrhi. 2014. *Corpus of Soqotri Oral Literature*. Vol. 1. Leiden: Brill.

Norrick, Neal R. 2015. 'Subject Area, Terminology, Proverb Definitions, Proverb Features'. In *Introduction to Paremiology*, edited by Hrisztalina Hrisztova-Gotthardt and Melita Aleksa Varga, 7–27. Warsaw: De Gruyter Open Poland. https://doi.org/10.2478/9783110410167.1

Peterson, J. E. 2004. 'Oman's Diverse Society: Southern Oman'. *Middle East Journal* 58 (2): 254–69.

Petrova, Roumyana. 2015. 'Contrastive Study of Proverbs'. In *Introduction to Paremiology*, edited by Hrisztalina Hrisztova-Gotthardt and Melita Aleksa Varga, 243–61. Warsaw: De Gruyter Open Poland. https://doi.org/10.2478/9783110410167.11

Risse, Marielle. 2015. 'Generosity, Gift-giving and Gift-avoiding in Southern Oman'. *Proceedings of the Seminar for Arabian Studies* 45: 289–96.

Robin, Christian J. 1981. 'Les inscriptions d'al-Miʻsâl et la chronologie de l'Arabie méridionale au IIIe siècle de l'ère chrétienne'. *Comptes rendus des séances de l'Académie des Inscriptions et Belles-Lettres* 125 (2): 315–38.

Rubin, Aaron. 2012. 'The Future Tense in Jibbali'. In *Grammaticalization in Semitic*, edited by Domenyk Eades, 193–203. Oxford: Oxford University Press.

———. 2014. *The Jibbali (Shaḥri) Language of Oman*. Leiden: Brill.

———. 2015. 'The Classification of Hobyot'. In *Semitic Languages in Contact*, edited by Aaron Michael Butts, 311–32. Leiden: Brill.

Serjeant, Robert B., and Ewald Wagner 1959. 'A Sixteenth-century Reference to Shaḥrī Dialect at Ẓufār'. *Bulletin of SOAS* 22: 128–32.

Sima, Alexander. 2005. '101 Sprichwörter und Redensarten im Mehri-Dialekt von Ḥawf'. *Zeitschrift für Arabische Linguistik* 44: 71–93.

———. 2009. *Mehri-Texte aus der jemenitischen Sharqiyyah: Transkribiert unter Mitwirkung von Askari Sa'd Hugayrān*. Edited, annotated, and introduced by Janet C. E. Watson and Werner Arnold. Wiesbaden: Harrassowitz.

Simeone-Senelle, Marie-Claude. 2011. 'Modern South Arabian'. In *The Semitic Languages: An International Handbook*, edited by S. Weninger et al., 1073–1113. Berlin: De Gruyter.

Smith, G. Rex (ed. and trans.). 2008. *A Traveller in Thirteenth-century Arabia: Ibn al-Mujawir's Tarikh al-Mustabsir*. Hakluyt Society, 3rd ser., 19. Aldershot: Ashgate.

Taylor, A. 1962. *The Proverb and Index to the Proverb*. Hatboro, PA: Folklore Associates.

Testen, David. 1992. 'The Loss of the Person-marker t- in Jibbali and Socotri'. *Bulletin of SOAS* 55: 445–50.

Thomas, Bertram. 1939. 'Four Strange Tongues from Central South Arabia'. *Proceedings of the British Academy* 23: 231–331.

Watson, Janet C. E. 2012. *The Structure of Mehri*. Wiesbaden: Harrassowitz.

———. 2013. 'Travel to Mecca in the Pre-motorised Period'. In *The Hajj: Collected Essays*, edited by Venetia Porter and Liana Saif, 96–99. London: The British Museum.

Watson, Janet C.E., Amer al-Kathiri. 2022. 'A Phonetically "Unnatural" Class in Central and Eastern Shehret (Jibbali)'. *Kervan: International Journal of Afro-Asiatic Studies,* 26 (1): 129–59.

Watson, Janet C. E., Gisela Tomé Lourido, Abdullah al-Mahri. 2023a. 'Epenthesis and Vowel Intrusion in Central Dhofari Mehri'. *Journal of Semitic Studies* 69 (1): 521–76. https://doi.org/10.1093/jss/fgad028

Watson, Janet C. E., Gisela Tomé Lourido, Barry Heselwood, and Amer al-Kathiri. 2023b. 'Pre-aspirated Sonorants in Shehret, a Modern South Arabian Language'. In *Proceedings of the 20th International Congress of Phonetic Sciences, Prague 2023*, edited by Radek Skarnitzl and Jan Volín, 3442–46. Prague: Guarant International.

Watson, Janet C. E., and Abdullah Musallam al-Mahri. 2017. 'Language and Nature in Dhofar'. In *Linguistic Studies in the Arabian Gulf,* edited by Simone Bettega and Fabio Gasparini, 87–103. «QuadRi»—Quaderni di RiCOGNIZIONI 7. Turin: Università di Torino, Dipartimento di Lingue e Letterature straniere e Culture moderne.

Watson, Janet C. E., and Miranda Morris. 2016a. 'Documentation of the Modern South Arabian Languages: Mehri'. Endangered Languages Archive (ELAR). http://hdl.handle.net/2196/e1220e3a-459f-4565-bb7c-5a748d01ef97, accessed 3 July 2024.

———. 2016b. 'Documentation of the Modern South Arabian Languages: Shehret'. Endangered Languages Archive (ELAR). http://hdl.handle.net/2196/04d404f9-85ad-4398-a901-29e8113f3bff, accessed 3 July 2024.

Wehr, Hans J. 1976. *A Dictionary of Modern Written Arabic*. Edited by J. Milton Cowan. Ithaca, NY: Spoken Language Services.

INDEX

adverb, 92, 141, 221, 225
ʕAkʂāḵ, 16
Akkadian, 14, 21, 224
al-Baleed, 1
al-Hallānīyya, 7
Ali al-Shahri, 2, 20, 25, 45 n. 35, 215
allophone, 32, 137, 172
Aloe dhufariensis, 79
alveo-palatal labialisation, 31, 42
ʕAmri, 16
analogical levelling, 225
Ancient South Arabian, 14
Arabic, 1, 3, 5–6, 14–15, 17–18, 24–28, 32 n. 29, 33, 44, 46–47, 49, 55, 58, 61, 63, 67–68, 71–72, 76, 81–82, 84–85, 88–90, 92–98, 101–3, 105, 107–11, 113–14, 116–17, 119–21, 127, 129, 132, 135–38, 143, 148–50, 155, 157, 162, 166, 170, 171, 172 n. 45, 175, 177–78, 179 n. 48, 181–83, 189–90, 191 n. 52, 193, 196 n. 57, 197, 202, 204, 209, 212, 220, 227, 229 n. 27
areal phenomena, 13
argument, 105, 121, 137, 142, 148, 184, 191
assimilation, 3, 20, 38, 56, 108, 118–19, 192, 198

bad, 61–62, 68, 73, 75, 77, 97, 103, 111, 121, 127, 130–31, 138, 144, 152, 157, 159, 162, 175, 177–78, 182, 189, 195, 198, 202, 213
Barʕima, 14
Baṭāḥira, 14, 17, 17 n. 17
Bedouin, 57
Bertram Thomas, 10
Calotropis procera, 181
camel, 2, 34, 37, 41, 60, 83, 134, 207, 224
cave, 24–25, 114
celestial body, 151–52, 189
Christ-thorn tree, 78
circumfix, 38, 219
circumstantial, 64, 159, 191, 210
coalescence, 54, 66, 95, 140 n. 36
competition, 188
compound, 18, 79, 158, 168, 183, 196, 226
conditional, 8 n. 5, 12
conjunction, 72, 116, 129, 137, 207
construct, 52, 62, 89, 203, 226
curse, 28, 66, 91, 180, 195–96, 198–99, 201, 209
Darbat Ali, 1
ḍaʕīf, 15
definite article, 11 n. 10, 36–38, 54, 60–62, 65–66, 69, 75, 79,

96, 108, 116, 124, 140 n. 36, 144, 145 n. 37, 154, 161, 169, 172, 174, 195, 201
deletion, 33–34, 37, 53 n. 5, 148–49, 170, 192, 207
demonstrative, 178, 182
denominative, 43, 85, 204
devoicing, 31–33, 105, 216
Dhalkut, 6
Dhofar, 1–5, 7, 15–16, 18–19, 24, 24 n. 24, 25, 57, 74, 110, 121, 127, 147, 151, 215
dialect, 1 n. 1, 18–19, 22, 31, 33, 45, 57, 59, 64, 78 n. 14, 81, 87, 94, 112, 119, 141, 173–74, 192–93, 199 n. 60, 201–3, 215–19, 224–25
dialectal
  areas, 18–19
  variation, 4, 15, 19, 27, 33, 87, 161, 188, 195 n. 56, 226
diminutive, 33, 69, 71, 89, 134, 142–43, 156, 172, 193, 198, 224–26
direct object marker, 40
divorce formula, 7
documentation, 6
dual, 7 n. 4, 39–40, 52, 53 n. 5
Egypt, 21
ejectivity, 29
emphasis, 29, 32
emphatic request, 194
folk belief, 67, 74, 77, 80, 91, 144, 157

Fulgence Fresnel, 7
Gabúb, 16
gemination, 9, 37, 56, 144, 169, 225
generosity, 73, 136, 179, 210, 220, 227
genitive exponent, 37–38, 61–63, 161, 218
glottalisation, 8, 32
glow-worm, 90
God, 73, 83–84, 96, 101, 132, 137, 143, 157, 169, 180–81, 189, 193, 206, 209 n. 64
grammaticalisation, 103, 201
guttural, 13, 35–36, 38, 55, 68, 106, 172–73
Gəblɛ́t, 14, 16–18
hairline, 194
Ḥaklī, 14–16
Hasik, 6
Hawf, 1 n. 1, 45
health, 173, 175, 183, 202, 206
Hebrew, 14, 221
Hikman, 14
hyena, 203
Ibn al-Mujawir, 7
idiomatic, 44, 114, 188, 195–96, 201, 210, 212
idle glottis, 13
illness, 76, 151, 162, 176, 186, 195, 220, 223
Indian Ocean, 1
infix, 8, 193, 222, 226
interdental, 29, 32

isogloss, 10–12, 20
Jabal Qamar, 18, 141, 225
Jabal Qara, 18–19
Jabal Samḥān, 18
Jeddah, 7
Jibbali Lexicon, 27, 53 n. 4, 193, 227
Kaṯīrī, 14, 15 n. 14
Ḳitán, 16
Kleinia saginata, 225
Kuria Muria, 6–7, 18, 40, 112
Kuwait, 5
Kašúb, 16
labour pains, 63, 220
lateral, 8, 29, 32
lexis, 22, 219
limp, 212–13
lip-rounding, 83
loanword, 94, 143, 148, 177, 182, 193, 196 n. 57, 204
lowering, 35
malefactive, 54
Maria Theresa dollar, 2
Mašāyix, 14
Masira, 7
Maʕšni, 16
measure, 88, 91, 212
Mesopotamia, 21
Modern South Arabian Languages (MSAL), 1, 3, 5–6, 8–14, 18, 27–28, 34–35, 111, 197, 200 n. 61, 210, 218, 221–24
 Baṯhari, 6, 10–11, 13
 Ḥarsūsi, 6, 10–11, 13, 27

Hobyōt, 6, 10–11, 13, 14 n. 12
Mehri, 1 n. 1, 6, 10–11, 13–15, 22, 27, 33, 45, 47, 49, 51–52, 54–62, 64–66, 69–71, 73, 75, 82–83, 84 n. 17, 85–89, 92–95, 97, 100–1, 103, 105–8, 111–13, 115–19, 121, 123, 125, 128, 133–34, 137–38, 140–44, 146–47, 153–61, 164, 209, 219, 221–22, 224
 Mehrising, 170, 219
 Mehrism, 37, 58, 208
Soqotri, 9–13, 49, 66 n. 10, 70, 89, 147, 222
monoconsonantal base, 211, 222
morphology, 8–9, 23, 40, 69, 209, 218–19
Muḥammad bin Sālim al-Kaṯīrī, 15 n. 14
Muʕǧam Lisān Ḍufār, 18, 26, 33
nasalisation, 31, 33–34, 101, 104, 124, 225
negation, 38, 50, 54, 96, 98, 112, 114 n. 26, 148, 219
nisbah, 17, 57, 92–93, 221
numeral, 8, 50, 72, 200
offspring, 180
oil, 5–6
Oman, 1–2, 6, 25, 84 n. 17
optative, 102, 144, 146, 164, 168, 183, 186, 196
palatalisation, 20, 49, 67
paragoge, 63
paremiology, 1, 20–21, 45, 124

participle, 11, 56, 58–59, 76, 78, 91, 97, 104, 120, 123–24, 126, 138, 156, 160–61, 169, 193, 222–24

passive, 44, 56, 60, 64, 67, 72, 76–77, 81, 98–99, 115, 124, 136, 140, 173, 193, 201, 218

pausal, 20, 63, 86, 166, 174, 216–17

personal name, 3, 49, 109, 117, 132

personal suffix, 36, 39–40, 58, 82, 84, 87, 106, 108, 137, 140–42, 154, 156, 165, 168, 183–84, 186, 196–97, 201, 207, 209, 211–13, 222

phonetics, 23, 215

phonology, 23, 215

poetic language, 2, 15, 19, 219

poverty, 39, 141, 204

pre-aspiration, 31–32, 65, 105

prefix, 8–9, 12, 36–38, 42, 50, 55–56, 64, 80, 100, 108, 114, 134, 146, 159, 166, 191, 198, 209–11

preposition, 40, 54–55, 65, 71–72, 79–82, 88, 96, 102, 106, 110, 132–33, 137, 141, 153, 156, 162, 164, 169, 197, 201–2, 211, 213, 218, 222, 225–26

pronoun, 39, 95, 111, 124, 154–55, 194, 207

protasis, 52

proverbial affix, 63, 144

proverbial markers, 21

Qara, 14, 18–19

Qatar, 5

quadriliteral, 8, 11, 42, 44, 125, 134

quinqueliteral, 8 n. 6, 9, 11, 42, 44

raising, 86, 190

reduplication, 8 n. 6, 9, 42, 150

relativiser, 37–38, 50–51, 53, 59, 63, 90, 99, 101, 106, 123, 125, 129, 134, 172, 188, 208, 210, 218

roasted millet, 90–91

Rubʿ al-Khali, 1

Sadḥ, 19–20, 28

Šaḥra, 14–16, 18

Ṣalalah, 1, 6–7, 19

Šammás, 16

Sarcostemma viminale, 217

Saudi Arabia, 1, 5

Ṣayhadic, 14

scoffing, 202

semantic shift, 220

Semitic, 5–7, 9–12, 14, 28–29, 34, 93, 184, 190, 200 n. 61, 218, 221–22

Sharbithat, 1

short, 28, 33–35, 43, 51, 55, 66–67, 79, 81, 94, 114 n. 26, 124, 172, 191, 194, 202, 215, 219, 224

Śḥərɛ̄t, 16–18

Sima, 1 n. 1, 45, 47, 51–52, 54–62, 64–66, 69–71, 73, 75, 82–83,

85–89, 92–95, 97, 100–1, 105–8, 111–13, 115–19, 122–23, 125–26, 128–29, 133–34, 137–38, 140–44, 146–47, 153–61
snail, 175
snake, 36, 144, 169, 175, 192
sonorants, 32
Soqotra, 5, 7, 25, 78
sorcery, 195, 223
stress, 52, 54, 98–99, 109, 204, 218 n. 18
strong, 8, 55, 67, 73, 99, 121, 124, 137, 147, 183, 188, 194, 197, 206, 223
subjunctive, 41, 54–55, 69, 96, 100, 102, 122, 133–34, 144, 146, 148, 161, 164–66, 168–69, 183, 186–87, 189, 196, 198, 209
Südarabische Expedition, 15
suffix, 8, 11–12, 36, 39–40, 50, 52, 53 n. 5, 58, 82, 84, 87, 99, 102, 106, 108, 137, 140–42, 154–56, 161, 165, 168, 183–84, 186, 196–97, 201, 207, 209, 211–13, 222
Šxawri, 15
syntax, 22–23
tall, 9, 194
Ṭawi Aʕtair, 19–20
The Language of Aad, 2, 24, 30–31, 46
topicalisation, 52, 99

transcription, 25 n. 26, 26, 27 n. 28, 29–31, 33, 42, 45, 46, 72, 122, 181
transhumance, 90
Ṭəbɔ́k, 16
uncle, 160, 200–1
variant, 4, 26, 39, 51 n. 1, 57, 74, 86, 97, 111, 126, 144, 147 n. 38, 157, 163, 169, 188, 193, 197, 202–3, 211, 221, 223–24, 226
verbal classes, 9, 11, 12, 40, 42–43, 52 n. 2, 55, 223
voiced, 29, 31–32, 34, 52 n. 3, 61
voiceless, 31–32, 37, 42, 108
vowel harmony, 20, 174
Wadi Darbat, 114, 215
weak, 9, 15, 32, 51, 58, 71, 78, 90 n. 18, 96, 98 n. 21, 125, 129, 133, 144, 152, 167–69, 173, 183, 187–88, 195, 199–200, 206, 211–12, 218, 221
wealth, 15, 69, 106, 187–88, 210
Wellerism, 24, 143
witch, 167, 196
Yemen, 1, 25, 45
əḥkilyɔ́t, 14–16

About the Team

Alessandra Tosi was the managing editor for this book and provided quality control.

Anne Burberry performed the copyediting of the book in Word. The fonts used in this volume are Charis SIL, Scheherazade New and Abyssinica SIL.

Cameron Craig created all of the editions — paperback, hardback, and PDF. Conversion was performed with open source software freely available on our GitHub page at https://github.com/OpenBookPublishers.

Jeevanjot Kaur Nagpal designed the cover of this book. The cover was produced in InDesign using Fontin and Calibri fonts.

Cambridge Semitic Languages and Cultures

General Editor Geoffrey Khan

www.ingramcontent.com/pod-product-compliance
Lightning Source LLC
Chambersburg PA
CBHW070325240426
43671CB00013BA/2365